# ISIS, IRAN
## AND
# ISRAEL

## C&L PUBLISHING

**WWW.ISISIRANANDISRAELBOOK.COM**

Publication date: February 2016

ISBN Print: 978-0-9862233-3-4

ISBN eBook: 978-0-9862233-4-1

ISBN ePDF: 978-0-9862233-5-8

Library of Congress Control Number: 2016931124

This publication is designed to provide accurate and authoritative information in regard to the subject matter covered. It is sold with the understanding that the author or the publisher is not engaged in rendering any type of professional services. If expert assistance is required, the services of a competent professional should be sought.

1. ISIS 2. Israel 3. Iran  4. Middle East 5. Terrorists 6. Persecution 7. Iran Nuclear Treaty 8. Russia

I. Mitchell, Chris II. ISIS, Iran and Israel

*ISIS, Iran and Israel* may be purchased at special quantity discounts. Resale opportunities are available for sales promotions, corporate programs, gifts, fund raising, book clubs, or educational purposes for churches, congregations, schools and universities. For more information contact Mel Cohen:

1000 Pearl Road
Pleasantville, TN 37033
931-593-2484

Have Chris Mitchell speak at your live event or by videoconferencing.
For information call Mel at 931 593-2484 or email Mel at mel@isisiranandisraelbook.com

Editors: Mel Cohen, Anne Severance

Cover design: Megan Van Vuren

Interior layout: Lynne Hopwood

Photos by Jonathan Goff

Publishing Consultant: Mel Cohen of Inspired Authors Press LLC www.                    .com

Publisher: C & L Publishing LLC

*ISIS, Iran and Israel* Website: www.isisiranandisraelbook.com

Printed in the United States of America

*Dedicated to Elizabeth, the "wife of my youth."*
*It's been said, "A good friend listens to your adventures,*
*and a best friend makes them with you."*
*Here's to our adventures, past, present and future.*
*Remember, the best is yet to come!*

# Acknowledgments

Winston Churchill said, "Writing a book is an adventure." Penning *ISIS, Iran and Israel* was no exception... although the companions on the adventure make all the difference. My wife Elizabeth joined me 37 years ago and, as Winnie the Pooh said, "As soon as I saw you, I knew an adventure was going to happen." Here we are nearly four decades into our friendship, and it's still true that "a good friend listens to your adventures; a best friend makes them with you." Here's to this adventure that's "in the book" and the new ones around the corner. Thanks for being my best friend and letting me go "around the corner."

Speaking of around the corner, our young tribe is now "around the world," launched out on their own adventures. Philip, Kathleen and Grace inspired *ISIS, Iran and Israel* from afar. Now Philip and his best friend, Caitlyn, have birthed a new generation and are launching out on their own new adventures with their fellow traveler Simone. My fellow travelers in the Mitchell clan—Kevin, Brian and Nancy (Clarke) and Jeanne—continue to encourage this sojourner scribe on his way home. We all remember Rick, whose new Heavenly adventure has already begun.

My adventure with CBN began more than a quarter of a century ago. Its vision to take the Gospel to the ends of the earth was a star to which I hitched my wagon all those years ago. More than a half a century into fulfilling its mandate to prepare the way of the Lord, Founder Pat Robertson, CEO Gordon Robertson and so many others are engaged in a labor of love and devotion to the One who birthed this Heavenly vision. Their faithfulness allows this reporter to step onto the front lines and find a front-row seat to His story. Behind CBN's worldwide team is an army of partners whose steadfast support and prayers make forays into Kurdistan and other destinations possible. Thank you!

Fellow companions on these expeditions are an extraordinary *CBN News* team from Virginia Beach to Washington DC, led by Rob Allman. Here, in the city of the Great King, a fabulous bureau—Julie Stahl, Tzippe Barrow, Yehuda Chamorro, Annika Kopp, Nissim Lerner, Colette Cheramie and Lesly Bertell—experience the awe of telling the stories of this age from the epicenter. Jonathan Goff, our intrepid cameraman, shared many of these adventures. His pluck, good humor, resourcefulness and Godliness got us through many predicaments and yielded outstanding results. On the field in Kurdistan, Pastor Majeed proved an invaluable resource, companion, friend and brother to his two sidekicks from the Holy Land. From America's heartland, John Waage added his invaluable Middle East expertise to our coverage.

Throughout the process, unsung, unseen and unheralded intercessors have held up my hands and heart through their steadfast prayers and intercession. Whether in the streets of Kirkuk, on the front lines of ISIS or at my computer in Jerusalem, their cries to the One who hears and answers have protected, encouraged and inspired this herald. Their prayers breathed life into *ISIS, Iran and Israel*. I benefit from those prayers whether whispered in the secret place or shouted amongst the Body. We all share in the fruit. This side of Heaven, their full story may never be told, yet He knows.

On the earth: the practical work of publishing lay on the capable, experienced shoulders of Mel Cohen, our publishing consultant from Inspired Authors Press. He's been the penultimate maestro, orchestrating all the various elements to bring *ISIS, Iran and Israel* to fruition. Anne Severance's copy editing guardrails kept this author from veering off the straight and narrow road of good grammar and proper punctuation. More importantly, her prayers and belief in this message and its power to bless inspired this scribe throughout the editing. Lynne Hopwood added her expert graphic design and creativity.

This tome owes its heart to those brave men and women throughout the Middle East who have endured unspeakable horrors, yet who remain faithful to their Lord Jesus. They are the heroes of our age, who stand in the face of terror and yet lift up their eyes to see their Redemption drawing nigh.

Finally, to the three most important Persons in my life: my Father, under whose wings I find shelter, who sets my times and seasons and whose Kingdom I long to see; to Jesus, who found me when I was lost and now steers me through the shoals of life and to the Holy Spirit, whose still, small voice comforts and guides. Their love is my beacon, guiding this homesick soul home. *Maranatha!*

# Contents

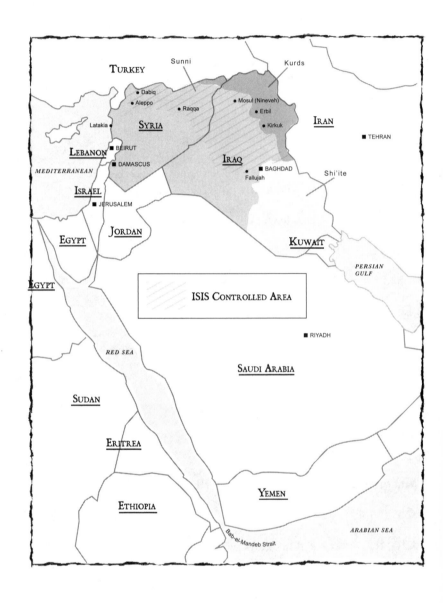

# A Perfect Storm

*"The warfare now taking place in Iraq and Syria is happening against a background of what the Americans call a 'perfect storm,' that is an assortment of events ... whose coming together creates an occurrence far more powerful than the sum of its parts."*

–Yaakov Amidror, "Perfect Storm: The Implications of Middle East Chaos[1]

The twin prop plane roared above Israel's Negev Desert. From the window, I could see the craggy terrain thousands of feet below. Purple-tinted mountains bracketed a trough of flat, barren land. Modern Jordan's border began at the foot of the mountains to the east where ancient Moab ruled. Other ancients like the Persians, Assyrians, and Romans once stalked these lands millennia ago. They came for conquest and war. Now I flew with a planeload of foreign and Israeli journalists toward Israel's lavish resort city of Eilat. We hadn't come for a holiday. Instead, one theme would resonate through a myriad of news outlets: after thousands of years, the winds of war still swirl throughout the Middle East. Israel's Government Press Office had provided the plane and invited us to see the latest evidence of how the Islamic Republic of Iran—descendants of those ancient Persians—is waging war against the modern-day children of Israel. Days earlier, Israeli commandoes had seized an Iranian ship hundreds of miles away in the Red Sea. The ship carried a large cache of weapons bound for Hamas and the Gaza Strip. Israeli and U.S. intelligence tracked the nefarious shipment all the way from Bander Abbas, Iran's main port. After a bumpy landing and a short bus ride to Israel's naval port, we got to see the contraband for ourselves. Two Israeli warships—the INS Hetz and Hanit—stood sentry over a dock arrayed with Syrian-made and Iranian-shipped weapons. Neatly lined across the pier sat 40 long-range missiles, nearly 200 mortars, and 400,000 rounds of ammunition. Iran hid the booty in the belly of the ship where shipping containers held the deadly cargo concealed in bags of cement marked "Made in Iran."

We could literally reach out and touch the missiles. They represented a major threat to Israel's home front. These modern-day equivalents of the bow and arrow put five million

Israelis—more than 60 percent of their population—in range. Our cameraman, Jonathan Goff, and I spotted IDF spokesman Lt. Col. Peter Lerner, who reported: "The Gaza terrorists don't have anything of this magnitude. Not of the weaponry, capability, not of the distance it can go. This would have made a huge difference if these rockets made it into the terrorists' hands. We did a good thing."[2]

Jonathan began videotaping the 40 forty M 302 missiles, each with a range of more than 120 miles or 200 kilometers. Just one could destroy a high-rise building. Reuven Ben-Shalom of Cross Cultural Strategies Ltd. told us on camera, "When you go to 200 kilometers, it's almost not important anymore. It reaches all the important targets in Israel."[3] We waited for Israeli Prime Minister Benjamin Netanyahu to address the Israeli and world press. Before he arrived, I walked to the edge of the dock and looked around. The setting seemed surreal. Behind me lay an impressive display of military hardware. Before me, resort hotels sparkled in the afternoon sun, para sailors glided high above the Rea Sea, and wind surfers plowed its crystal waters. These vacationers seemed oblivious to the implements of war just a few feet away.

With an Israeli navy boat patrolling near the dock, Prime Minister Netanyahu showed up. Along with his Defense Minister "Bogie" Ya'alon, he walked by the shipping container with cement from the Hormozgan Cement Company that veiled its deadly companion cargo. He looked over the 14-foot-long missiles; the shiny olive-colored mortars and stacked boxes of ammunition. On his way, he grabbed one of the 400,000 bullets and put it in his pocket. I assumed he kept it as a souvenir or an object lesson. Before a battery of cameras and reporters, he began: "This shipment reveals the true face of Iran. The weapons on this ship were destined for terrorists in Gaza who are committed to Israel's destruction. The goal was to have these weapons rain down on the heads of Israel's citizens. The ship was organized by Iran, dispatched by Iran, financed by Iran. The missiles were loaded by Iran in Iran."[4]

Netanyahu, a master communicator, reiterated a recurring theme throughout his tenure as leader of the Jewish state: "Iran, a brutal regime, has not abandoned its deep involvement in terrorism, its systematic efforts to undermine peace and security throughout the Middle East, and its ambition to destroy the State of Israel."[5]

He singled out what he called the hypocrisy of Western diplomats. "This determination to ignore the truth that was exposed once again with the capture of the ship is first of all hypocritical. I heard a few faint condemnations of Iran from the international community after we intercepted this murderous shipment. We even saw representatives of the world powers shaking hands and smiling with the heads of Iran's regime at the same time we were unloading these missiles here in Eilat!"[6]

As an American, Israel's prime minister then delivered what for me, was the takeaway for the U.S.: "Does anyone truly believe that Iran has given up its plans to develop nuclear weapons or long-range ballistic missiles that are capable of carrying nuclear warheads to Europe and the United States?"[7]

I pondered that question and agreed that Western leaders —and my home country's leaders —ignored or greatly underestimated Iran's nuclear program at our peril.

"The missiles that we uncovered today were intended to strike at the citizens of Israel. The intercontinental ballistic missiles that Iran is developing are intended to strike at the citizens of the West. Come to think of it, Iran might not need ICBMs. Just as they concealed these weapons in containers on this ship, they could tomorrow conceal in other containers the ultimate weapon, nuclear weapons, which they could ship to any port in the world."[8]

His conclusion: the world needs to wake up!

"So my message today is simple," he continued. "Those engaged in self-deception must awaken from their slumber."[9]

Tuesday, March 11, 2014, marked our rendezvous on that Eilat dock. More than seventy years earlier, another Prime Minister echoed warnings of a similar danger. Winston Churchill, before he assumed leadership of Great Britain, admonished at another time when the world slept and another leader and nation—Adolf Hitler and Nazi Germany—prepared for war: "I look with wonder upon our thoughtless crowds disporting themselves in the summer sunshine, and upon this unheeding House of Commons, which seems to have no higher function than to cheer a minister and all the while, across the North Sea, **a terrible process is astir, Germany is arming!**"[10]

Churchill delivered his warning in 1932. Throughout the 1930s, he kept raising his "voice in the wilderness" about a gathering storm poised to engulf the world in a world war. His exhortations became a clarion call between WWI—the "war to end all wars"—and WWII. Some Israeli leaders believe we live in a similar time. For example, then IDF Chief of Staff Benny Gantz described the Iranian weapons seizure as one more example of the "war between wars."[11]

## "AN ASSORTMENT OF EVENTS"

The Iranian nuclear threat stands as just one of many dangers during this era. Retired Israeli General Yaacov Amidror once prepared the annual threat assessments for the Israeli military. He now serves in one of Israel's most respected think tanks. Amidror described the current configuration of the Middle East as a "perfect storm." He calls it "***an assortment of events** that, on the face of it, seem not to be connected in advance, [yet] whose coming together creates an occurrence far more powerful than the sum of its parts.*"[12]

The rise of ISIS provides one of those "assortments of events." It menaces the region and dispatches killers to murder and terrorize major Western cities like Paris. Its gruesome Friday the 13th attack in November 2015 killed 130, wounded hundreds more, and marked France's "9-11." French President Hollande called it an "act of war." Yet the Islamic State still controls land the size of Great Britain, spews out videos promising to strike America, and commands the allegiance of perhaps multiplied thousands of "home-grown" terrorists strewn throughout the free world. Since their barbaric splash onto the world stage in the summer of 2014, their caliphate has gained followers throughout the Middle East and northern Africa and has lured adherents from such faraway places as California and Mississippi.

Deterred but not defeated by an incessant bombing campaign, this fanatical and largest Islamic terror group of our time will require "boots on the ground" before they can be dislodged. The ascent of Russia into the Middle East is another "event." In September 2015, Russia's leader, Vladimir Putin, forged his way into the middle of Syria's more than four-year-old civil war. This action represented Russia's biggest foreign intervention in decades and signaled a much greater regional role for the former Soviet Union. Following his own agenda, Putin began a bombing campaign against ISIS but a more robust one against the foes of Syrian president, Bashar Assad. These foes turned out to be allies of Turkey, the U.S., and the West. It complicated an already complex situation.

Retired U.S. General Jay Garner told me in Erbil, Kurdistan, that Russia's entry into the Syrian civil war introduced a new danger to the region. "In the air, it will be a big problem if he puts fighter aircraft in there and they begin to put in air strikes against rebel forces while we're putting in air strikes against Assad forces. How do you de-conflict all that? It's a tinderbox."[13]

Garner's foreboding came to pass. Just eleven days after the Paris attacks, Turkey shot down a Russian SU-24 fighter jet over the Turkish-Syrian border. Turkey claimed it violated Turkish air space. Russia insisted the jet safely remained within Syrian territory. Both nations provided evidence supporting their versions. After the attack, Russia suspended military contact with Turkey and Russian President Putin bellowed that the incident was a "stab in the back," promised "significant consequences" to Turkey, and declared Russia would not tolerate "such atrocities."[14] Turkish President Erdogan responded he would defend their borders and allies in the region.

In Washington, U.S. President Barack Obama urged calm while Brussels convened an emergency NATO session. Since Turkey is a NATO member, the organization could invoke Article 5 that states an attack on one member is an attack on all. This carried the potential of a direct military confrontation between the U.S., other NATO members, and Russia. Putin raised the stakes even higher when he dispatched his S400 air defense system and the possibility of an unwitting strike against coalition aircraft. Another "event" spread throughout the region. The two monoliths of Islam—Sunni Saudi Arabia and Shiite Iran—wrestled for dominance throughout the Middle East. Proxy wars between the two peppered the region. On the Arabian Peninsula, Iran and Saudi Arabia were battling over the country of Yemen and control of its strategic waterway, Bab Al Mandab. That choke point leads to the Red Sea and the Suez Canal and carries a substantial flow of the world's oil supply. This Sunni/Shiite rivalry, which goes back thirteen hundred years – percolated throughout the region until Saudi Arabia executed a top Shiite cleric, Sheik Nimr on January 2, 2016. They claimed he fomented opposition to their regime. His execution sparked riots throughout the Shiite world culminating in Tehran where an Iranian mob ransacked the Saudi embassy while shouting "Death to the house of Saud." Iran's Ayatollah Khamenei promised "divine revenge."[15] As a result, Saudi Arabia cut diplomatic relations. The tense relationship that had been percolating began to boil. The race for nuclear weapons leavens their duel. On July 14, 2015, in what could be the document defining our generation, the U.S., five other world powers, and Iran signed a nuclear deal. While adherents of the deal say it will prevent Iran from getting a nuclear bomb, critics charge it all but guarantees the Ayatollahs of the Islamic Republic will become a nuclear power. Some believe it gave Iran a head start on its nuclear race with Saudi Arabia. The agreement also stirred up fresh speculation that Israel could launch a military strike on Iran's nuclear facilities and sparked fears of nuclear proliferation with "nuclear trip wires" crisscrossing the region. After the pact, a real-life "Game of Thrones" emerged in the Levant. Just before the signing, longtime enemies Israel and Saudi Arabia met for the first time in public. This new alliance marked a profound geo-political shift in the Middle East and pits the Sunni Arab nations and Israel against the Shiite axis of Iran, Syria, and Hezbollah.

This Sunni/Shiite divide provides one of the keys to understanding today's Middle East. Amidror wrote, "It is impossible to understand the Middle East at this time without taking into consideration the deep, centuries-old rivalry between Sunnis and Shiites, and the historic change that took place as a consequence of the (1979) revolution in Iran, a change that to this day is the strongest driving force on the Shiite side of the struggle. This change has found expression and will continue to do so everywhere in the Middle East where there is competition between Shiites and Sunnis."[16]

While bitter rivals, many Sunnis and Shiites anticipate the imminent return of their versions of the Islamic Messiah, the Mahdi. This apocalyptic Islam animates the Sunni branch of Islam through ISIS and Shiite Islam through Iran. Both ideologies believe it is their duty to hasten his return by laying a foundation of chaos and turmoil. One more cloud creating this "perfect storm."

## WAR CLOUDS ON THE HORIZON

Other clouds include Syrian President Assad fighting his bitter and deadly civil war against ISIS and a myriad of Islamist groups. The result of this war in human terms has been catastrophic. Nearly 300,000 have died, four million Syrians became refugees, and nearly eight million are "internally displaced."[17] "The country formerly known as Syria" has become a breeding ground for Islamists, the ground zero for a proxy war for Sunnis and Shiites and a sea of human misery and debris. It churned a tsunami of refugees that crashed over the borders of Europe. The war the West refused to stop for years nevertheless ended up on its doorstep. One small boy's tragic death on a Turkish beach triggered a global outpouring of compassion to help and house a modern-day exodus of Syrians and others from the Middle East to Europe. Others warned it's an Islamic invasion with yet-to-be-seen catastrophic consequences for the future of the continent. Israel itself—where war can begin in a matter of hours—is preparing to fight on several fronts. For example, to Israel's north, it has fought two wars with Lebanon and is preparing for a third.[18] Israel's Home Front Command recently "briefed . . . 257 local authorities in Israel about a possible conflict with Hezbollah, which has the capacity to fire 1,000 to 1,500 rockets a day and a massive stockpile of more than 60,000 rockets."[19] According to Israel's Channel 2: "The Israel military is (also) preparing for a possible ground operation on the Syrian side of the Golan Heights."[20]

CBN's Scott Ross saw firsthand what's happening on Israel's southern border. Hila Fenlon took Ross on a tour of the front lines between Israel and the Gaza Strip. Fenlon lives in Moshav Netiv Ha'asara, the closest Israeli community to the Gaza border. It's a community within mortar range of Hamas. As they approached the front, shots were fired from nearby. "What's that?" Ross asked. Fenlon replied, "Probably Hamas practicing somewhere." Sensing the nearby danger, she advised, "I think we might want to go away (from here) actually." She added, **"This is where Hamas is practicing for the next war, right now, as we speak."**[21]

Given all these threats, Israel's Home Front Command "believes that the next war will be more challenging than the previous ones."[22] While no one knows when the "next one" will come, the region already has at least four wars igniting the Middle East.

Just like the pre-WWI landscape, the conflicts make for a bewildering array of enemies and allies along various battle lines. Into the midst of these fiery conflicts, a number of developments are kindling throughout the Middle East that could escalate any or all of these fires into a Mideast conflagration. Given this chaos, an increasing number of world leaders—from a Muslim king to the head of the Vatican, and commentators from conservative talk radio to the liberal *New York Times*—scan the world's landscape and see a much larger storm on the horizon.

## ECHOES OF 2014

When Turkey shot down a Russian SU-24 warplane over the Turkish-Syrian border on November 24, 2015, many compared that incident to the assassination of Archduke Franz Ferdinand on June 28, 1914, by Serbian nationalist Gavrilo Princip. That shot triggered WWI. Some wonder if a Sidewinder missile, launched by a Turkish F-16, has triggered the next.

Even before that incident, Jordan's King Abdullah called the fight against the Islamic State "a third world war by other means."[23] Given the world's increasingly deadly landscape, Pope Francis warned, "Even today, after the second failure of another world war, perhaps one can speak of a third war, one fought piecemeal, with crimes, massacres, destruction."[24]

After the Russian/Turkish episode, former Congressman and conservative commentator Allen West wrote, "Go back and read all of the diplomatic discussions that happened after Archduke Ferdinand's assassination, quite similar. In the end, they stopped talking, drew lines, mobilized, and commenced fighting. . . . We now have a French carrier group deployed and a Russian naval cruiser with orders to defend Russian troops. Ladies and gents, we can dismiss this, but we're on the verge of a world war."[25]

Conservative talk show host Rush Limbaugh opined, "Did you see where Turkey shot down a military jet of Archduke Ferdinand? Archduke Ferdinand's military jet shot down over ... It's just my way of saying what everybody thinks. You know, it's amazing to me, it really is . . . How? I don't know, what's the word?

Unified? So you have Turkey shoots down a Russian jet and you look at one place, you look at a hundred places and they say, 'This is exactly how World War I started.' O, my God! O, my God! World War I!"[26] The liberal *New York Times* ran this op-ed by their International Affairs and diplomacy columnist, Roger Cohen. Cohen explained the situation with a fictitious conversation between a mother and young child. The child asks how World War I began. The mother describes the complicated environment:

> Mother: "There were things called empires. They controlled vast territories full of different peoples, and some of these peoples wanted to rule themselves rather than be governed by a faraway emperor."
>
> Child: "O.K."
>
> Mother: "The Austro-Hungarian Empire was one of them. It had lots of grand palaces in its capital, Vienna, where people danced at fancy balls. It governed parts of a poor corner of Europe called the Balkans, where its rule was disliked. One day in 1914, the heir to the Austro-Hungarian throne and his wife were assassinated in a Balkan city called Sarajevo by a young man, a Bosnian Serb, who wanted the freedom of the south Slavs from imperial rule."

From the complicated geo-politics of pre-WWI, the mother went on to describe the maze of geo-politics in the Middle East today beginning with Syria.

> Mother: "Syria has broken up, like the Ottoman Empire. Russia is bombing some enemies of the Syrian tyrant. America is bombing the throat-slitters. So is France. Turkey shot down a Russian plane. Russia is angry. The Kurds want the state they didn't get 100 years ago. Saudi Arabia is fighting a region-wide war against Iran. That war is most intense in Syria, where hundreds of thousands are dead." The mother pauses, and then concludes: "Sometimes little things get bigger. There's a spark . . . and it's a big mess."[27]

When things get bigger; when there's a spark and there's a big mess, these developments in the Middle East affect your life. What happens in the region can shake stock markets around the world, lead to a greater Western military intervention in the region; spark a confrontation between major powers or flood immigrants to your country (if it hasn't already). Former Israeli Ambassador to the U.S., historian, and now member of Israel's Knesset, Michael Oren, explained what happens when the Middle East ripples to the shores of the U.S. "If anybody in the United States thinks that they can turn their back on the Middle East and walk away, then they are kidding themselves. The Middle East is not like Vietnam, where you can pull your troops out and go home and be pretty confident that the Viet Cong are not going to follow you to wherever you're going— Chicago or Florida. The Middle East is going to come after you. The Middle East is coming to a neighborhood near you and the United States will remain connected, both strategically and financially, to the Middle East. So there's no detaching."[28]

*ISIS, Iran and Israel: What You Need to Know about the Current Mideast Crisis and Coming Mideast War* probes the subject. It's a way for you to attach to the Middle East.

As a journalist and, perhaps more importantly, a watchman on the wall, I've had the privilege of seeing the Middle East through the perspective of a number of people: People like retired U.S. General Jay Garner who warned of the dangers of Russia's expansion in the region or another retired General, William "Jerry" Boykin, who explained one of Russia's hidden agendas. U.S. Senator Tom Cotton (R-AR), who is concerned about the nuclear deal he believes could set the stage for a disastrous Mideast war. Author Tom Doyle, who recounted the stories of men and women ready to die for the Gospel. He says their remarkable faith in the face of death and dangers have earned them the biblical salute "for whom the world is not worthy." Middle East expert Joel Rosenberg warned of a "catastrophic capitulation" by the U.S.; he sees the prophetic puzzle pieces of Ezekiel 38 and 39 falling into place. I have also heard the perspective of the tender soul of a ten-year-old Kurdish girl named Myriam, with a heart big enough to forgive ISIS, the ones who "despitefully used" and persecuted her and her family.

This book also affirms that "Aslan is on the move" in the Middle East. This reference to Aslan, a type of Christ in the *Chronicles of Narnia*, refers to the movement throughout the region where thousands of souls—many of them former Muslims—are accepting the Good News of Jesus as they look forward to His coming Kingdom and their coming King. While ISIS swept through the area, raping and pillaging, many Christians in Syria and Iraq stood in their path. Some say "genocide" is the word to describe what happened to the 2000 year-old Church in the very cradle of Christianity. Yet many of these believers in Jesus refused to deny their Savior and paid their "last full measure of devotion." Martyrdom came to the Middle East.

The genesis of the title of this book came around a kitchen table in Michigan as we discussed what's happening in this region. It's an area that sets the tone for the globe. I hope it finds a way to a discussion around your kitchen table.

The conversation begins on the front lines of the free world.

 QR Code for CBN News video: "Iran's Weapon Cache: 'Awake from Your Slumber'"

 QR Code for CBN News video: "Turkey, Russia Headed for a Military Faceoff?"

# On the Front Lines of the Free World

*"The difference is that they are fighting to die.*
*We are fighting to live."*

–General Karzan, the Peshmerga[1]

*Dohuk, Kurdistan*

We got an urgent call from General Karzan of the Kurdish military known as the Peshmerga. Peshmerga is a Kurdish word that means *"those who face death."* These cadres of Kurdish men and women have lived up to that motto for more than a year facing ISIS, the darkest horde to walk the earth in our lifetime. In fact, the Peshmerga have been the one military force capable of standing up to the ISIS onslaught.

We had met Karzan the night before at a hotel in Dohuk to arrange our interview. He greeted me with the traditional Middle Eastern handshake and kisses on both cheeks. I wasn't expecting him to be dressed in civilian clothes. Although we had set up a room to do an interview, the General apologized, saying that he first needed to get permission. Abby Abildness of Healing Tree International had arranged this meeting via email. From our first greeting, it was clear her work with the Kurds had earned her great favor. The General said, in effect, "Any friend of Abby's is a friend of mine." These kinds of relationships are invaluable in the Middle East, especially on this Kurdish trip.

When we sat down to discuss the subjects of our interview, the General made a call to his superior. Permission granted. The interview, however, would have to be the following day, he explained, adding that he would be happy to take us to the front lines.

Rising, he invited us outside in the fresh Kurdish air. We gathered at a table next to the hotel pool. Others were enjoying a late evening meal or the ubiquitous tea with sugar. I liked this man—engaging, warm, and eager to make sure our needs were met as his guests. We sat there for nearly two hours discussing the current situation of the Kurds in this year after ISIS. Given such a pleasant atmosphere, one could hardly imagine that a savage Islamic troop lay less than an hour's drive from Dohuk, while we lounged around a pool in peace.

Dohuk is one of Kurdistan's (ancient Assyria's) largest cities, about a two-and-a-half-hour drive west of Kurdistan's capital, Erbil. More than a million people call Dohuk home and after ISIS captured large swaths of northern Iraq, thousands of refugees swelled its population even more. Mountains hug the city on all sides, and the Tigris River runs nearby. Four thousand years of history run through it, too. At one time, the Assyrians, Babylonians, Ottomans and British all vied for this strategic city.

## ROAD TO NO MAN'S LAND

The next day Karzan wants us to meet him right away on the outskirts of the city. We arrange a rendezvous point and head out. I'm in the car with Pastor Majeed, our guide/driver/friend/translator and brother in the Lord. Majeed has been our trusted and invaluable companion on each of our trips to Kurdistan. His love of his people, knowledge of the land and deep faith have carried us through many ordeals. Jonathan Goff, our CBN News cameraman extraordinaire, sits in the back with his gear. Goff is like a MacGyver, who can not only fix most things and solve most problems, but is an artist with his camera.

Karzan is anxious and calls us several times, wondering how long before we arrive. Twenty minutes later, we see his SUV and pull over. He wants one of us to ride with him. I volunteer. Even though he can't speak much English, and my Kurdish is limited to *Pash*—their word for "thank you"—we manage to communicate . . . a little. We're on our way to his section of the line separating his soldiers and ISIS. It's about 3 p.m. and we're racing the clock and the sun.

Soon we're outside the city, passing rolling hills capped with fuzzy, reddish-brown grass, studded with thousands of rocks. We pass a sign—Mosul 45km (kilometers). I assume we're not going to head that way. ISIS controls Mosul. I'm glad the General carries a side arm. I also mentally rehearse what to do if we ever run into an ISIS ambush. I assume the General's gun (I think it's a Glock) will only take us so far. Then I wonder how fast a Land Cruiser can go. How quickly can he shove it into reverse? I know the General is familiar with the lay of the land, and he wouldn't deliberately court unnecessary danger. But we're out in the middle of nowhere, in a gray area between the black of ISIS and the white of the Peshmerga. I have no frame of reference as to how far we've gone, the distance we have yet to cover, or even where we are. Nevertheless, I try and calculate how far we've driven and how far it might be to the front lines.

We pass several checkpoints. At one, we see soldiers wearing helmets, not caps. It's a sign we're getting closer to the front lines and ISIS. I'm struck by how young and boyish one of the soldiers looks, almost out of place for such times as these. We traverse a maze of earthen berms and drive on. This land seems like a no man's land. The terrain is flat now. Feels like the badlands of some Western movie. Desolate. Abandoned. *It's not the end of the world, but you can see it from here,* I muse. We pass several dilapidated billboards. I wonder who those are for. *Who ventures out this far to read them?*

Since only an occasional vehicle comes the other way, most of the time the General cruises down the middle of the road. With the temperature at 41 degrees Celsius or 105 degrees Fahrenheit outside, we're grateful for the comfort of his air-conditioned Land Cruiser.

Haze and sand clutch the horizon. We pass villages. The General points out one called Mamara. More signs for Mosul. We're getting closer.

We ride in silence much of the time or wrestle through the General's broken English: his attempts to communicate; my attempt to interpret. But we make do. We see flocks of sheep, stray dogs and kids beside the road. *Where do they live?* I wonder. *What's their life like?*

Then we pass several villages with different histories. One village had sided with ISIS. Bad choice. It's destroyed. It reminds me of the biblical term *Ichabod*, "the glory has departed." We pass two other abandoned villages. Those people had fled to the relative safety of nearby Dohuk.

We've been on the road now for about 45 minutes. The atmosphere seems eerie, tension-filled. The General continues his descriptions of the area in his broken English: "ISIS and Peshmerga fought here. Twelve Peshmerga died there. That hill, we killed ISIS fighters, ten. Six more died there." Even though the landscape is desolate, it's also blood bought.

This is obviously not a tourist destination. We pass through one village that must have been the site of a major battle. "Over six hundred ISIS fighters died in the battles," the General continues. "They attacked more than thirty times. Of the six hundred, more than one hundred and fifty came from other countries . . ." He drops his voice and mutters, almost to himself, "What kind of power does ISIS have to send foreign fighters over here?"

## MOSUL DAM: WEAPON OF MASS DESTRUCTION

Finally, we see a sign for the Mosul Dam, 2km. A welcome harbinger. One year before, we had attempted to get close to the Mosul Dam. At that time, when ISIS had swept through and swallowed up much of this territory, they'd captured what might have been their biggest weapon of all, Iraq's largest dam. The nightmare scenario for the world has been a terror group getting its hands on a weapon of mass destruction. This dam was a WMD.

Now, just a two-hour drive from Erbil in northern Iraq, ISIS had done just that. When it captured the Mosul Dam, experts knew the group had a new weapon in its terror arsenal. At the time, we'd met with a Kurdish civil engineer Adwa Jaji. He'd told us terrorist control of the dam was a frightening prospect. Why? Because the huge structure, which in the best of times was called "the most dangerous dam in the world," by the U.S. Army Corps of Engineers, represented a ticking time bomb in the hands of ISIS.

"I think now it's too dangerous," Jaji had warned. "Even if it's not exploded by ISIS, the dam would destroy itself because there is nobody to make necessary repairs. The dam is poorly designed and was built on unstable soil that needs periodic infusions of grout to keep it safe. If ISIS fails to maintain the dam, it could burst. And if it gives way, it would send a 60-foot-high wall of water downstream to Mosul that could reach all the way to Baghdad. According to the information we have, maybe 500,000 to 600,000 people could be killed in one day.[1]

The thought was sobering. And even if ISIS did not destroy the dam, the group could have held the country hostage with the threat of an ecological catastrophe.

Yet, in one of the bright spots in an otherwise bleak picture in the summer of 2014, the Peshmerga retook the dam. It proved a significant victory. U.S. airstrikes played a key role in the offensive. The Pentagon announced the military hit a number of ISIS positions near the dam. Now we were grateful to see, up close and personal, the site we'd hoped to see one year before.

Before we reached the dam, however, General Karzan pulled into what was obviously their regional headquarters. We got out and he motioned for us to follow. We passed the sentries and walked into the sandbag-shielded building. The General greeted several other officers, and I guessed by the insignia on their shoulders, he outranked them all. Then he led us into another room where we met his commanding officer, Major General Bahjat Arab.

General Arab met us with a somber, serious gaze. He struck me as a man with a crushing weight on his shoulders. He carried the burden for this area between ISIS and the thousands of people we had just left behind. Most had probably never met him or even knew him. But they could enjoy tea around a hotel pool on a warm summer's evening because of leaders like him and his "rough men with rifles."

## "FIGHTING FOR THE WHOLE WORLD"

Contrary to our expectations, we quickly realized I'd be interviewing General Arab rather than General Karzan. Making a mental adjustment, we began to set up for the interview. Since the setting didn't look very military—a couch with big pillows in a black-and-white checkerboard pattern—I asked the General if we could move to his office. He declined and we sat tight.

We began the interview by asking how the battle was going one year after ISIS.

"There's a big difference from one year ago," General Arab said. "The Peshmerga re-captured many areas from ISIS." (We had seen the evidence in the past hour.) "Don't forget, right now the Peshmerga are fighting for the sake of the whole free world."[2]

"It's very clear: No one stands against ISIS. Look at what happened to the Iraqi army. Look at what happened to them."[3] We found out in a briefing later that when ISIS took over Mosul the previous year, they did so with about 800 men and ran off two Iraqi divisions. While they had already infiltrated the city and co-opted some of the population, their victory was stunning against what some labeled a "checkpoint army."

"No one fought ISIS," he continued. "Only the Peshmerga. So this is why I can assure you, if we leave a place, ISIS will come and take it at once. But we fought a good fight, and this is why the Peshmerga are fighting . . . for the sake of the whole world."[4]

The war veteran painted a sobering picture of ISIS: "If the other people in the world want to know the danger of ISIS, let them come here and go to Mosul. See what happened to the Yazidis or the Christians. . . . ISIS destroyed their culture and history. They only left the history of ISIS and their own people and nation. So the very same thing will happen to the whole world. If we let ISIS go out, they'll destroy everything."[5]

General Arab explained why the Peshmerga suffered early defeats at the hands of ISIS: "We didn't have the weapons, so this is why when ISIS came, we lost the battle. Unfortunately, most of the most advanced and newest weapons were in the hands of ISIS because they took them from the Iraqi army. ISIS fought against the Peshmerga with the weapons they seized."[6]

This weathered veteran blamed the Baghdad government for the lack of advanced weapons. He didn't say so, but it's been U.S. policy to funnel all weapons to the Kurds through Baghdad. Arms sent to Baghdad designated for the Kurds rarely make it. He further confirmed a report we had heard before. Baghdad forbade the Kurds to buy weapons on the open market. "We could have bought weapons from outside of Iraq, but they didn't allow us to do that."[7]

In the face of this lack of sufficient, advanced weaponry, the General described what they had to do to maintain those they already possessed. "Sometimes we have to repair one weapon by using parts from another. This is how we've used the old weapons to fight against ISIS."[8]

He lamented the early exodus of U.S. troops from Iraq in 2011 and what followed. "It was too early for them to leave because they didn't establish control, but they left anyway. They simply should have divided Iraq because the Shiites and the Sunnis cannot live with the Kurds. Even if ISIS disappeared, the Arab Sunnis cannot live with us anymore. All the Arabs look down on us as a second-class nation and a second-class people. We say, 'We are brothers. Let us live in peace.' But they show by their actions that we are *not* brothers."[9]

The General went on to express gratitude to the United States, but with a caveat: "We're very grateful to the people of the United States of America and the government. But we remember what happened in the revolution of 1975. . . ." (At that time, the U.S. abandoned the Kurds in what was called the Algiers Accords. Some historians believe their revolt and hopes for independence collapsed as a result of the U.S. betrayal.)[10] "The American government just set us aside and forsook us," he continued. "We have a Kurdish proverb that says: 'The one who has been bitten by the snake, he is also scared of a black cable.' So we have history with the United States and hope they don't repeat the same experience with the Kurds. We'd love to tell the American people that the Kurds are the only true friends they have in this area."[11]

We ended our interview by telling the General that many Christians both support and pray for the Kurds. He replied: "We will honor your prayers and respect your love for us, and we hope that you can continue to pray for us so God may protect us. Please pray for us to overcome ISIS and also becoming independent." With a chuckle, he added "And pray that Kurdistan becomes the 52nd state of the United States."[12]

With that, the General thanked our team for coming thousands of miles "to take our problems, our issues and our situation to other parts of the world. We appreciate what you are doing."[13]

They allowed me to pray for them, asking God's protection over these generals and the soldiers who shoulder the great responsibility of keeping the free world free. We asked Him for wisdom and strategies for these new friends and allies. Then we offered our goodbyes and headed back to the SUV.

## GARDEN OF EVIL

This time, the General sits in the passenger seat and his driver takes over. Jonathan notices an RPG (Rocket Propelled Grenade) in the back of the SUV.

Within a few turns, we see the massive Mosul Dam. Suddenly we cross the fabled Tigris River.

The Book of Genesis says the river was located near the Garden of Eden: *"Now a river went out of Eden to water the garden, and from there it parted and became four riverheads. The name of the first is Pishon; it is the one which skirts the whole land of Havilah, where there is gold. And the gold of that land is good. Bdellium and the onyx stone are there. The name of the second river is Gihon; it is the one which goes around the whole land of*

*Cush. The name of the third river is Hiddekel (Tigris); it is the one which goes toward the east of Assyria. The fourth river is the Euphrates" (Genesis 2:10-14).*

Yet we're not in paradise. It feels more like the Garden of *Evil.* General Karzan explains that ISIS blew up the bridge over the Tigris. The Peshmerga had to construct a steel span to connect the two concrete sides. "ISIS is like a fire," the General says. "They're not against a specific ethnicity, people or religion. They're against everything."[14]

We speed on our way, crossing through several checkpoints. On the way, he points to a village. "We know some families in this village where the father, brother and sons are with ISIS right now. But what shall we do?"[15]

Not everyone, though, is sympathetic to ISIS. Suddenly we approach an intersection with a number of cars and dozens of people. He explains that these Arabs have come to demonstrate in support of the Peshmerga. With obvious pride, the General says, "They are really very glad to live with the Kurds and under our control. Look at them and how they express their shared life with us."[16]

Many people line the road, several of them waving Kurdish flags. We drive on.

On the way, we pass an area that the General warns is extremely dangerous. He says it was very difficult to recapture this area from ISIS.

After a few more minutes, we slow down and turn right.

Our white SUV Land Cruiser chugs up a steep road chiseled out of the barren Kurdish land. The road is filled with loose stones that look like the kind used in a gravel drive. When we reach the top of the first rise, we can see a second hill up above. It's the base. There are two roads to the top. The General tells his driver to avoid the one closer to the ridge; there could be snipers, he warns.

Thankfully, we take the road more travelled and drive up to the base and through the entrance. The camp is surrounded on all sides by high earthen walls topped with sandbags. We stop, get out and the soldiers come up to greet their General. He cautions us not to take any pictures inside the base; we can only point our cameras away from the camp. They don't want ISIS to get a hold of any information that could harm them.

While the soldiers welcome their commander, the driver takes the time to proudly show us his hand that's missing a finger. He says he lost the finger and also took a bullet to his side during a battle with ISIS. I'm impressed.

We turn to greet the rest of the soldiers, these guys on the front lines.

The General introduces us to the officers of the base and then leads us around a trailer to one side. I notice it's pock-marked with what appears to be holes made by shrapnel. We pass the trailer, and suddenly we see the view from the base. Rimmed by haze and dust, it's a panoramic vista of the front lines. You can see for miles.

We walk along a narrow dirt path to an observation hut. Topped by a steel roof and enclosed on three sides by sandbags, the hut has two small openings, one directly to the front, and another to the side.

It doesn't get much closer to ISIS.

General Karzan explains our view and Majeed interprets. "You know the distance between us and ISIS is only five hundred meters. In some places the distance is a kilometer. The villages that you see belong to ISIS, all of them."[17]

During the General's explanations, we hear two explosions. He explains that they fire mortars a few times a day. "This is the only way they can show they are still active. But any attack will be beaten back, one way or the other. Sometimes they try to attack our position, but we give information to the U.S. so they can strike ISIS from the air. The planes usually come, but if they don't, we will attack. When ISIS attacks our front line, the jihadis believe they are attacking the front line of Europe."[18]

Majeed gives me a studied look. "Do you get what the General is saying? ISIS believes that, as you say, this is the line between the free world and the enemy. . . . This is why when they come to fight against the Peshmerga; they think they are approaching the border of Europe."[19] Even though we're more than one thousand miles from Europe, ISIS sees this remote outpost as Europe itself.

We shoot a quick stand-up:

THIS IS THE FRONT LINE BETWEEN ISIS AND PESHMERGA. ISIS FIGHTERS ARE ABOUT 500 METERS FROM THIS POSITION. MANY SAY THIS IS A KEY SECTOR BECAUSE IT

CONTROLS THE MOSUL DAM. BUT MORE
THAN THAT, IT IS THE BATTLE LINE, THE
FAULT LINE BETWEEN THE FREE WORLD
AND ISIS.[20]

From this overlook, I get the distinct sense that this, indeed, is the front line between the free world and the tyranny of ISIS. Overlooking the sweep of land linking us with ISIS, I pray a quiet prayer that the Peshmerga will hold the line for this free world.

It's time to go. We walk back off the ridge. Someone has arranged a time to sit down for tea behind the pock-marked trailer. There's always time for tea, even on the front lines. However, I still haven't figured out why their tea comes in small, thin glasses with no handles. The tea is usually so hot it burns your fingers before you can get it to your mouth. But it's still refreshing—even on the front lines.

We meet some of the officers. One of them is the soldier who coordinates the air strikes between the Peshmerga and the U.S. He says the air strikes are pivotal in the battle with ISIS. Soon we will be leaving. But before we do, Jonathan and I step back around the corner overlooking ISIS territory. We shoot a stand-up to end our story, using this soldier's final words:

THE PESHMERGA SAY A DECISIVE FACTOR
IN THE BATTLE AGAINST ISIS HAS BEEN
U.S. AIR STRIKES. BUT WITH MORE ARMS,
AMMUNITION, AND HEAVY WEAPONS,
THEY SAY THEY CAN MAKE EVEN MORE
ADVANCES AGAINST THE ISLAMIC STATE.
CHRIS MITCHELL, CBN NEWS, ON THE
FRONT LINES WITH THE KURDISH
PESHMERGA.[21]

As we drive back down the steep hill, I ask the General about the lights that are set up on the ridge just below the observation hut.

"Those lamps light up the hill during the night," he says. "One of ISIS's tactics is to try to infiltrate the base with suicide bombers. We need to see them before they can breach the walls of the base." It's a lesson from this war, which the General sums up in one sentence: "They are fighting to die; we are fighting to live."[22]

## TERROR IN JERUSALEM

Once again, terror struck the heart of Jerusalem at the Damascus Gate on 2/3/16. Three Palestinians terrorists armed with automatic weapons, explosive devices and a will to murder opened fire on two policewoman. One policewoman died, a second was wounded and a city shook from yet another terror attack. Hamas called them heroes destined for Paradise. But it's one more tragic example of Islamic terror striking the free world from the Old City of Jerusalem, the cafes of Paris or offices in the town of San Bernardino.

CBN News Story: "Kurdish Army Holding the Line Against ISIS."

CBN News Story: "Mosul Dam a Ticking Bomb in Terrorists' Hands"

# Back to Makhmur

*"ISIS came into a hospital and told the doctors to remove the kidneys of twenty Kurdish babies. The doctors refused. ISIS then took the doctors to the hospital roof and threw them off."*

*- Kurdish Man's report from Mosul[1]*

*Erbil, Kurdistan*

We're in the heart of Erbil, the capital of Kurdistan, but soon we'll be on our way to a town about a 45-minute drive outside the city. Our destination is Makhmur. In the summer of 2014, it sat at the epicenter of fierce fighting between the Islamic State and the Peshmerga. Back then, we arrived in Makhmur just one day after the Kurdish military secured the city from ISIS. Since then, ISIS and the Peshmerga have wrestled for control of this strategic municipality. Thankfully, the Peshmerga control most of the area around the town. But if ISIS broke the line and captured this key battleground town, from there it's a straight shot to the capital, Erbil, directly into the heart of Kurdistan.

Before we leave Erbil, we pick up Masoud, a Peshmerga sniper. He asked his Kurdish commander if we could meet American volunteers stationed in Makhmur. With his dashing good looks, Masoud looks like he should be cast in a movie. Instead, he's on the front lines with an enemy no more than thirty miles from his home. He brings along his sniper rifle with scope and stashes it in the back. He tells us later its range is about a mile.

We drive through an industrial area on the outskirts of town, and soon Erbil is behind us, Open road lies ahead. On the way, we talk to Masoud about the war. We ask him what ISIS is like.

"I've never seen anything like them in the world," he says, shaking his head. "They are animals! How is it acceptable," he asks, "for them to sell girls as sex slaves? Or take them from town to town, or allow a group of men to have sex with one young girl?" He and the Peshmerga, he says are "fighting for our honor and for our women." He feels that when ISIS is finished with sex slaves in nearby Mosul, they'll try to capture more territory to feed their sexual appetite.

He warns that Erbil itself is riddled with ISIS sleeper cells, just lying in wait for the right opportunity. He describes the temper of the city as frayed, anxious, and on edge. He feels one beheading on the streets of the city would send people scurrying. They have already seen and experienced too much. He hints if Makhmur fell, Erbil would flee.

It's U.S. airstrikes that have held the line, he says. Whenever and wherever ISIS moves, the fighter jets can strike. But he's worried about the winter. During the summer, skies are clear and ISIS's movements are restricted. But when inclement weather comes with its limited visibility, that's when ISIS can attack. He suspects ISIS has plans in the coming months.

Finally, we reach the hill just before Makhmur. This rise offers a panoramic view of the city and stirs up memories from our last visit. We drive down the road framed by two large ridges. In the city, we pass a number of trucks loaded with wheat waiting to dump their golden cargo into the local granary. It's one sign of life in an otherwise deserted town. The main reason for our foray into Makhmur is to meet with some of the American volunteers we've heard who are fighting alongside the Kurdish military. Masoud says they're operating from his base. We pass through town and come to the Peshmerga base. We wind through the security barriers and approach the gate. Just as we arrive, the Americans are on the other side of the gate and just about to leave the base.

We get out and greet them. All of a sudden, we find out the Peshmerga commander didn't tell the Americans we were coming. I explain we're CBN News and ask if we can talk with them. It's clear they don't want to talk. In fact, it feels like they'd rather not be seen. Their leader says he has to get permission from his chief before he can talk. We ask if we can call his boss. "No" comes the curt reply. He takes my phone number and says they'll call us. From the tone of our conversation, I have little to no confidence we'll ever hear from them. With that, they get back in their SUVs and speed away. The whole conversation lasted about two minutes. To this day, the encounter is a mystery.

With that rebuff, we reset our schedule for the day. We head back to the overlook and shoot a stand-up describing some of the challenges the Kurds face:

> THE KURDISH MILITARY HOLD A MORE THAN SIX-HUNDRED-MILE LINE AGAINST ISIS. THAT INCLUDES TOWNS LIKE MAKHMUR BEHIND ME, WHICH CONTROLS ACCESS TO ERBIL, THE CAPITAL OF KURDISTAN.[2]

We also shoot an interview with Masoud about how the Peshmerga are holding up. We wrap up. It's lunchtime and we head back to Erbil. Majeed knows where we can get great kabobs, but we have no way of knowing that we'll soon lose our appetite.

## "BLOODY WOLVES OF ISIS"

Back in the city, we park the SUV and walk down a narrow side road. On the way, we pass a woman and her child. Majeed explains they're refugees from Syria, one more sign of the fractured Middle East. We turn the corner onto a crammed street, navigate the traffic, and step up to the restaurant.

Majeed introduces us to the owner. He's a short, stocky man with a round face, big glasses and a kind, welcoming face. Immediately, I like him. He invites us in. It's not a big place but it's hopping. Several waiters bark out orders. Over in one corner is the kitchen. In the heart of the kitchen is a long tray of hot coals, where the kabobs sizzle and cook. It's the kind of place we relish. No pretense, just good food and fast service—fast food, Kurdish style.

The waiters bring us pickles, tomatoes, olives, and yogurt. These are all part of the one-item menu—just kabobs, side dishes and hot bread. We all order two kabobs. They're delicious! We're also introduced to a spice unique to Kurdistan. It's got a sweet, lemony flavor that adds to the kabobs. We like it so much the owner gives Jonathan and me a bottle as a gift.

After lunch, he comes over and talks about the situation. He's afraid. He tells us his business has fallen by 60 percent. "But I pay my employees every day because they need the money," he says, then leans over and drops his voice. "The city is surrounded by the bloody wolves of ISIS, wolves that don't even care about children." He motions to a customer, who comes over to our table and confirms his statement.

"In Mosul," the customer says, "ISIS came into a hospital and told the doctors to remove the kidneys of twenty Kurdish babies. The doctors refused. ISIS then took the doctors to the hospital roof and threw them off."[2] We sat there, stunned. We couldn't independently verify the story, but it fit ISIS's barbaric modus operandi. It's also why these kinds of stories from a city just fifty miles away are rattling the nerves of the Kurdish population.

We saw that rattling firsthand just one block away from the restaurant. After saying our goodbyes to the owner, we went to videotape the open air market down the street. In the distance, Erbil's ancient Citadel rose above the city. The Citadel is thought to be the oldest continual settlement in the world and estimated to be about seven thousand years old.

On the surface, it looked like any other open air market. It hummed with activity—shopkeepers, shoppers, and workers—even in the 47-degree Celsius or 117-degree Fahrenheit heat. But Majeed said there's another story beneath the surface. He pointed out that much of the furniture spread out around the traffic circle and the appliances for sale were being sold by people trying to leave the country. They need the money. He said some are even selling twenty-five-thousand dollar cars for ten thousand.

It's quiet desperation.

## PRO-AMERICA IN THE MIDDLE EAST

Across town and earlier in the week, we heard from two retired U.S. war veterans that the Kurds need more help to quench that gloom, especially as they man the frontline of the free world.

We met one of them, retired U.S. Colonel Richard Naab at the oil company office, where he now works as a consultant. We sat down in the company's conference room. I enjoyed Naab's direct, no-nonsense manner. He struck me as someone you'd want on your side in a battle. His history with the Kurds goes back nearly a quarter century. In 1991, Naab took part in "'Operation Provide Comfort,' a series of U.S. operations aimed at defending Iraqi

Kurds fleeing their homes in the aftermath of the First Gulf War."[3] That's when he first recognized the special character of the Kurds.

"They're good people and very good people to have in your corner. And they're very important for this region. They're very loving, giving, dedicated people. I admire their strength of character, their courage. They're tough. I admire their strength of purpose. They've been through some tough times. And they won't give up."[4]

## HE SAYS THEY ADMIRE AMERICA.

"They love America more than I think some Americans do. The Kurds are our friends. They need our help. They love America, and we're letting them down. We should be full force with them."[5]

Naab believes that by helping the Kurds, the U.S. would be helping itself. "These people are fighting for their lives. And in a way they're fighting for our future lives, because if they can kill this radical Islam here, it doesn't migrate to the States."[6] Yet Naab knows the hardship his friends face. With limited equipment and stretched lines, the Peshmerga face an implacable foe on a more than six-hundred-mile front. That front stretches all the way from deep inside Iraq to the east and along the Syrian Turkish border to the west. He says, "It's a lot of ground to hold. The Kurds simply need better weapons to fight ISIS."[7]

That's a theme we've heard often, a theme echoed by Retired General Jay Garner when we sat down with him. Garner, too, has a long history with the Kurdish people. He "first got to know the Kurds during his stint as Commanding General, Joint Task Force Bravo during Operation Provide Comfort in northern Iraq after Desert Storm."[8] During that Operation, he worked with Colonel Naab.

He says, Kurdistan in the heart of the Middle East, is a General's dream: "Think about it: You have a country of about four or five million people who are totally pro-American, more so than we're pro-American. They're in one of the most strategic locations in the world in the Middle East for us. To the east is our enemy Iran. To the south is our enemy Shiite Iraq. To the west is our enemy Syria. And to the north is what we call a NATO ally, Turkey, which gives us great lines of communication. For a military guy, it's a military guy's dream. You're in a perfect place where you can strike out of there and hit any of your enemies, and you have support from your ally to the north. And on top of that, it's oil-rich, which means something. Why we don't look at that strategically and wrap our arms around that is beyond me."[9]

Garner points out U.S. air power turned the tide of the battle and is still pivotal in the fight against ISIS. What hasn't happened is delivery of the weapons and equipment the Kurds need in the trenches. For example, he described a typical ISIS attack.

"What happens is ISIS takes like a dump truck, and they pack it with explosives and put a driver in it. In front of the truck, they weld sheets of metal six to eight inches apart. And so when they start driving toward the Peshmerga lines, the heaviest thing the Peshmerga have is an RPG, which is a chemical round. And you fire that RPG and it hits that first piece of metal and it burns through. It hits the second piece of metal and starts breaking up the chemical jet. It hits the third piece of metal and it dissipates. So it never penetrates in the truck and the truck gets right in the lines. And the suicide driver detonates it, and it causes havoc in the lines of the Peshmerga. So we could give them our systems like our Javelin or our Tow (both anti-tank weapons) and things like that which would destroy those (trucks). But why we don't do that, I don't understand."[10]

He adds they need heavy machine guns and mobility. With more than six hundred miles of front lines to cover, he says they need a rapid reaction force to respond to a well-coordinated ISIS attack. Armored Humvees, armored personnel carriers and what's called an MWRAP (Mine-Resistant Ambush-Protected) vehicle designed to withstand IEDs (improvised explosive devices) could help even the battlefield. He added these are the same kind of vehicles the U.S. army is destroying in nearby Afghanistan as part of its withdrawal.

But why would the U.S. and its allies fail to arm the Kurds, the most motivated and capable ground force facing the Islamic State? One Middle East analyst says to look toward Iran. "Under the administration, the strategic assumption of U.S. Middle East policy is that the U.S. should strengthen and curry favor with Iran. Iran fears an independent Kurdistan in Iraq and Syria because of the likely impact such a state will have on Iran's large Kurdish minority. Consequently, the U.S. is refusing to directly arm the Kurds in their war against Islamic State in Iraq and Syria."[11]

Con Coughlin, the defense editor from *The Telegraph*, reported the U.S. blocked Middle East allies from flying weapons directly to the Kurds. "High-level officials from Gulf and other states have told this newspaper that all attempts to persuade Mr. Obama of the need to arm the Kurds directly as part of more vigorous plans to take on the Islamic State of Iraq and the Levant (ISIL) have failed."[12]

It's a policy he reports that angered at least one Arab government official: "If the Americans and the West are not prepared to do anything serious about defeating ISIL, then we will have to find new ways of dealing with the threat. With ISIL making ground all the time, we simply cannot afford to wait for Washington to wake up to the enormity of the threat we face."[13]

Couglin points out the Peshmerga are successful in their fight against ISIL. "But they are doing so with a makeshift armory.

Millions of pounds worth of weapons have been bought by a number of European countries to arm the Kurds, but American commanders, who are overseeing all military operations against ISIL, are blocking the arms transfers."[14]

Ironically, Garner says, the Peshmerga face one of the best-equipped armies in the world, thanks in part to the U.S. and Russia. "We equipped the Iraqi Army with some of the most modern equipment in the world. And they fled. They had less than a thousand people enter Iraq last August and four divisions—four divisions, 65,000 Iraqis—fled and left their equipment on the ground: new tanks, new artillery pieces, new Bradleys (fighting vehicles). I mean, overnight we made ISIS the best-armed terrorist organization in the world; in fact, one of the best-armed armies in the world. A similar thing happened to them in Syria where the Syrians ran, and they got all the Russian equipment the Russians had given. They came here and the Iraqis ran; they got all the modern American equipment. So they have the best of both East and West, in terms of military equipment. And the only people stopping that right now, as I said, is the Peshmerga . . . so we ought to give that Peshmerga force the weapons they need to fight ISIS."[15]

Since ISIS plunged deep into northern Iraq, the Peshmerga fought back to a stalemate. But Naab says the U.S.-led coalition can't win the war from the air alone.

"No, we're not winning yet. You can't destroy an insurgency with air power only. You just can't. You have to do it like the YPG (Kurdish People's Defense Units) are doing it. Go door to door. You know, root 'em out. It's the only way. I thought we'd learned that in Vietnam. You can't do it with bombs, in sort of an antiseptic warfare. You can't do it."[16]

He says Americans need to know who their friends are in the Middle East. "I hope Americans understand we have some real friends here, and we don't want to betray them again. We pulled the rug from underneath them before. Let's not do that again."[17]

Garner says Iraq and Syria are like Humpty Dumpty. They will never go back together again. "It's lunacy to believe that you could put Iraq back together again. To put it back together again and expect different results is fantasy. What I think you're going to have for a long period of time is this: You're going to have an Iranian part of Iraq—that's a Shiite Iraq. You're going to have an ISIS caliphate part of Iraq—that's Sunni Iraq, and you're going to have an independent Kurdistan. And the sooner we recognize that and understand that and wrap our arms around the Kurds and support them, the better off we'll be."[18]

It might help keep the "bloody wolves of ISIS" at bay.

CBN News Story: "Military Experts: Want to defeat ISIS? Arm the Kurds"

# ISIS:

## Inside the Caliphate

*"They're there for one reason and one reason only: to die for the caliphate and usher in a world without infidels. That's their strategy, and it's been that way since the seventh century. So do you really think that a few Special Forces teams are gonna put a dent in that?"*

~ Peter Quinn, Homeland[1]

Jonathan and I, along with three others, drove up to the entrance of one of the region's best private security companies. Taking note of the guards and other security arrangements, I could immediately tell these guys were good. Really good! With bullet-proof vests, automatic weapons at the ready, and everyone clear-eyed and at attention, they all looked the part. When our vehicle stopped for the security check, I noticed there were no dogs to sniff for explosives or mirrors to check underneath the car, which was typical at other checkpoints. Later we found out they'd scanned the underside of our SUV as we waited. They compared that scan with a computer analysis of the underside of the make, model and year of the same vehicle. If any irregularities were discovered—like a bomb—they would know instantly.

We came around to the entrance where the company's chief of security greeted us. A former Special Forces alumnus, he led us inside the highly protected building. Everything inside, except for the offices, was covered by cameras. In a briefing room, where a floor-to-ceiling map covered the wall, he introduced us to their staff intelligence expert. The expert—with years of experience in the region—proceeded to give us an update on the current battle between the Islamic State and the Peshmerga, the Kurdish military. Here's one give-and-take:

> "IS (Islamic State) may launch spoiling attacks anywhere in this sector which they did yesterday. They attacked south of Dibbis ... they attacked Bashir and they attacked somewhere in the Dokuk sector."
>
> 'Were they successful?'
>
> 'Those were spoiling attacks, in my estimation.'"[2]

Black ISIS flags dotted one side of the battle line. On the other side, Kurdish flags represented Peshmerga positions. ISIS controlled the major cities of Sinjar, Tall Afar and Mosul. Kurdish centers of Duhok, Erbil, Kirkuk and Makhmur lay in the hands of the Peshmerga. I can't divulge who gave the briefing, where it was, or who was with Jonathan and me. Yet the briefing provided an up-to-the-minute analysis of the skirmishes along the more than six-hundred-mile front.

The map looked like one you might see in a World War II movie, with Nazi insignias on one side and U.S. and Allied flags on the other. More than seventy years ago, the might of Nazi Germany, with aspirations of worldwide domination, arrayed itself against the Allied nations contending for the freedom of Western civilization. Now ISIS has inherited the ignominious mantle of the Nazis, trying to snuff out liberty around the globe.

When ISIS captured Mosul in the summer of 2014, the world woke up to this Islamic predator. They might have seen it coming. After all, ISIS captured the strategic and well-known town of Fallujah in January of 2014. Perhaps President Obama's comment comparing them to a "JV team" after that victory helped keep the world asleep. But when hundreds of thousands fled ISIS, the alarm clock of their scourge across Syria and Iraq could not be ignored. By the summer of 2015, ISIS controlled land the size of Great Britain with an estimated 7 to 9 million people under their control.

But exactly who is ISIS and what do they want?

## THE INFIDEL'S GUIDE TO ISIS

It would seem to be an easy question, but Islamic scholar Robert Spencer says denial of the true nature of ISIS is blinding many in the West to the real answer. That's why he wrote the book, *The Complete Infidel's Guide to ISIS*. I asked Spencer about that book on our weekly TV "Jerusalem Dateline" program. He explained that the overwhelming majority of Western leaders on both sides of the Atlantic insist that ISIS is not Islamic. "I think there is so much misinformation and disinformation about ISIS at the highest level that it's hamstringing our ability to deal with it. And it's a universal thing. It's not just the President of the United States who says ISIS has nothing to do with Islam, but the entire government, the opposition party, the Prime Minister of Great Britain, virtually every authority in the Western world is in denial."[3]

U.S. President Barack Obama, however, issued perhaps the most famous denial. He addressed the American people on September 10, 2014, declaring, "Now let's make two things clear: ISIL is not 'Islamic.' No religion condones the killing of innocents. And the vast majority of ISIL's victims have been Muslim. And ISIL is certainly not a state."[4]

But others disagreed. For example, following the president's address, a man with a unique insight into this issue begged to differ. His name was Brother Rachid and he brought impeccable credentials to the debate. He grew up in Morocco and, with his Middle Eastern upbringing and Islamic education, he respectfully corrected the president in a rebuttal posted on YouTube:

> Dear Mr. President, with all due respect, sir, I must tell you that you are wrong about ISIL. You said that ISIL speaks for no religion. I'm a former Muslim. My Dad is an Imam. I spent more than twenty years studying Islam. I hold a Bachelor's degree in religious studies. And I'm in the middle of my Master's degree in terrorism studies. I can tell you with

confidence that ISIL speaks for Islam. Allow me to correct you, Mr. President, ISIL is a Muslim organization. Its name stands for Islamic State, so even the name suggests that it is an Islamic movement.

Their leader, Abu Bakr al-Baghdadi, holds a PhD in Islamic studies. I doubt you know Islam better than he does. He was a preacher and a religious leader in one of the local mosques in Baghdad. ISIL's ten thousand members are all Muslims. None of them are from any other religion. They come from different countries and have one common denominator—Islam. They are following Islam's prophet Muhammad in every detail ... ISIL is just one symptom. If it disappears, other ISILs will be born under different names. You might ask then: Why does ISIL kill other Muslims? The answer is that they consider them infidels, not Muslims. Do you know that all four schools in Islam agree that if a Muslim stops praying, he should be asked to repent and if he does not, he should be killed? Do you know Muhammad tried to burn his own companions when they stopped coming to prayers? So anything that qualifies a Muslim to be an infidel can be a reason for killing him, even neglecting to pray (*Sahih Muslim Book 5, Hadith* 321, http://sunnah.com/muslim/5/321).[5]

Into this debate fraught with political correctness, Graeme Wood of *The Atlantic* wrote a timely and at the time controversial article called "What ISIS Really Wants." His research was exhaustive: "I read every ISIS statement I could find, including fatwas and tweets and road signs, and I front-loaded my mornings with execution videos in hopes that by bedtime I'd have forgotten enough of the imagery to sleep without nightmares. I picked through every spoken or written word in search of signals of what ISIS cares about and how its members justify their violence. I also asked a small group of its most doctrinaire overseas supporters for guidance, and they obliged."[6]

After his extensive research, he concluded:

The reality is that the Islamic State is Islamic. Very Islamic. Yes, it has attracted psychopaths and adventure-seekers, drawn largely from the disaffected populations of the Middle East and Europe. But the religion preached by its most ardent followers derives from coherent and even learned interpretations of Islam.[7]

Wood found that ISIS followed the pattern set by Islam's founder Muhammad.

> Virtually every major decision and law promulgated by the Islamic State adheres to what it calls, in its press and pronouncements, and on its billboards, license plates, stationery, and coins, "the Prophetic methodology," which means following the prophecy and example of Muhammad, in punctilious detail.[8]

The question—Is ISIS Islamic?—is central for the enemy, the West, and the world. While many Muslims abhor and reject ISIS, others do not, with devastating consequences. One person who has seen the human wreckage left in the Middle East by ISIS is Turkish-born Sister Hatune Dogan. She traveled to the United States to warn Americans and send them a wakeup call. She told CBN News Terrorism Expert Erick Stakelbeck:

> We know that in Islam, there is no democracy. Islam and democracy are opposite, like black and white. And I hope America will understand. America today has the power that they can stop this disaster on the earth, with other Western countries. I'm not coming here for a holiday. I'm coming here to bring a voice to the voiceless so that the world can hear their voice. They don't have a voice. I am the channel for them.[9]

She went on to expose the ultimate goal of ISIS:

> The mission of (Abu Bakr) Baghdadi, of ISIS, is to convert the world completely to the Islamic religion and bring them to Dar Al Salaam (House of Peace), as they call it. And Islam is not peace, please. Whoever says ISIS has no connection to Islam or something like this is, he's a liar. ISIS is Islam; Islam is ISIS.[10]

## ISIS AND THE CALIPHATE

The signature moment for ISIS came on July 5, 2014. The head of ISIS, Al-Baghdadi, climbed the stairs of the minbar (pulpit) in the Great Mosque of al-Nuri in Mosul. He addressed the waiting faithful, announced the formation of a new Islamic Caliphate, and made history. Al-Baghdadi studied Islamic history, claimed to be the descendent of the Islam's Prophet Mohammed, and earned the nickname "jihadist philosopher." He declared himself "Caliph Ibrahim," the leader of the Umma, the Muslim community. He also renamed ISIS (Islamic State of Iraq and Syria) as the Islamic State.

Al-Baghdadi's declaration sent shockwaves throughout the Middle East. When I heard the news, I knew this was a significant moment. For nearly one hundred years, many Muslims dreamed of the restored caliphate. One Islamic analyst told me, "It is their dream, but it will not happen." Now it was unfolding before the eyes of the world.

Here's some of what Baghdadi said on that fateful day:

O Muslims everywhere, glad tidings to you and expect good. Raise your head high, for today—by Allah's grace—you have a state and caliphate, which will return your dignity, might, rights, and leadership. It is a state where the Arab and non-Arab, the white man and black man, the Easterner and Westerner are all brothers. It is the caliphate that gathered the Caucasian, Indian, Chinese, Shami, Iraqi, Yemeni, Egyptian, Maghribi (North African), American, French, German, and Australian. . . .Therefore, rush, O Muslims, to your state.[11]

What then is a caliphate? Robert Spencer writes,

"The caliphate in Islamic theology is the Islamic nation, embodying the supranational unity of the Muslim community worldwide under a single leader, the caliph, or 'successor'—that is, the successor of Mohammad as the spiritual, political, and military leader of the Muslims."[12] He adds: "As the successor of Mohammad, the caliph does not hold the Prophet's status as an exemplar, but he does command the obedience of all Muslims, and loyalty to him transcends all ethnic and national loyalties."[13]

This fealty above and beyond national allegiance has eclipsed the luster America, Europe, and other Western countries have had in the hearts and minds of a number of Muslims.

"ISIS is quintessentially Islamic. It's not just an Islamic group. It styles itself as being THE Islamic group, the caliphate. They are guided by the example of Mohammad and the teachings of the Quran which mandate warfare against and subjugation of unbelievers. The only earthly authority to which any Muslim owes allegiance according to Sunni Muslim theology is to the caliph. This has proven already to be an extraordinary powerful claim."[14]

The declaration of the caliphate rang out like a siren song to Muslims worldwide.

## EXPANSION OF THE CALIPHATE

While some quarters of the Muslim world rejected Baghdadi's declaration, others saw his announcement as the fulfillment of their dreams. It inspired Islamic groups from Afghanistan to Yemen, including Nigeria's infamous terror group Boko Haram, to pledge allegiance to the new caliph and his caliphate. These pledges exponentially spread the influence of ISIS throughout the Middle East and Africa. Lt. General Vincent Stewart, head of the Defense Intelligence Agency, presented a sobering assessment of the spread of the Islamic State: "Particularly concerning has been the spread of ISIL beyond Syria and Iraq. With affiliates in Algeria, Egypt, Libya, the group is beginning to assemble a growing international footprint that includes ungoverned and under-governed areas."[15]

Not only did they acquire franchises and the allegiance of Islamic groups throughout Africa and the Middle East, some saw their ideas hemorrhage throughout the region like a disease. The general director of the Palestinian branch of The Bible Society believed ISIS might have inspired violence in Jerusalem and the Palestinian territories. He said, "The dark ideology of ISIS is spreading all over the region like cancer."[16]

In just more than a year, this cancer both spread and metastasized.

"Last year, fighters belonging to the Islamic State in Iraq and the Levant (ISIL), a group once part of the same organization responsible for the 9/11 attacks stormed into Iraq, conquered half that country, declared itself both a state and a Caliphate and set about to slaughter and enslave thousands of Christians, Shi'a, and members of Islamic minority sects. Fifteen months later, ISIL's influence has spread far beyond the Levant and Mesopotamia. A thousand foreign recruits converge monthly on its operational cynosure. Hailing from some fifty countries. They exceed by a factor of ten the average monthly flow of foreign fighters to Iraq at even the height of the war there a decade ago. . . . The cumulative effect has been that we've stood on the sidelines as a new, more pernicious hybrid threat has emerged—a threat that erodes any meaningful distinction between terrorism, insurgency and limited conventional warfare. **ISIL is something the world has never seen before."**[17]

It's true the world has never before seen a group like ISIS. They control vast amounts of land, oversee four million people in Iraq and another four to five million in Syria. These eight to nine million make up their main recruiting base. Ninety percent of their recruits come from Iraq and Syria, while the more highly publicized disenfranchised and radicalized youth come from surrounding Middle East countries and the West. And while they recruit, they also get down to the business of governing. "Once in control, the Islamic State imposes strict Sharia law. But unlike some other jihadist groups, it seeks to actively govern, providing services like water, roads and a judicial system."[18] And they are maintaining their financial equilibrium. "The Islamic State takes in more than $1 million per day in extortion and taxation."[19] "The Islamic State's oil infrastructure, especially refineries, has been targeted by the United States-led airstrikes. Oil revenue has fallen to about $2 million per week, but the group is not dependent on oil income."[20]

In terms of fighters on the battlefield, estimates vary, but some put the number at between thirty-five and fifty-five thousand actual fighters. They're fighting now as light mobile infantry, not just like guerrilla terrorists. In sum, they are the largest, wealthiest terror group ever in history.

## ATROCITIES IN THE NAME OF ISLAM

This largest, wealthiest terror group in history has sent mind-numbing and heart-stopping videos of the barbaric atrocities. No one is spared, the young or the old. Here are just two from a myriad of examples:

Islamic State militants beheaded 81-year-old Kahled al-Assad, one of Syria's most prominent antiquities scholars in the ancient town of Palmyra, then strapped his body from one of the town's Roman columns.[21]

For this and the copious other beheadings, ISIS cites two verses from the Quran: "Your (Mohammad's) Lord revealed to the angels: 'I am with you, give the believers firmness; I shall put terror into the hearts of the disbelievers. Strike above their necks and strike their fingertips"[22] (Sura 8:12). "So, when you meet those who disbelieve, smite (their) necks till you have killed or wounded many of them" (Sura 47:4).[23]

Beheading is so ingrained in the religious culture of ISIS; they are passing it on to the next generation, even toddlers. One ISIS video "shows a very young child dressed in signature Islamic State gear, brandishing a large knife and beheading a teddy bear. The child receives kudos and encouragement from an adult in the background."[24]

ISIS has also resurrected the practice of crucifixions:

Two boys under the age of 18 were crucified by Islamic State in the streets of the Syrian city of al-Mayadin for not observing the laws of Ramadan, the Syrian Observatory for Human Rights reported. . . . The children, who were charged with the crime of 'not fasting on Ramadan,' had placards around their necks announcing their crime was committed 'with no religious justification' … the boys had reportedly been caught eating.[25]

They cite Sura 5:33 from the Quran as their religious justification: "Those who wage war against God and His Messenger and strive to spread corruption in the land should be punished by

death, crucifixion, the amputation of an alternate hand and foot
or banishment from the land: a disgrace for them in this world,
and then a terrible punishment in the Hereafter" (*The Qur'an*, Ox-
ford UP, 2004).[26]

## ISIS'S TO-DO LIST

But these atrocities are just the beginning of their to-do
list. Intelligence officials discovered a secret Islamic State document. The screed compares to Hitler's *Mein Kampf*. It's called, "A
Brief History of the Islamic State Caliphate (ISC), The Caliphate
According to the Prophet" and "lays out their intent, their goals
and objectives, a red flag to which we must pay attention. . . .The
document serves as a Nazi-like recruiting pitch that attempts to
unite dozens of factions of the Pakistani and Afghan Taliban into a
single army of terror. It includes a never-before-seen history of the
Islamic State, details chilling future battle plans, and urges al-Qaeda to join Islamic State."[27] Its tone is direct: "Accept the fact that
this caliphate will survive and prosper until it takes over the entire
world and beheads every last person that rebels against Allah. This
is the bitter truth, swallow it."[28]

They also revealed a six-phase battle plan to "end the
world":

• **Phase 1 "Awakening" 2000–2003**: Islamic State calls
for "a major operation against the U.S. to provoke a crusade against
Islam."

• **Phase 2 "Shock and Awe" 2004–2006**: Islamic State
will lure U.S. into multiple theatres of war, including cyber-at-
tacks, and establish charities across the Muslim and Arab world to
support terrorism.

• **Phase 3 "Self-reliance" 2007–2010**: Islamic State will
create "interference" with Iraq's neighboring states with particular
focus on Syria.

• **Phase 4 "Reaping/extortion/receiving" 2010–2013**:
Islamic State will attack "U.S. and Western interests" to destroy
their economy and replace the dollar with silver and gold and expose Muslim governments' relations with Israel and the U.S.

• **Phase 5 "Declaring the Caliphate" 2013–2016**: Not much detail offered here. The document just says, "The Caliphate According to The Prophet."

• **Phase 6 "Open Warfare" 2017–2020**: Islamic State predicts faith will clash with non-believers and "Allah will grant victory to the believers after which peace will reign on earth."[29]

Rabbi Abraham of the Simon Wiesenthal Center for Human Rights warned: "We did a lousy job predicting what Hitler was going to do in the 1920s, 1930s—honestly, we blew it. . . . It's hard to take seriously or believe that such hatred was real or would be possible. They made jokes about Jews, degraded Jews, but nobody believed that they would be capable of what they were saying. So now, when groups, like [Islamic State] come along and say they are going to do A, B, and C, you have to take them for their word."[30]

Others feel the West needs to take ISIS at their word in regard to weapons of mass destruction. German journalist Jurgen Todenhofer spent ten days with ISIS and lived to tell his tale. He came out with this chilling warning: "The terrorists plan on killing several hundred million people. The West is drastically underestimating the power of ISIS. ISIS intends to get its hands on nuclear weapons." He called the group "a nuclear tsunami preparing the largest religious cleansing in history."[31] According to Australia's foreign minister, ISIS is taking steps toward that goal. She reports, "ISIS has seized enough radioactive material from government facilities to suggest it has the capacity to build a large and devastating 'dirty bomb.'"[32]

## AN INCONVENIENT TRUTH

It is an inconvenient truth that the world is facing an Islamic group bent on world domination with a thirst for WMDs and at war with the West. Yet our current leadership doesn't seem to employ the first maxim of this or any war: KNOW YOUR ENEMY! They refuse to recognize the religious context our enemies employ in waging this war.

A scene from the Showtime TV series called *Homeland* brought that reality into sharp focus. Peter Quinn leads a special ops team on the ground inside Syria. He returns to Washington to brief his superiors. He sits at the head of a large conference room filled with military brass and his civilian superiors, while his boss grills him about the "strategy":

BOSS: Our strategy working?

QUINN: What strategy? Tell me what the strategy is. I'll tell you if it's working. (Silence) See, that right there is the problem, because they – they have a strategy. They're gathering right now in Raqqa by the tens of thousands. Hidden in the civilian population, cleaning their weapons, and they know exactly why they're there.

BOSS: Why is that?

QUINN: They call it the end times. What do you think the beheadings are about? The crucifixions in *Deir Hafer*, the revival of slavery, you think they make this (bleep) up? It's all in the book, their (bleep) book, the only book they ever read. They read it all the time. They never stop. They're there for one reason and one reason only: to die for the caliphate and usher in a world without infidels. That's their strategy, and it's been that way since the seventh century. So do you really think that a few Special Forces teams are gonna put a dent in that?

BOSS: Well, what would you do?

QUINN: You're offering me a promotion?

BOSS: I'm offering you a hypothetical.

QUINN: Two-hundred thousand American troops on the ground indefinitely to provide security and support for an equal number of doctors and elementary schoolteachers.

BOSS: Well, that's not going to happen.

QUINN: Then I better get back there.

BOSS: What else? What else would make a difference?

QUINN: Hit reset.

BOSS: Meaning what?

QUINN: Meaning, pound Raqqa into a parking lot.[33]

We're witnessing seventh-century Islam reborn in an army with twenty-first century weapons. This resurrected army is marrying state-of-the-art social media technology to spread its propaganda to a global audience. They are at war with us and the stakes are no less than what the world faced during World War II. As world-renowned Islamic scholar Bernard Lewis once told me: "What's at stake is the survival of our civilization."[34]

CBN News Story: "Nun: 'Islam is ISIS. Whoever Says Otherwise Is a Liar'"

# The Siren Song of
# ISIS

*"My son said, 'They told us beautiful women,
money, nice cars, fancy villas, the Garden of Eden.
But there's nothing of that.'"*

~ Said Musallam, father of a 19-year-old executed by ISIS[1]

We kept looking for the address. It wasn't easy to find. Jonathan Goff, Julie Stahl, and I drove into Neve Yaakov, an unfamiliar Jerusalem neighborhood. I've been in most every area of the city, but this section baffled me. What made it more difficult was the fact that all the apartment buildings looked alike. They were alike! The approaching darkness didn't help.

Finally, we found the address of the apartment building— our elusive destination. We had come to interview a grieving man and witness a family in mourning. We walked from the parking lot, around the building, and up to the entrance. A death notice greeted us at the front door. The building resembled the kind of apartment buildings found throughout the city—a bit run down, spartan, no frills. We walked up the stairs, knocked on the apartment door, and stepped into a cloud of gloom.

We pushed our way through the gloom. Inside, I cringed a bit. I would have traded this story for a covered dish and sympathy. We didn't have a covered dish with us, but we did bring sympathy.

People crammed the small living room. A picture of the deceased hung on the wall. Women stood in the kitchen, eying this latest press contingent. The family in this cramped apartment had drawn journalists from around the world. Men stuffed the couch from one arm rest to the other. The man of the house rose. He greeted us as he had so many other members of the press before. In spite of the fact that we were meeting for the first time under these difficult circumstances, I hoped we could offer some comfort.

His name was Said Musallam. *Said* means "happy" in Arabic, but now sadness clung to his shoulders like an unwelcome cape. He worked as a bus driver for Egged, Israel's national bus company. The men on the couch were colleagues. These Jewish men came to stand with Said and his Muslim family. When we arrived, they stood up, offered their condolences to their co-worker, kissed him on both cheeks, and departed.

When they left, we sat down with Said, set up our camera, and began our interview. Said repeated the story he had already told a number of times that day. In the background, I spotted Said's wife, casting furtive glances in our direction. She wore the same sad yoke as her husband. Her body language blared she wanted no part of this or any other interview. The wound burrowed too deep. She disappeared into the back section of the apartment where more family members clustered.

Bleary-eyed and unshaven, Said recited his dreadful tale.

During his bus route, he had received a call. "Did you see the news?" someone asked. He had not. Then someone sent him a picture. When he saw the picture, he immediately knew it was over. The picture showed his son Mohammad in an orange jumpsuit. "I already knew from watching television that this is the uniform they use when they're going to kill somebody."[2]

The picture came from a thirteen-minute ISIS video. In grisly detail, it documented Said's son's last few moments on earth. His execution spelled the end of a story tragically repeated in Jerusalem, throughout the Middle East, and around the world.

Said told us ISIS used the Internet to lure and deceive their son into joining their cause.

He fell prey to the siren song of ISIS.

"My son said, 'They told us beautiful women, money, nice cars, fancy villas, the Garden of Eden. But there's nothing of that. They hardly give us money to buy food in the village. So I want to return home'."[3]

Home for Mohammad meant Neve Yaacov, a mixed Jewish-Arab neighborhood in Jerusalem. Inside that home, his parents didn't know what dark ISIS influences had begun to penetrate his 19-year-old mind. ISIS hooked Mohammad with dreams of the caliphate and reeled in this impressionable young man to its death cult. Without telling his family, Mohammad flew to Istanbul, crossed the Turkish border into Syria, and joined ISIS. Soon his dreams spun into a nightmare.

When the ISIS promises mutated into lies, he called home from Raqqa, the capital of the Islamic State, and plotted his escape. Said sent him money to finance the breakout. It didn't help. Homeward-bound and tantalizingly close to freedom, ISIS captured Mohammad at a Turkish checkpoint. It was then Said saw his son in that infamous orange jumpsuit.

They accused him of being a spy for the Mossad, Israel's spy agency. Sitting there in his fog of grief, Said denied the accusation. "Mohammad is a good man. He doesn't work with the Shin Bet or the Mossad. There's nothing like this. He's a little kid. ISIS said that about him because he wanted to return to his Dad and to Israel."[4] In fact, Israel's Defense Minister Moshe Ya'alon took the unusual public step of denying Mohammad spied for Israel.

The misled 19-year-old met his doom at the hands of a 12-year-old boy. ISIS called him one of the "cubs of the caliphate." He shot Mohammad in the head, then three more times while crying "Allah Akbar" ("Allah is greatest"). An older ISIS fighter then boasted, "Here are the young lions of the Khilafah (Caliphate). They will kill the one sent by the foolish Mossad to spy on the secrets of the mujahidin and the Muslims." In the video, other fighters bragged, "We are looking towards Jerusalem. We will liberate Jerusalem from your filth, by Allah's permission. Today we say to you the Islamic conquests have begun and the Jews have become frightened because the promise is near." They encouraged others to attack Mossad agents: "We've revealed to you some of the names and pictures of the spies in Jerusalem and so make those who recruited them see their blood flow."[5]

ISIS reveled in Mohammad's blood and trumpeted their victory. Earlier in the video, Mohammad "confessed" and described how the Mossad recruited him. In the February issue of Dabiq, their monthly magazine, they featured an interview with Mohammad. His father said, "They did not want to let him leave because if he comes back, he might be caught by the Israelis and tell them what he had seen. So they wanted to get rid of him."[6]

Near the end of our interview, Said sent a warning to moms and dads worldwide. "My wife and I both say to everyone to watch their kids' computers and their phones and check them all the time. Check who they're talking to and who they're with. Check them all the time."

As we left, Said showed us a flattering picture of his son, his features glimmering with promise. On Said's face, I could see a father's pride riddled with heartache. He had wanted his son home. Now the lifeless body lay in some unknown Syrian field.

Tragically, the warning for his Mohammad came too late.

## THE MELODY OF ISIS

Like many young Arabs, Mohammad got swept up by the Internet propaganda and the growing influence of ISIS in places like Gaza and the West Bank. Israel's Shin Bet security service and police believe that more than thirty Israeli Arabs have joined the Islamic State in the last two years.[7] But it's not just Israel; it's a worldwide phenomenon. According to the 2015 "Global Terrorism Index" published by the Institute for Economics and Peace:

The flow of foreign fighters into Iraq and Syria continued in 2014 and 2015. The current estimates are that since 2011 between 25,000 and 30,000 fighters from 100 different countries have arrived in Iraq and Syria. The flow of foreign fighters is still high with estimates suggesting that over 7,000 new recruits arrived in the first half of 2015. This highlights the attraction of these jihadists groups is still strong.[8]

What drives these thousands of men and women to migrate to this ISIS dungeon of darkness? What's the melody playing in this Islamic siren song?

Part of that answer lies in that history-making summer of 2014 when the ISIS song rose to an oracle of triumph and the caliphate was born. Al-Baghdadi's declaration of the caliphate struck a global harmony. It's hard to overestimate how potent a song he created in the minds of many Muslims throughout the world. His announcement marked the first caliphate since 1924. In 1517, the Ottoman Empire established the last caliphate that lasted for more than four hundred years. Caliphs ruled from its seat of power, Istanbul at the time. Successful caliphs sat in the Topkapi Palace overlooking the Straits of Bosporus, the gateway from East to West. For centuries, they presided over a vast empire. But in 1924, Turkey's President Kemal Ataturk, in a move designed to create a secular— not Islamic—state, abolished the caliphate. Since then, the dream has remained just that . . . a dream.

In our interview from our Jerusalem studio, Robert Spencer, the author of *The Complete Infidel's Guide to ISIS*, told me the declaration of the caliphate earned the devotion of many Muslims around the world. The longer it exists; it continues to transmit a song with a classical Islamic theme. "They do say this is the perfect Islamic state. This is the Islamic State where Islamic law is fully in effect. Nowhere else in the world can that be said. This is the Islamic State where there is the caliph. Nowhere else in the world can that be said. All these things are based on Quranic teaching and Muslims know this."[9]

This powerful claim propelled the terrorists of San Bernardino, the killers in Paris, and motivates the ones the world has not yet seen. While it exists, the caliphate continues to transmit its deadly signals. It explains why Tashfeen Malik, before her murderous rampage in California, pledged allegiance to her Caliph Al-Baghdadi. The *Long War Journal* explained why:

"Assuming that Malik did swear allegiance to Baghdadi as has been reported, her behavior is entirely consistent with what the Islamic State's propagandists tell believers to do. For example, the 12th issue of the Islamic State's English-language magazine *Dabiq*, which was titled 'Just Terror,' specifically told any would-be follower to "record his will, renew his bay'ah (oath of allegiance), carry the Khilafah (Caliphate) banner, and strike the crusaders and their pagan and apostate allies wherever he can find them, even if he is alone'."[10]

ISIS also sings another chorus to their potential proselytes. They claim rulership over a pivotal part of the Middle East. It's called al-Sham.

"Geographically, al-Sham, or the Levant, refers to the area that includes Jordan, Syria, Lebanon and the territory of Palestine. Theologically it has great significance in Islamic eschatology: al-Sham is deemed to be the site of the last jihad between true Muslims and the forces of the infidel led by an anti-Christ-like figure. Judgement [sic] day will be preceded by a series of battles culminating in the city of Dabiq in northern Syria. **As a result, ISIS is sending a very clear message to potential recruits: if you had a desire to be a jihadi to secure your own salvation, this is your very last opportunity as they have captured the territory of al-Sham, and the final jihad has begun.**"[11]

That's why geography is so important to the battle with ISIS. In early January 2016, the U.S.-led coalition announced the Islamic State had lost thirty percent of its territory. Baghdad-based spokesperson Col. Steve Warren said they were in a "defensive crouch."[12] One on-the-scene reporter noted ISIS was "in a state of retreat."[13] It's a key to defeating ISIS, recapture the land of the Caliphate. It's a vital point made by Jay Sekulow in *The Rise of ISIS*. "A Caliphate requires territory, and if a Caliphate stops expanding—or suffers battlefield losses that even shrink its reach—it can lose authority and legitimacy ... just as nations require territory, so does a Caliphate ... if ISIS loses its territory, 'all those oaths of allegiance are no longer binding.'"[14]

Yet it still controls enough land to send out its potent invitation to the "**final jihad.**" It can seduce the most unlikely. This *New York Times* article described a young couple from the belly of the Bible belt, Starkville, Mississippi:

"She was a cheerleader, an honor student, the daughter of a police officer and a member of the high school homecoming court who wanted to be a doctor. He was a quiet but easygoing psychology student. His father is a well-known Muslim patriarch here, whose personable air and habit of sharing food with friends and strangers made him seem like a walking advertisement for Islam as a religion of tolerance and peace.

"Today, the young woman, Jaelyn Young, 19, and the young man, her fiancé, Mohammad Dakhlalla, 22, are in federal custody, arrested on suspicion of trying to travel from Mississippi to Syria to join the Islamic State. Friends and strangers alike said it was difficult to imagine two less likely candidates for the growing roster of young, aspiring American jihadists."[15]

But Jaelyn and Mohammad represent just two of the hundreds of Americans hearkening to this siren song.

## THE ENEMY IS WITHIN

On February 25, 2015, FBI Director James Comey raised the alarm of this expanding crisis with the National Association of Attorney Generals.

"So why do I tell you this? To explain to you why this remains at the top of the FBI's list and to explain to you why the conversations I have with our state and local partners in all 50 states matter so much today. **Because ISIL in particular is putting out a siren song through their slick propaganda through social media that goes like this: Troubled soul, come to the caliphate. You will live a life of glory. These are the apocalyptic end times. You will find a life of meaning here fighting for our so called** caliphate. **And if you can't come, kill somebody where you are. That is a message that goes out to troubled souls everywhere; resonates with troubled souls; people seeking meaning in some horribly misguided way.**"[16]

He described the breadth of the problem:

"Those people exist in every state. I have homegrown extremist investigations in every single state . . . so we have investigations of people in various stages of radicalizing in all 50 states. I tell my state and local partners this is about all of us being connected tightly to each other. This isn't a New York phenomenon or Washington phenomenon. This is all 50 states and in ways that are very hard to see."[17]

He said the local "boots on the ground," the police, would be the country's first line of defense:

"Because it's highly unlikely that it's going to be a federal agent who will first see or hear about someone acting in strange ways on social media or acting in a strange way in a religious institution or education institution or in the community. It's going to be a deputy sheriff; it's going to be a police officer who knows that neighborhood. The Joint Terrorism task forces that we have set up all over the country are in some ways more important today than they were at 9-11 because of the nature of this threat; so all of us leaning forward to push info to each other and to make sure that if we see something it quickly gets to the right place. It's critical to respond to this threat. So counter-terrorism remains at the top of our list and our relationships represented around this square are critical to dealing with the threat in the way that it's changed."[18]

The numbers behind this morphing threat are chilling. An extensive report by Sebastian and Katharine Gorka, "ISIS: The Threat to the United States," dispensed the cold statistics:

Eighty-two individuals in the United States affiliating with ISIS have been interdicted by law enforcement since March 2014.

 More than 250 individuals from the United States have joined or attempted to join ISIS in Syria and Iraq.

 The FBI currently has nearly 1,000 ongoing ISIS probes in the United States.

 ISIS Pied Pipers like Ali Shukri Amin and Ahmad Musa Jibril had nearly 4000 and 38,000 Twitter followers' respectively.[19]

The timely report noted that the young—like 19-year-old Mohammad in Jerusalem—seemed most vulnerable. "Sixty-three percent of those arrested were between 15 and 25. This should be of particular concern to lawmakers, parents, teachers and community leaders, given the vulnerability of youth and ISIS's cultic appeal."[20]

Spencer says ISIS targets the haven for the young—social media—and paves a digital highway for jihad. "They are very sophisticated in their use of the internet, Twitter or Facebook. But the main thing is not so much the means by which the message is conveyed but the message itself. And that message is powerful among American Muslims because it is so deeply rooted within Islamic tradition."[21]

While some ISIS disciples seek to join ISIS on the battlefields of Syria and Iraq, not everyone can physically join the Middle East caliphate. These "home-grown terrorists" or so-called "domestic plotters" present a daunting challenge. "Of the 59 people they identified in their study, 31 were foreign fighter aspirants, 11 were facilitators and **17 were domestic plotters**. Again, if the total number of supporters is into the thousands, that presents the United States with a very serious domestic threat that could easily lead to multiple Paris attack-type scenarios."[22]

When they wage jihad on the home front, they're heeding the battle cry of ISIS leaders like Abu Mohammad al Adnani. He declared in September 2014: "So rise O *muwahhid* (monotheists).

Rise and defend your state from your place wherever you may be. Rise and defend your Muslim brothers, for their homes, families, and wealth are threatened and deemed lawful by their enemies."[23]

His murderous screed continued:

"Strike the soldiers, patrons, and troops of the *tawāghīt* [those who cross the limits of Allah]. Strike their police, security, and intelligence members, as well as their treacherous agents. Destroy their beds. Embitter their lives for them and busy them with themselves. If you can kill a disbelieving American or European—especially the spiteful and filthy French—or an Australian, or a Canadian, or any other disbeliever from the disbelievers waging war, including the citizens of the countries that entered into a coalition against the Islamic State, then rely upon Allah, and kill him in any manner or way however it may be. **Do not ask for anyone's advice and do not seek anyone's verdict. Kill the disbeliever whether he is civilian or military.**"[24]

This is the fiery fuel behind the massacre at San Bernardino, the worst terror attack on U.S. soil since 9-11. The home front—schools, shopping malls, neighborhoods—have become the front line in this global war and part of the new twenty-first century battlefield.

## HOMELAND INSECURITY

What could this twenty-first century battlefield look like?

One Hollywood screenwriter with boots on the ground—literally—both in Israel, and in the U.S. came up with a chilling scenario of that potential theatre of war. Dan Gordon, an IDF veteran, lived through a number of the Middle East battlegrounds in his career as a soldier and an IDF spokesperson. A trooper of six wars, he combined his front-line experience and writing skill into a thrilling novel called *Day of the Dead*. It showed how ISIS could use a deadly tactic from Israel's archenemy Hamas to strike America.

During its war with Hamas in the summer of 2014, Hamas dug dozens of tunnels inside Israel to kill, kidnap, and terrorize Israelis. They infiltrated Israeli territory and shocked residents along the border with Gaza. Hamas dug some of those tunnels more than a mile long, sixty feet deep with multiple exits. Thankfully Israeli soldiers thwarted those attacks and destroyed more than thirty of their tunnels.

With Jerusalem's Jaffa Gate behind us, we met with Gordon. He told us about his book and the inspiration behind it.

"I've been a soldier now for 40 years, which is a long time, and the most terrifying thing that I've ever seen is the advent of the terrorist tunnel attacks that happened last (2014) summer."[25]

He called his book a wakeup call to the U.S.

"The country that is most vulnerable to that attack is my other homeland, the United States of America; far more vulnerable because there are terrorist tunnels that exist already. They're called drug-smuggling tunnels and they run from part of Mexico into California to Arizona and to Texas."[26]

For example, both former FBI agent and Republican Senator Lindsey Graham (R-SC) warned those tunnels could be used as an underground highway for ISIS. Gordon says the drug tunnels would bond ISIS and the Mexican drug cartels in an unholy alliance.

"They don't even have to dig them; they just have to rent them from Mexican drug cartels. They have billions of dollars, that's a language all the drug cartels understand."[27]

Gordon says ISIS studied Hamas during the summer of 2014.

"They watched what Hamas did. They saw why it failed. They know how it can succeed. What people don't realize is the Middle East for ISIS is their R & D lab, their Silicon Valley to what they want to do in the United States."[28]

He warned that southern border cities and towns like San Diego are vulnerable.

"The reason the United States is so vulnerable is that we don't have the surveillance over that border like Israel does. We don't have our most elite military units on constant patrol on the U.S.-Mexican border. If you want to talk about juicy targets for ISIS, half the Pacific fleet is at anchor in San Diego."[29]

Ironically, military bases can be vulnerable targets.

"Because of U.S. policy, it's against regulations for any US personnel to carry a weapon on the U.S. military installation. That's why a fat psychiatrist named Major Nidal was able to kill 13 people with two pistols and wound a couple dozen more. Imagine what trained ISIS terrorists can do. You take out 20 rent-a-cops or 20 shore patrol MPs, you own the base. What did ISIS do in Paris with three terrorists and Charlie Hebdo? They paralyzed a city. They killed scores of people. Imagine if you had a thousand terrorists, six truck bombs. In two hours, you can dwarf 9/11 and Pearl Harbor combined."[30]

As an author, Gordon also wrote the book to entertain. One reviewer said Gordon gets into the mind of a terrorist like no one since Tom Clancy, but Gordon says his book has things Clancy never included in his thrillers.

"It's a big Tom Clancy, wonderful, international espionage, great read. It's the first book that I know of that has a born-again Christian, graduate of Liberty University—a female James Bond. At the heart of that book is faith. At the heart of that book is something that you and I both experience together, which is that you may think that you're in control, but the One who is in control at all times is the Almighty. A faith that there's a perfect design and a perfect Designer who's reachable through prayer, whose heart and door is always open to us to receive us."[31]

Gordon refutes the idea that his book gives ideas to ISIS. He points out they've already got the blueprints.

"I guarantee you as someone who's spent 40 years in the Middle East in six wars and part of them in a unit that dealt with terrorism, ISIS has people in the United States right now scouting locations, just like you would do for a movie. It takes, people think oh, a terrorist attack happens because they get off the boat and go and attack something. A terrorist attack will take months if not years to set up. I guarantee there are people right now examining US cities and, like any military, there are a number of young, hot commanders who are saying: 'I have a great idea' and who are presenting their plans to the general staff of ISIS. One of those plans is going to get accepted and one of those plans is going to get implemented and, if I'm looking at the most logical plan, it's in that book, *Day of the Dead*."[32]

"What people have to understand is ISIS has to do it. It's not a question of do they want to do it, will they do it. They've got to do it. ISIS declared the caliphate. They claim to be anointed by the Islam's prophet Mohammad and by Allah. Well, if you're anointed by Allah, you have to hit the Great Satan. You have no choice."[33]

Gordon says the U.S. needs to wake up to this clear and present danger.

"We need to make some changes right now. We need a ready response team along that border 24 hours a day that's ready to move inside of ten minutes. We need increased surveillance, which we don't have. We need not just eyes in the air; we need eyes on the ground. We need increased intelligence. If you're underground, you're impervious to surveillance. Drones can't see you; satellites, all the technological advantages we have in the United States are useless. You're in a tunnel. Ancient warfare. It's how King David took Jerusalem. That's how old it is."[34]

Another ancient tactic ISIS uses is terror: "Strike terror (into the hearts of) the enemies of Allah and your enemies" (Sura 8:60).[35] This weapon of war is a means to their end—world conquest: "Fight then against them till strife be at an end, and the religion be all of it Allah's" (Surah 8:39).[36]

It might not be what many Muslims practice or what some Muslims believe, but these jihadists are following—many times to the letter—what the Quran says and the examples Mohammad set.

In light of this, the Gorka report reached its sobering conclusion: the U.S. and the world are facing an unprecedented threat, the siren song of ISIS:

"The United States, indeed the world is facing a threat unlike any it has seen. The old rules of engagement no longer pertain, and terror is the order of the day. Citizens are as vulnerable (if not more so) than soldiers. If we want to prevent the loss of more lives, we must acknowledge the seriousness of this threat. That does not mean making Muslims register or banning all refugees, but neither does it mean continuing with the status quo. There is much that can be done by law enforcement, by intelligence and by citizens to keep America safe and yet also free."[37]

CBN News Story: "ISIS Underground Highway at America's Doorstep?"

CBN News Story: "Father of Slain ISIS Teen: 'My Son Was No Spy'"

# Escape From Darkness

*"Describing their situations is very, very hard because some of the girls have told us they have had their hands tied for three months. They've been harassed and forced to have sex. . . . Imagine having sex with a mother in front of her son and then killing the son."*

~ Hadi Doubani, Director, Yazidi Affairs[1]

We drove out of Dohuk, "T," a male Yazidi nurse, came along with Pastor Majeed, Jonathan, and me. "T" had arranged interviews in one of the major UN refugee camps for Yazidis. His help would be invaluable in navigating a world we knew little about. We left the streets of the city and traversed rolling, barren hills. The route took us southwest, closer to ISIS. The direction also led to tales of woe, terror, and yet redemption in the land now populated by thousands of Yazidis.

This ethnic group had captured the attention of the world in the summer of 2014 when ISIS overran their main city of Sinjar and surrounding villages. They massacred thousands. Thousands more found refuge on Mount Sinjar. They escaped ISIS but ran directly into the searing Iraqi sun and severe lack of food and water. Exposure to the unforgiving elements killed hundreds more on that mountain. The rest made the trek to refugee camps, sometimes a nearly hundred-mile walk through relentless terrain.

We met many of them during the heat and heart of their deadly encounter with ISIS. Sitting inside a stifling UN tent, one Yazidi man told us both Christians and Yazidis suffer the same fate in the Middle East. With a hand motion indicating slitting his throat, he said, "They slaughter us like sheep."[2] I still vividly remember sitting on the ground with three young Yazidi boys. With their ordeal freshly written in their eyes, they told us ISIS gave one neighborhood friend—a young 14-year-old girl—the choice to "convert or die."[3] She chose to die.

More than one year later, the slaughter is over for many Yazidis, but they still face an uncertain future. This tribe ended their exodus in UN camps sprinkled throughout Kurdistan. Now most languish in refugee camps like the one we'd set as our destination. Kurdish forces, bolstered by Yazidi volunteers, recaptured Sinjar in mid-November 2015. It gave some hope of returning one day. But a number of their women and young children, captured in the summer of 2014, were still in the claws of ISIS.

Driving over a rise in the road, we caught our first glimpse of this indigenous people. Hundreds dotted the roadsides. Dozens of makeshift stalls lined the road, unlikely vendors selling wares—a crude but organic economy. Dust swept the landscape. Litter blew about aimlessly. The scene appeared chaotic, yet some hidden order seemed to stitch the social fabric together. Like a symphony, where everyone knew the score. We had come to listen to their music.

"T" asked us to stop so we could pick up someone. He got out and returned several minutes later with a 14-year-old boy. I forget his real name, but we called him "Mamo." He would help "T" make our way into and out of the refugee camp. A cheery and savvy young chap, he had reddish-brown hair and a round face that gave him the look of a permanent smile and friendly appearance. At the time, his countenance gave no indication of having barely escaped a terrifying nightmare of his own.

We drove another half mile and turned right into the entrance of the Kankle UN refugee camp. Spread before us was a sea of white tents with UNHCR emblazoned on their flaps. UNHCR stands for United Nations High Commissioner for Refugees. In just a short time, thousands of Yazidis had gone from living in their ancient homeland to crowding into UN refugee camps like this one. Cars streamed in and out as we drove up to the entrance. "T" explained to the guard who we were and stated our mission. The guard replied he had no record of our arrival, so "T" went to the main UN office to argue our case.

In the meantime, we talked with Mamo, who had been captured by ISIS. As he began to share some of his experiences, I sat stunned by his chilling stories and quickly decided to see if his family would allow us to do an interview. He was just a kid, but ISIS wanted to make him a part of the next generation of the Islamic State, intent on taking over the world. We'd find out more details of his ordeal in a couple of hours.

## "NAZDA"—ISIS SEX SLAVE

When "T" returns with the camp's permission, we pass through the front gate, turn a sharp left, carefully maneuver through a deep gully (very glad for our 4x4) and drive up to the tent where "T" had arranged our interview. The back of their tent faces the gravel street. We walk between this tent and their next-door neighbor's tent just a few feet away. The UN has arranged these tents for survival, not privacy. I realize these rudimentary conditions provide shelter, bathing and living conditions for a whole family. It's home . . . at least, for now.

Our presence sparks a lot of activity. It's not every day a camera crew shows up. The buzz among the neighbors is palpable. As is Kurdish custom, we take off our shoes and walk up the few concrete steps. Inside is a concrete floor rimmed by thin mats. I'm impressed that these tents have some permanence, but I question how much protection they'll offer several months from now during the harsh Kurdish winter.

We greet four generations of this Yazidi family: the grandmother, mother, the young girl we have come to interview, and a few of the younger children. I notice the young girl is dressed in more modern attire than the traditional garb of her seniors. In a few moments, the patriarch strides in. He's a big man with a grizzled face, chiseled by years under the Middle Eastern sun. He greets us with a handshake. His hand swallows mine. He sits down with an air that suggests he's king of this canvas castle. He tells us he's honored by our visit. We return the honor. He tells us ISIS recently set him free because of his old age. One more sign how ISIS has dramatically altered the course of this Yazidi family and their people.

A small fan whirs behind us as we all sit down on mats. The fan takes the edge off the more than one-hundred-degree heat. I had no idea what they'd do to blunt the cold. Bedding is piled up at one end of the tent. This space—just under 250 square feet[4]—is a bedroom, living room, and dining room, all in one. The UNHCR designs their tents for five people; I sense their family is much bigger. A soccer game is playing on an old TV set. A concrete wall—about three to four feet tall—gives some stability to their home. The rest is covered by canvas with the ubiquitous UNHCR stamp. I'm usually a UN critic, but I'm grateful this agency provides the basics to so many needy people worldwide. I wonder where these Yazidis would be and what difficulties they'd face without the UN.

We set up for our interview. We decide to call this 19-year-old Yazidi girl "Nazda." For her protection, we hide her identity with a veil over her face. I'm struck by how unaffected she seems by her ordeal. Nazda looks like any number of young women anywhere in the world. Someone you'd expect to be looking forward to marriage and a family. Yet, against her will, she became part of the darkest society on the face of the earth—sex slavery inside the Islamic State.

She begins to share some of the details of her crucible experience: In August 2014, ISIS captured her along with nearly two thousand other Yazidi women. The women were moved from place to place and then separated into smaller groups. During one division, the women were put in one group, virgin girls in another.

The slave market brought its own terrors. "When they were selling us, the buyer would come in to take his slave. If any of us refused, they would beat us very badly. No one went with the buyers willingly."[5]

Nazda spent ten months as a sex slave. An Arab man from Mosul bought her from ISIS for the equivalent of eight hundred U.S. dollars.

She describes her owner: "The man was really, really bad. He treated me like an animal. He had four wives and they had no sympathy for me . . . everyone treated me as a slave. I was beaten and treated very badly."[6]

She quickly learned, along with the other slaves, that they couldn't trust anyone in Mosul, either.

"Unfortunately, even the people of Mosul accept the situation. Yazidi girls couldn't say to the people there that we've been captured by ISIS. Because if a Yazidi woman would plead with a taxi driver, 'I'm Yazidi, please take me to a safe place,' the driver would do the opposite and take her back to ISIS."[7]

ISIS also tried to convert Nazda to Islam.

"They told us we were blasphemers and our religion was not true," she explains. "They told me, 'Islam is the true religion.'"[8]

As we sat, gripped by her story, Nazda said ISIS dealt harshly with anyone who tried to help any of the captured Yazidi women. One incident stood out.

"They brought three men into the ISIS court. They had been accused of helping some of the women who had become Yazidi sex slaves. They killed them and beheaded them in front of us. They told us this would be the fate of anybody trying to help us."[9]

"T" had requested that we not ask Nazda any personal questions about her sexual treatment. He didn't want to trigger any flashbacks. We'd readily agreed.

But here in the twenty-first century, how does ISIS justify their use of sex slaves? According to Jihad Watch, they cite the Quran from the seventh century:

"The seizure of infidel girls and their use as sex slaves is sanctioned in the Quran. According to Islamic law, Muslim men can take 'captives of the right hand' (Quran 4:3, 4:24, 33:50). The Quran says: "O Prophet! We have made lawful to you your wives to whom you have paid their dowries, and **those whom your right hand possesses of those whom Allah has given you as spoils of war**" (33:50).[10]

"Quran 4:3 and 4:24 extend this privilege to Muslim men in general. The Quran says that a man may have sex with his wives and with these slave girls: The believers must win through, those who humble themselves in their prayers; who avoid vain talk; who are active in deeds of charity; **who abstain from sex, except with those joined to them in the marriage bond, or those whom their right hands possess**, for they are free from blame" (see Quran 23:1-6).[11]

## MESSAGE FROM NAZDA

Near the end of our interview, I asked Nazda what message she would send to the world.

"My only request is that the rest of the world would come together to save the Yazidis under the control of ISIS. I also want to send a message to ISIS that they cannot destroy all of the Yazidis all over the world."[12]

Nazda escaped her plight by feigning sickness and went to the hospital in Mosul. There she got a cell phone and called her family. She ran away and, after seven hours on foot, found the Kurdish military—the Peshmerga—and freedom.

"When I saw the Peshmerga, I became so happy! I knew I had just spent ten months under ISIS control that was so difficult. It was my pleasure, my great pleasure to re-join my family!"[13]

Nazda relishes her happy ending, but her joy is braided with heartache. Two cousins—and hundreds more Yazidi women—still wither under the dominion of ISIS.

I asked how we could pray for her.

She replied, "If you can lift up prayers to save and rescue the rest of the girls who are with ISIS—this is my only desire."[14]

Sobered, we finished our interview, thanked Nazda and the rest of the family. It was hard to leave. After hearing such a raw, unvarnished testimony, I wanted to turn back the ISIS clock and change the tortured past of this family. But now, like multitudes of others, they're part of this Middle East history, careening though one of its most sad and tragic chapters.

We walked up the street to the top of the hill overlooking the camp. Majeed and "T" discussed further the plight of the Yazidis while Jonathan and I videotaped a stand-up:

AFTER ISIS CAPTURED SINJAR, THE MAIN CITY OF THE YAZIDIS, MOST OF THEM LIVE IN CAMPS LIKE THIS. NEARLY TWENTY THOUSAND LIVE IN THIS ONE ALONE. BUT A FEW HERE HAVE MADE THE HARROWING ESCAPE OUT OF THE HANDS OF ISIS.[15]

Yazidi kids—like kids everywhere—flocked to our camera. Cameras and kids simply go together. Jonathan loves kids and lets them mug for the camera. After our stand-up and more video, we walked back down the hill. Along the way, we passed young men playing dominos, intent on their game. In contrast to the kids, they hardly looked up. We saw an old woman cleaning her 250-square-foot home, teenage girls giggling at the sight of strangers walking through the camp, and a gaggle of old men discussing whatever old men discuss. Resilient young kids were playing, oblivious to their refugee status.

Suddenly, I looked at the sea of white tents soiled by desert sands and wind. I wondered: *What is the future of these people? Their lives are a shell of what they used to be.* It felt overwhelming. Then it hit me. The panorama before me appeared to be a sign Jesus described as the end times. On the Mount of Olives in Jerusalem two thousand years ago, He'd said there would be "wars and rumors of wars" (Matt. 24:6). Wars create refugees. It may not have been a revelation to others, but that moment—at least to this reporter—unveiled one facet of the times in which we live. Furthermore, I thought, refugees need help. They need His love, a love that compels us to reach out to this uprooted segment of humankind.

## MAMO'S STORY

After my brief epiphany, we got back into Majeed's 4x4. We drove outside the camp to interview Mamo at his relative's house. By now, the Iraqi sun was racing to its rendezvous with the horizon. We, too, sped to finish our interview before daylight vanished. As in the case of Nazda, we wanted to conceal Mamo's identity. Jonathan sat Mamo in a chair with the sun behind him, placing the boy in silhouette.

We learned that ISIS had captured Mamo along with hundreds of other young Yazidi boys in the summer of 2014. Then his indoctrination began:

"They insulted us and told us we were unclean," he shared. "They accused us of being blasphemers, unbelievers who didn't believe in Islam or Allah. They taught us the Quran and also trained us how to use heavy weapons . . . later, they told us we should be jihadists just like them and convert to Islam."[16]

Their goals were clear, Mamo said.

"To convert us, then to make us into jihadist and then kill our own people, the Yazidis. They were encouraging us to become jihadists just like them to get Allah's pleasure and do whatever he requires of us."[17]

ISIS also warned Mamo and the rest of the children about their global goal.

"They said, 'We will not leave any place—even a small part of the world—without Islam.'"

Earlier, Nazda had told us the same tale. "They said they are not simply a state of Mosul, or Raqqa, or anywhere else. They said, "The Islamic State is not a small state. It is a big state and can cover the whole world."[18]

Mamo, too, witnessed the cruelty of ISIS.

"One of the most frightening things that I have ever seen was when one of their followers was captured. They accused him of spying on ISIS for the Kurdish fighters of Syria. That was why they beheaded him in front of the children."[19]

The brainwashing lasted for months.

"We felt really bad, really bad because, you know, our brain has been washed. It was very dangerous."[20]

After months of this training, Mamo miraculously escaped by convincing his captors he was ill. They put him with his mother, which gave them both an opportunity to flee.

After the sun set and our interview ended, we went into the house. We found that Mamo's uncle, Abdullah, lives in this house. Abdullah acts as a go-between for captured Yazidis and their captors. In short, he smuggles people—a present-day Oskar Schindler, the German businessman who rescued thousands of Jews from the Nazis during WWII.

He explained his job qualifications. "Before ISIS took over Sinjar, I used to buy and sell things inside Syria. Now, with these relationships in Syria, I rescue people."[21]

By the time we met with Abdullah, he had already freed 138 captives.

Smart phones are the main tools of his trade. He uses them to communicate with his Syrian contacts. He also showed me a screen shot from a captured ISIS cell phone, displaying Twitter accounts where ISIS fighters communicate with each other when buying and selling sex slaves.

Given this knowledge, we videotape a stand-up inside the dimly lit room. I show pics on two cell phones and explain:

THESE ARE TWO PICTURES OF WHAT MAMO ESCAPED. OVER HERE, YOU CAN SEE THIRTY-TWO YOUNG YAZIDI BOYS, POSING WITH THE ISLAMIC STATE FLAG. HERE, A GRADUATION SERVICE. ISIS WANTS THESE BOYS TO BE YOUNG JIHADISTS OF THE NEXT GENERATION OF THE ISLAMIC STATE.[22]

Abdullah was passionate about his mission, and showed me why. On his cell phone, he pulled up a picture of an ISIS graduation service for young boys like Mamo. Pointing out one of the kids, he said, "That's my nephew." *What heartbreak for an uncle or a father,* I thought. His nephew lived perhaps only a few miles away and was being reprogrammed into a whole new life. I wondered if they'd ever see him again. And if they did, what would he be like? Would he ever escape the grip of ISIS? Would he become a future jihadist? Would they convince him to turn against his own people? Or would his brainwashed young mind ever again know the innocence of youth?

I asked Abdullah how much it costs to rescue someone.

"It depends," he says. "Sometimes we bring them out for free; sometimes, for just a thousand dollars; sometimes, five thousand."[23]

He's motivated by the joy he feels when a captive is set free. We also learn that Nazda, who walked seven hours to freedom, is his niece.

"If you could just be there and document when the rescued victims come out from the control of ISIS and see their relatives again. . . . If you could, you'd work hard like me because you'd know how beautiful it is to rescue them and reunite them with their families."[24]

Abdullah is just one of many go-betweens to rescue Yazidis. They coordinate their work with the Kurdish office of Yazidi affairs. Before we left, he gave us directions to find their office the next day back in Dohuk. In the dark Kurdish evening, we said our goodbyes to Abdullah, Mamo, and several other family members, knowing we had heard first-hand accounts of those who come face to face with ISIS.

## HADI'S HEARTBREAK

The next day we searched for the Yazidi affairs office. After several attempts, we finally found the small building. Inside, about a dozen people worked on a large-scale human reclamation project. The Kurdish government set up the office to help rescue the nearly six thousand captured Yazidis. We met Hadi Doubani, the director, who welcomed us and offered us the customary tea. We enjoyed the tea while Majeed and Hadi discussed the current situation in Kurdish, and Jonathan set up for our interview.

As we began our interview, Hadi struck me as an efficient but somewhat detached bureaucrat. I was wrong. Hadi prefaced his remarks with an explanation of the Yazidi people. Then he began to describe the horrific stories he hears.

"Some of the girls have told us they have had their hands tied for three months; they've been harassed and forced to have sex. . . . Imagine having sex with a mother in front of her son and then killing the son."[25]

When he described the plight of one 13-year-old girl, he took out his phone to show us her picture, then dropped his phone and broke down. Through tears, he explained, "I tried very hard to rescue this girl. Five times she was married. She's also been put in prison."[26]

But Hadi and his office enjoy a measure of success. So far, he and his team have helped more than two thousand women escape. Their first mission: to rehabilitate them psychologically from the mental horrors of being in the clutches of ISIS. "T" later explained the chief Yazidi religious leader helped in that rehabilitation. He issued an edict that Yazidis should not shun these women because of their sexual mistreatment but instead, pay them honor.

Success stories make Doubani's efforts worthwhile. But he pleads for more help. "Is it acceptable that the international community or the UN, who know that nearly six thousand people—people who have been kidnapped by ISIS and who experience persecution, harassments, and are treated like animals—keep silent? They don't make any steps to help."[27]

The Kurdish offensive that retook Sinjar might alleviate some of this suffering, but hundreds of Yazidis still remain prisoners in the grasp of ISIS. Men, women, boys, and girls swept up in the darkness of our age.

CBN News Story: "Escaped Yazidis Share Chilling Tales of ISIS Captivity"

CBN News Story: "For Yazidis, Christians: 'They Cut Us Like Sheep"

# For Whom the Bell Tolls

*"They don't want any Christians to live in Iraq. They want to kill them all, have them leave or become a Muslim."*

- Raged, an Iraqi Christian Refugee[1]

For Ammar and his family, the bells tolled at midnight.

"It was very strange that the bells rang at that time. The loudspeakers that belong to the church called out, 'All of you; go out from Qaraqosh. ISIS is coming and there is no one to protect you.' So I took my family, my wife, my children, and we left."[2]

They left into an unknown future and left behind home, belongings, and their livelihood. We interviewed Ammar and other families for a story on the plight of Iraqi Christians after the scourge of ISIS cut a swath through their homeland. Most got out with only the clothes on their backs. I sat just a couple of feet away from Ammar, but I felt our lives were so different we might as well have been thousands of miles apart. He now lives as a sojourner in a strange land, his fate determined by forces and people outside of his control. His kind but watery eyes told a tale of hardship and yet steadfastness in the face of the stiff winds of adversity. I admired his fortitude and obvious love for his family. His story radiated a willingness to protect and provide for them despite his crushing circumstances.

Sixty thousand other Christians like Ammar fled for their lives from Qaraqosh. They formed just one contingent of thousands of believers in Jesus throughout Iraq who now found themselves homeless and stateless. Many headed to Erbil, the capital of Kurdistan. Others escaped to Dohuk, a Kurdish city near the Turkish border. Months later, some made it to Amman, Jordan's capital, and its surrounding towns. That's where we met Ammar and his family.

We also greeted mothers like Raged, who told us what her life has been like since that night the bells tolled. "It's very, very difficult. It's like when you're sleeping and you're dreaming. It was a big surprise. Even now, we can't believe this is happening to us. It's like a dream. Everything was so normal. Our life was so comfortable and, suddenly, everything changed."[3]

Her life—now a nightmare—changed when Islamic terrorists arrived with their deadly goal.

"They don't want any Christians to live in Iraq," a teary-eyed Raged explained. "They want to kill them all, or have them leave or become Muslims."[4]

Most of the Christians in Qaraqosh never saw ISIS. They left when the bells rang. But those who came face to face with ISIS were given four choices. First, they could leave the houses they had lived in for years. Second, they could pay what is called the Jizya tax for non-Muslims or infidels. Third, they could renounce their faith in Jesus Christ and convert to Islam. Finally, they could choose to die by the sword.

We met some believers who were given the choice of denial or death. They refused. Seham, a wife and mother, told me, "He died for us on the Cross. I can't deny Jesus. I can't deny Him."[5] When I hear such a robust profession of faith from someone who had to make that grisly choice, I often wonder, *How would I respond?*

My gut churned when I heard their stories. But I knew my distress was nothing compared to their heartbreak as they recounted what happened to their once blossoming and now shattered lives.

Kareem, Raged's husband, shared one bright story in a litany of grim ones. His weathered face brightened when he told us his family escaped their persecutors: "Jesus made for us a miracle.

He saved my family. I have a wife and three daughters that He saved! He saved them from ISIS."[6]

Kareem and Raged beamed with pride when they introduced us to their pretty young girls. Other Iraqi parents, however, sadly have suffered a horrific fate when ISIS captured their daughters and sold them as sex slaves.

While Kareem, Raged, Ammar, and Seham, along with several other families, are still without a country, they fared better than most. A Christian humanitarian group—the Foundation for Relief and Reconciliation in the Middle East—provided a nice house where several families could live comfortably.

At the end of my interview with Ammar, I asked him, "How can people pray for you?" Ammar expressed a big-hearted view when he asked for prayer not only for himself but for the others who were worse off than himself. "Pray for us. We are in a very hard situation here," he said. "Life is very difficult, especially here in Jordan. There is no work. We—the Iraqi people—are not allowed to work. So we want them to pray for us. Me, I'm good. But there are so many (others) living in camps—in Erbil, in Iraq, and here in Jordan."[7]

## THE COMMUNION OF SAINTS

We drove through the narrow, crowded streets in the Ankawa neighborhood of the capital city of Erbil. I marveled how Majeed, our guide/driver/friend and brother in the Lord, navigated his SUV through these environs. With cars parked on both sides of the street, he had to carefully maneuver. With just inches to spare many times, I often just held my breath.

We arrived at the church we had come to visit, where the pastor had saved us a parking space. We greeted him and a small contingent from his congregation. We would be videotaping his evening service to find out how some Christians there have fared after more than a year since ISIS.

Soon we're standing in a cramped apartment. It's the bottom floor of a three-story building, not unlike the triple-decker I lived in at one time in Boston—except this is a stone, not a wooden building. Ordinarily, it would have been the living and dining rooms. Now chairs fill the room wall to wall. I guess about fifty to sixty people are squeezed into the narrow space. I find a spare seat and wait while Jonathan begins to videotape the service.

I find the music off key, the words unfamiliar, and I don't know these people. But I do recognize the familiar sense of the Holy Spirit. He pervades the service. While I don't "know" these people, I "know" they're my brothers and sisters. Despite the language and cultural barrier, the color of the skin or the different features, it's true that wherever you go in the world, the Body of Christ remains one family. His Spirit binds us together in the One who promised never to leave or forsake us. For many here, however, that promise has been severely tested. I realize that most of those in this service used to pray and worship just about fifty miles away in Mosul or Qaraqosh. Now, their former churches and homes might just as well have been on the moon. A great gulf exists between where they stood and those towns just about an hour's drive away. ISIS fills that gulf.

During the worship time, I try to soak in the atmosphere. I know the feeling will eventually fade away, but I want to remember and savor this moment. I feel like I am here to be a conduit from these people back to those in the West. It is a rare privilege and opportunity to be with these believers. I get to hear their hearts and feel their plight. Most have lost nearly everything and yet they're here, still faithful, worshipping and serving the Lord. I want to tell their story.

Before the music ends, I step outside, and Jonathan and I shoot a brief stand-up for the story we're planning:

MANY CHRISTIANS WHO FLED ISIS ARE NOT IN THE LARGER REFUGEE CAMPS. INSTEAD, MOST LIVE AMONG THE NEIGHBORHOODS THROUGHOUT KURDISTAN AND HERE IN ERBIL. THIS IS WHERE ONE OF THE CHURCHES MEETS FOR THEIR WORSHIP SERVICE.[8]

After the worship, Abu Fadi, their pastor, begins his message. About halfway through the service, the lights go out. No one is concerned however; it's a common occurrence in post-ISIS Erbil. Without missing a beat, he continues his sermon on how to hear the voice of the Holy Spirit. The lights come back on. After his message, they end their service with communion. I'm struck how this sacrament knits the family of God anywhere in the world to the Head of the Church, Jesus. Two thousand years ago, He instructed His Body to remember Him through the celebration of communion. Two thousand years later, this persecuted church in northern Iraq still follows His example. One day He has promised to celebrate it with His church in His coming Kingdom.

## THE COST OF FOLLOWING CHRIST

After communion, they asked me to come up and speak. After all, they didn't get a lot of visitors from the outside world. I was humbled to stand before these brothers and sisters who had suffered so much for their faith. I brought greetings from Jerusalem and told them that Christians around the world are praying for them. They smile and nod their heads when they hear that. I searched for good words, comforting words in the hope I can sprinkle their weary hearts with hope and courage.

Before we left for Kurdistan, Julie Stahl, our Jerusalem-based correspondent, felt we should buy crosses for the believers we'd meet. It was an inspired idea. She bought 100 small crosses. We passed them out. I told them the olive wood crosses had come from the Bethlehem area. You should have seen the respect and honor they paid those crosses. One elderly man lifted it up like a beacon. Women kissed it and held it tightly.

With the service over—like churches around the world—refreshments suddenly appeared. Children raced around and played, women served the tea and cookies, and men talked. We found out most had come from Mosul, ancient Nineveh. Others came from the Christian town of Qaraqosh like Ammar, whom we met in Jordan. Most had similar stories about ISIS. Laith Ganem said as he was leaving Mosul, ISIS had a checkpoint at the edge of the city. "They put a gun to my head and demanded, 'Whatever you have in your pockets, take it out.'" Wisam Jubrael said, "One of our neighbors told us they killed my cousin because he was a Christian. They told us we had to leave."[9]

Their transition from a normal life to refugee status has been hard. "In such circumstances, it's really hard for families to live all together," Sabah Jamil confirmed. "For example, we came here and found out we'd be living in a small apartment with five or six families. It was very difficult for us."[10]

When we sat down to interview the pastor, I realized I knew him! I had interviewed him before, in the summer of 2014. At the time, he led several families on a mini-exodus out of the clutches of ISIS. More than a year later, he's still tending his flock: "When we first came here, for about eight months, I was asking all the charity organizations, humanitarian organizations to go and visit the people. The only reason behind it was giving out the Word of God to the people, so God showed me His Word is not only words, but actions."[11]

Yet fear still stalks many of these wounded souls. Rota Mosa, a widow with two daughters, told us, "I don't know if the people know, but actually we're still scared. We need those (Christians around the world) to pray for us, that God will remove fear from our hearts. We're living here and still very close to the front lines of ISIS. The situation is not really helpful. When our children go to school, they cannot get high marks or a good degree because they're scared in their hearts. Right now, I cannot leave my children alone because I'm afraid of the people that surround us. I really need for people to pray for us."[12]

She added, though, that she's thankful. "God has saved us and moved us from Qaraqosh to here. That means He was faithful to us. But right now, we need to be faithful, so please pray for us to have a faithful heart."[13]

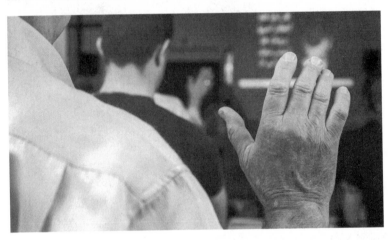

Laith Ganem, that short, stocky man with a ready smile who said ISIS put a gun to his head, beamed with pride when he boasted how believers responded to their crucible: "I'm really very proud of the Christians because the Christians, they left everything behind and they followed Christ. They left their money, their jewels, their wealth. They left everything for the sake of Christ."[14]

Wisam emphasized the need and power of prayer: "The Christians of Iraq need the other parts of the world to pray for them because they are really in need spiritually, physically, and emotionally. They really need to pray for us to live in peace and experience the peace of Jesus."[15]

After several of these interviews, I saw young ten-year-old Myriam. Like tens of thousands of others, I had first seen her on a YouTube video that went viral. A reporter from Sat 7—a Middle Eastern Christian satellite channel— met Myriam in one of the many refugee camps four months after her family fled ISIS. Her childlike faith and spiritual maturity in that interview inspired believers around the world, including myself. Despite her circumstances, she forgave her ISIS tormentors. We knew she'd be there at church, along with her father and sister. Of all the people I expected to see in Kurdistan—military generals, government officials, soldiers or experts—I looked forward to meeting her most of all. When you read some of her interview with Sat 7 journalist Essam Nagy, perhaps you'll understand why:

• ESSAM: What's the thing that you miss most from Qaraqosh?

• MYRIAM: We used to have a house and were entertained, whereas here we're not. But thank God, God provides for us.

• ESSAM: What do you mean God provides for you?

• MYRIAM: God loves us and wouldn't let ISIS kill us.

• ESSAM: You know how much God loves you, don't you?

• MYRIAM: Yes, God loves us all, not just me. God loves everybody.

• ESSAM: Do you also think God loves those who harmed you, or not?

• MYRIAM: He loves them, but He doesn't love Satan.

• ESSAM: What are your feelings toward those who drove you out of your home and caused you hardships?

• MYRIAM: I won't do anything to them. I will only ask God to forgive them.

• ESSAM: And can you, too, forgive them?

• MYRIAM: Yes.

• ESSAM: But that's very hard—or is it easy—to forgive those who made you suffer?

• MYRIAM: I won't kill them. Why kill them? I'm just sad they drove us out of our homes. Why did they do that?

• ESSAM: I hope you go back to a home that's better than your first home.

• MYRIAM: If God so wants. Not what we want, but God, because He knows.

• ESSAM: Don't you sometimes feel sad? Do you feel Jesus had forsaken you, for example?

• MYRIAM: No. Sometimes I cry because we left our home and Qaraqosh, but I'm not angry at God because we left Qaraqosh. I thank Him because He provided for us, even if we're suffering here, He provides for us.

• ESSAM: You taught me so many things.

• MYRIAM: Thank you. You taught me things, too.

• ESSAM: What did I teach you? You taught me.

• MYRIAM: You didn't teach me, I mean, you felt for me. You felt for me. I had some feelings, and I wanted people to know how the children here feel.

• ESSAM: Do you know that Jesus will never forsake you?

• MYRIAM: He will never forsake me. If you're a true believer, He will never forsake you."[16]

This endearing give-and-take lifted the hearts of people worldwide. Surrounded by the debris of war and devoid of the comfort of home, this little girl still kept her heart fixed on Jesus, "the Author and Finisher of her faith." When we sat down with Myriam for a brief interview, I sensed a powerful anointing on this angelic young girl. Her father translated as she expressed her childlike faith: "Whatever situation we are in, it is because God allowed it. We don't know how to deal with this life unless we have Jesus with us."[17]

Myriam is living out what Jesus taught in His Sermon on the Mount:

"*You have heard that it was said, 'You shall love your neighbor and hate your enemy.' But I say to you, love your enemies, bless those who curse you, do good to those who hate you, and pray for those who spitefully use you and persecute you, that you may be sons of your Father in heaven; for He makes His sun rise on the evil and on the good, and sends rain on the just and on the unjust. For if you love those who love you, what reward have you? Do not even the tax collectors do the same? And if you greet your brethren only, what do you do more than others? Do not even the tax collectors do so? Therefore you shall be perfect, just as your Father in heaven is perfect"* (Matthew 5: 43–48).

For those in the West, Myriam and the other suffering Christians are a reminder that *"if one member suffers, all the members suffer with it"* (1 Cor. 12:26). They're also a living admonition that as the author Milton once wrote: "No man is an island, entire of itself; every man is a piece of the continent, a part of the main. If a clod be washed away by the sea, Europe is the less. . . .I am involved in mankind, and therefore never send to know for whom the bell tolls; **it tolls for thee.**"[18]

CBN News Story: "Iraqi Christians Flee ISIS, Find Refuge in Jordan"

CBN News Story: "Christian Refugees: 'Please Pray for Us"

Sat 7: "Myriam's Story and Song"

# Under the Shadow of Islam

*"Christian communities being totally slaughtered and murdered and driven out and a whole ethnic cleansing of the Middle East to wipe out Christianity, and Western leaders just look the other way. It's totally crazy that the churches are not speaking out; that the politicians are not speaking out; that there aren't demonstrations in the street."*

~ Yaakov Kirschen, "Dry Bones" Cartoonist[1]

Late fall, 2014: I got an unexpected phone call. One of the world's best-known political cartoonists wanted to talk. He had an idea, thought I should know about it, and wanted some help. The call took me by surprise. I'd admired his work for years from a distance, and I felt honored to be speaking with "Mr. Dry Bones" himself.

"Dry Bones" is actually Yaakov Kirschen. He began his daily editorial strip called "Dry Bones" in January 1973. The *Jerusalem Post, New York Times*, LA Times and a host of other publications around the globe have run his work. He laces his simple but profound cartoons with satire, wit and, above all, cutting truth. He often says more in one cartoon than op-eds do in hundreds of words. His art form—refined over more than four decades—communicates raw realities in just a few sentences.

For example, in one cartoon, he shows two jihadists. One proclaims: "We Islamists are not just a bunch of Jew-hating terrorists."

"You're not?"

"Of course not! We also murder Christians!"[2]

Kirschen left Brooklyn, New York, in 1973 and moved to Israel. Inspired by the Book of Ezekiel, he named his cartoon "Dry Bones."

"When I came to Israel and decided I would start doing a cartoon, I thought . . . well, I needed a name like 'Kirschen's Korner,' with Korner spelled with a K, and I kept thinking what should it be? Then I realized that one of the things that had brought me to Israel was my reading of the Book of Ezekiel. And in that book, this guy Ezekiel who lived 2600 years ago saw a vision of what was the far future. And that was of a time when it looked like the world had destroyed the Jewish people but at that point we would come out of our graves, and the image he saw was of a valley filled with dry bones . . . and these bones came together like the knee bone connected to the shin bone and all like that. And in that imagery, he saw the rebuilding of the Jewish state. He saw the coming together, the ingathering of the Jewish people. He saw the rebuilding of the cities and the planting of the trees and, therefore, if I was going to do a cartoon about what was happening today, all I could do would be to add to what he had seen incredibly 2600 years ago, and so I had decided to call it 'Dry Bones'."[3]

For more than forty years, Kirschen (known to many as simply "Bones") aimed his political commentary at Islamic terrorists and anti-Semites. Now he called to let me know he'd taken on a new cause. He turned his cartoon spotlight on what "Bones" called one of the worst problems in the world today—the persecution of Middle East Christians. He wanted help to tell a story about his fledgling Internet campaign, one he hoped would open the eyes of the world to the all-out attack on these Christians. After spending time with a number of Middle Eastern brothers and sisters who were forced to "convert or die" or see their churches destroyed, I readily agreed. If someone like "Dry Bones" wanted to trumpet their plight, it was a story worth telling. We agreed on a date and time to meet.

## FIGHTING BACK

Several days later, our cameraman Jonathan and I arrived at Kirschen's home studio. Tucked away at the end of a street in a Tel Aviv suburb, the place immediately had the feel of an artist's retreat. It looked like a rumpled but comfortable shirt. He cheerfully greeted Jonathan and me and then introduced us to Sali, whom he called his "LSW." That translated into "long-suffering wife." Sali painted, so these two artists filled their eclectic home with her paintings and his cartoons. Kirschen and his "LSW" sprinkled our time with self-deprecating good humor. We began a delightful day.

We sat down in his cluttered studio and started our interview. We heard his passion and outrage on behalf of persecuted Christians: "Christian communities are being totally slaughtered and murdered and driven out and a whole ethnic cleansing of the Middle East—to wipe out Christianity—and Western leaders just look the other way."[4]

Kirschen viewed the situation as a Jew who knows what it means to be silent in the face of evil. He couldn't fathom the apathy of the Western church to what he called a Holocaust facing Middle East Christians. "I think the unusual thing is the apathy. It's totally crazy that the churches are not speaking out; that the politicians are not speaking out; that there aren't demonstrations in the street."[5]

This widespread indifference provoked Kirschen to turn up the volume and use his cartoon megaphone. To attack this lethargy, he enlisted his "LSW" and their intern Michael into a Gideon's army. Sali served as the entire shipping and fulfillment departments. This trio launched an Internet campaign to rally support for persecuted Christians. He hoped to turn "Dry Bones" fans into members and then activists. "People have to find a way to fight back against this, and if our churches and our Jewish organizations and our political leaders are willing to go along with the willful re-writing of history; if they are willing to go along with just looking the other way while the Christians in the Middle East are totally slaughtered and wiped out, then we the people need to do something."[6]

We completed our interview, said goodbye to this merry band, and later produced a story on their campaign. We met "Bones" just before the Christmas season, and this Jewish artist penned two cartoons on behalf of the suffering Christians in the Middle East. We ended our story with them: One cartoon said: "Santa Claus will have it easy this year. Just about the only place left in the Middle East with Christians left to visit is the Jewish state."[7] Another pleaded: "A Christmas wish for Christian communities across the Middle East: May the world hear your cries for help."[8]

## NO MORE RELIGIOUS FREEDOM

Those cries for help Kirschen so eloquently expressed could have come from the Christians in the Syrian town of al-Karenten. In August 2015, the Islamic State captured the area. They allowed the Christians to live, but only if they signed the document below. This written agreement, forced from these Middle Eastern Christians at the threat of death, is something few believers in the West could comprehend:

1. *Christians may not build churches, monasteries, or hermitages in the city or in the surrounding areas*

2. *They may not show the cross or any of their books in the Muslims' streets or markets, and may not use amplifiers when worshiping or during prayer.*

3. *They may not make Muslims hear the reciting of their books or the sounds of church bells, which must be rung only inside their churches.*

4. *They may not carry out any act of aggression against ISIS, such as giving refuge to spies and wanted men. If they come to know of any plot against Muslims, they must report it.*

5. *They must not perform religious rituals in public.*

6. *They must respect Muslims and not criticize their religion.*

> *7. Wealthy Christians must pay an annual jizya of four gold dinars; middle-class Christians must pay two gold dinars, and the poor must pay one. Christians must disclose their income and may split the jizya into two payments.*
>
> *8. They may not own guns.*
>
> *9. They may not engage in commercial activity involving pigs or alcohol with Muslims or in Muslim markets, and may not drink alcohol in public.*
>
> *10. They may maintain their own cemeteries.*
>
> *11. They must abide by ISIS dress code and commerce guidelines."*[9]

ISIS based their document on a seventh-century agreement known as the Pact of Umar. Umar bin Khattab, the second Muslim Caliph, conquered Jerusalem in 638. After he captured the city, he drew up a list of conditions by which Christians could live under Islamic rule. What we're seeing in Syria today is a return to seventh-century Islam.

For the Christians living in al-Karenten, the agreement is part of "dhimmitude." Dhimmitude allows Christians to live alongside Muslims but only as second- or even third-class citizens. Christians have suffered this status on and off within the Islamic world for 1400 years. As the document says, submit or else:

> They may dwell in the shade of Allah who will pray for their protector and grant him peace until the day that Allah brings his word [at the end of time], as long as they adhere carefully to the conditions in this document. If they do not keep any part of what is written in this document, they will have no more protection and the Islamic State can do to them what it is allowed to do to militants and objectors.[10]

What the Islamic State allows itself to do for "militants and objectors" is murder them. The document cites the Quran as its source:

> Fight those who do not believe in Allah or in the Last Day and who do not consider unlawful what Allah and His Messenger have made unlawful and who do not adopt the religion of

truth from those who were given the Scripture—[fight] until they give the jizya willingly in submission.[11]

In an ISIS video message posted online about the document, an ISIS spokesman issued a brazen call to other Christians:

> To conclude, this is a message to all the Christians in the East and West, and to America, the defender of the cross: Convert to Islam, and no harm will befall you. But if you refuse, you will have to pay the jizya tax. As our Sheikh Al-'Adnan said: The payment of the jizya is a thousand times less than the Christian investment in the futile war against the Islamic State.[12]

Christians in the village signed the document on August 30, 2015. Todd Daniels, Middle East Regional Manager for International Christian Concern, warned it represented yet another blow to Christianity in the Middle East. He said,

> The release of this agreement once again highlights the intent of the jihadists of ISIS to create a society in which only those who follow their strict interpretation of Islam have any sense of freedom. These restrictions nearly eliminate the presence of Christianity in this region.

## TWENTY-FIRST CENTURY CRUSADE

Throughout their caliphate, ISIS leaders continued their campaign to eradicate any trace of Christianity. *These are a few examples of their "crusade":*

> The twisted terror group today released a video showing its barbaric militants razing the ancient Mar Elian monastery to the ground, even digging up and desecrating the bones of a Christian saint. There were reports that fighters had also kidnapped the monastery's abbot, Father Jacques Mouraud, and a church volunteer, Botros Hanna, who are both now feared dead.[14]

> The Islamic State (IS) in Iraq has turned Christian homes in the city of Mosul, northern Iraq into military headquarters for the organization. Some of these houses were kept as stores

of weapons and factories for making improvised explosive devices after IS seized them. Other houses were given by the organization to its newly married members in Mosul. In the same context, IS members have stolen all Christian homes in the Nineveh Plain area, which were inhabited by more than 125,000 Christians.[15]

Sources of the Assyrian Observatory for Human Rights . . . said that elements of the terrorist organization turned all the churches of the city to mosques, except those which they blew up. The courtyards and corridors of churches were filled with sheep and cows for the purpose of slaughtering them on the occasion of Eid al-Adha.[16]

The so-called Education Office of the Islamic State (IS) announced the start of the 2015-2016 school year. . . .The curricula contain texts that describe Christians as infidels who must be fought.[17]

What makes ISIS's actions even worse? Their actions inspire other Islamic groups around the world.

Dr. David Curry, President of Open Doors, a group that monitors religious freedom worldwide, warned, "So you have the Islamic State, their tactics, their methodology now being adopted by Boko Haram, by Al-Shabaab and others, and so I think this means that, while this year was the worst ever, things look very troubling for years to come."[18]

Some observers believe the eradication of Christianity in the Middle East is a replay of the attempt to eradicate Judaism in Europe in the middle of the twentieth century.

Middle Eastern Christians are being exterminated by Islamic State, or ISIS, simply because they are Christians. As Jews were forced to wear the yellow Star of David in Nazi Germany, Christian homes are marked with the Arabic letter "N" for Nazarene. Iraqi Sister Diana Momeka testified to the House Foreign Affairs Committee in May that "ISIS's plan is to evacuate the land of Christians and wipe the earth clean of any evidence that we ever existed.[19]

## CALLING IT WHAT IT IS

**Genocide** is a word used more and more by Christian leaders to describe the situation in the Middle East for the church, leaders like Pope Francis:

> Today we are dismayed to see how in the Middle East and elsewhere in the world many of our brothers and sisters are persecuted, tortured and killed for their faith in Jesus. In this third world war, waged piecemeal, which we are now experiencing," he continued, a form of genocide is taking place.[20]

Congress is using that word, too:

Rep. Anna Eshoo, a Democrat from California, and Rep. Jeff Fortenberry, a Republican from Nebraska, co-chair the Religious Minorities Caucus on the Middle East. They introduced a resolution that read in part:

> Expressing the sense of Congress that those who commit or support atrocities against Christians and other ethnic and religious minorities . . . and who target them specifically for ethnic or religious reasons, are committing, and are hereby declared to be committing "war crimes," "crimes against humanity," and "*genocide*."[21]

Eshoo, a Chaldean Catholic, defended the use of the word.

> A genocide, because the oldest of the Christian communities are really being wiped out and there are so many other religious people of religious backgrounds that are going with them, too. I think that unless we call this and name this what it is, that we will be judged poorly and so it's with sadness that I say that we have legislation to call this genocide.[22]

Fortenberry described a dire situation for Middle East Christianity:

> The ancient faith tradition lies beaten, broken, and dying. Yet Christians in Iraq and Syria are hanging on in the face of the Islamic State's barbarous onslaught. This is genocide. The international community must confront the scandalous

silence about their plight. Christians, Yazidis, and other religious minorities have every right to remain in their ancestral homelands.[23]

Some Congressmen, like Texas Republican Ted Coe, say the White House and President Obama have left a void about the plight of Middle East Christians.

Christians are in trouble throughout the Middle East and northern Africa – I hope this administration dials up concern for Christians. . . . I don't know what the administration thought, that things couldn't get worse or whatever.[24]

Former Republican Frank Wolf of Virginian said,

Does this administration care? This is genocide.[25]

He noted when ISIS beheaded twenty-one Coptic Christians in Libya, the White House referred to them as simply "twenty-one Egyptians."[26]

In Erbil, I asked retired General Jay Garner what the Obama administration has done—or not done—for Middle East Christians. He said,

I don't know of one utterance coming from our government about the persecution of Christians in the Middle East. The only thing I've heard, the only quasi-religious statement I've heard the president say several times is that ISIS is not Islam. I don't know what . . . he thinks the "I" stands for, but there's been no dialogue at all about the terrible, terrible, terrible persecution of Christians in the Middle East, and I think that's tragic.[27]

Despite the inaction of the Obama administration, some are stepping in the gap to help Middle East Christians facing genocide. Two unlikely allies—one from a Washington D.C. think tank and the other from the world of entertainment—are teaming up to aid these Christians.

Nina Shea, the director of the Center for Religious Freedom at the Hudson Institute, and Mark Burnett of "Survivor" fame are teaming up to aid those Christians who need to find a new home. I met with Shea in CBN News' Washington D.C. studio. She said the world in good conscience cannot ignore them:

> They need to know that Christians are facing genocide. They need to help these Christians. They need to help them with their prayer and with aid to leave. ISIS stripped them of all their property. When they went into exile, they went into safe havens that will not give them residency status, that will not give them worker authorizations. So they have no money. So it's a very bleak picture.[28]

They plan to resettle these Christians in comfortable surroundings and hope their proposal may offer a way out for many caught in a heart-wrenching dilemma. They can't go home—ISIS has taken their property—and they can't work to support their families.

> We've decided that for the most-needy cases, they need to leave; they need to start their lives over. They need to be resettled in countries that would give them work authorization that would allow them to rebuild their lives. For the Armenians, Armenia; . . . for Orthodox communities, we're looking at Orthodox countries, maybe Georgia, maybe Russia, maybe some places in Eastern Europe. For Protestants, we're looking at the Western countries.[29]

While the numbers are staggering, Shea adds that Christians face an even greater danger.

> Now, the difference with Christians is that they . . . underneath the conflict, they're not just running from a conflict. They're running from targeted persecution against them.[30]

Shea calls on the Church not only to pray, but to get involved.

> The Church of the West and the free world, Latin America, needs to pray all the time, I mean, not just once a year, but pray every Sunday in congregation for these persecuted Christians. And if they can, [they should] contact their political representatives and the candidates running for office to say the United States should take its share of Christians as well.[31]

## CRIES FOR HELP

Who are these Christians and what are their cries for help?

I met a number of them on the dusty streets of the Anka-wa refugee camp just on the outskirts of Erbil. We came to one of the camps that houses about five thousand Christian refugees. The camp is a fusion of cars, kids scurrying on bikes, children playing, and people sitting on their front stoops. Caravans—small trail-ers—are stacked end to end and make up the backbone of the camp. They're the new homes for these refugees who used to live just an hour's drive away.

Without any work, it's easy to see how boredom could set in. When we join the mix, our camera is a welcome interlude and an instant attraction. Especially when we start to ask questions about their condition, they want to talk. They want the world to know what they're going through.

One Christian woman lamented, like Job, that living in Iraq has been one lifelong ordeal. With frustration etched on her face, she told us:

> Every day we're experiencing or living with crisis: economic crisis and financial crisis and explosions; the war with Kuwait, the war with Iran, the war with ISIS, the war with terror. We have spent all of our days with problems, with wars and battles. This is how we have lived and we continue to live. Now we're living in these caravans.[32]

One man declared that no one wants to remain in the camps, or Iraq. He said,

> "The Christians with financial ability have already left the country and the people you see here don't have the means to leave."[33] He said many Christians had moved to the Nineveh Plain, ironically to be safe. Then ISIS came. Now they face an uncertain future: "We don't know what will happen.[34]

During our visit, we ran into Myriam, the ten-year-old we interviewed at church. She giggled like any young girl playing jump rope with her sister. They didn't have a real rope, so they used an electrical cable. It worked. Jonathan videotaped the two playing. Then he packed away his camera and began to amuse the girls with his juggling ability. Soon a bunch of small kids gathered to see the show.

After Jonathan's show, we interviewed Myriam's father Walid about what it's like living in the camp. He said it's a listless existence for people who are used to working, providing for their families, and being productive.

We're still inside our country, but we feel that we have no aim for our life. We want something to show us we have an aim to live. I don't know where, anywhere there is a job, because we are people of life. We are not the kind of people to stay in a caravan for all of our life as a refugee. As a person, I don't like it. Even if they will give me better than this place in the name of refugee, I don't like it. I am free. I have to be a free man wherever I live. I want to work. If not for me as an old man at sixty, then there are young people that want to work. They want to establish a new family. They don't have aim. Even they can't marry because they don't have money to make a life. Because a new life they need money, furniture, something. From where do they have all these things if he doesn't have good work and a good salary and what they call making money to make a life for themselves?[35]

With the sun already set, the lights on, and with cars driving by, he asked for prayer.

Pray for us in the name of God our Savior in their heart to tell their governments. I would love for you to visit us in our city once upon a time. God's people are alive people. We are not dead people. We were having a lot of money, of good healthy (and) wealthy living. And that is why I want to get the people in the world to look to us. To look to us.[36]

CBN News Story: "Jewish Cartoonist Confronts 'Holocaust' of Mideast Christians"

CBN News Story: "Christians Facing Genocide Need Your Help Now"

CBN News Story: "Abandoned? Mideast Christians Overlooked in the War on Terror"

# Aslan Is on the Move

*"They say Aslan is on the move . . . perhaps has already landed."*

- Mr. Beaver, from C.S. Lewis,
*The Lion, the Witch, and the Wardrobe*[1]

C.S. Lewis enthralled generations of readers with his seven-book children's series, The Chronicles of Narnia. Lewis created Aslan, a noble lion, as his main character. In chapter 7 of *The Lion, the Witch and the Wardrobe*, he's introduced by Mr. Beaver: "They say Aslan is on the move . . . perhaps has already landed."[2] The impact was immediate to everyone who heard: "And now a very curious thing happened. None of the children knew who Aslan was any more than you do; but the moment the Beaver had spoken these words, everyone felt very different."[3]

The series inspired both young and old, who often read the stories to their children. Aslan represents Jesus Christ and, just as Aslan was "on the move" in Narnia, Jesus is on the move in the Middle East. Not just ISIS.

## BEHIND THE ISLAMIC CURTAIN OF IRAN

A group of us ringed the long table, standing behind our chairs. The head of the home offered a quiet prayer of thanks for the food and for the guests assembled from different parts of the Middle East . . . Israel, Iraq, and Iran. After his prayer, we sat down to a simple but delicious meal. The women and children had prepared a hearty menu of chili, white and yellow rice, bread, and sodas. Several kids sat at one end of the table; the adults, at the other in this family-friendly atmosphere.

We'd just returned from a two-hour prayer and worship service in a local church. For the Westerners who came from the safety of Israel, the U.S., or the relative security of Kurdistan, the gathering was edifying, yet an experience we've enjoyed many times. But for five Iranians, the experience shot through their souls with a Heaven-sent breath of fresh and free spiritual air.

"It was incredible!" they exclaimed. "The happiest day of our lives will be when there are more followers of Jesus!"

They came from Iran to take part in three days of Bible study and training. During the meal, we asked our new Iranian friends what life was like inside the Islamic Republic of Iran. While we already knew that the regime oppressed, imprisoned, and tortured Christians and opponents of the government, hearing their personal accounts brought a new reality. Between second helpings of chili and rice, we heard sobering testimonies about the challenges they face every day.

We can't tell you their names, but our Iranian friends included a mother and daughter, a single man, and a married couple. For the purposes of this story, we'll call them by the names of the children from *The Lion, the Witch and the Wardrobe*: Lucy, Susan, Edmund and Peter. To round out the five, I'll add one more name, Joy. We felt compelled to know more about what life was like in a country just a few hundred miles away, but centuries ago in time. And so we listened to life behind the Islamic curtain of Iran.

First of all, we found out they have police nearly everywhere and for nearly everything. For example, religious police scrutinize women's veils to make sure they conform to Iranian standards. You can be fined if the *hijab* (a veil covering the head and chest of Muslim women) doesn't cover enough of the face. Many hate the veil. In fact, the women told us as soon as they crossed the border out of Iran, they threw off their veils. Their repulsion to the hijab runs deep.

We learned how deep a little later when we interviewed these women. For their own protection, we asked them to put on a veil to hide their identity. If it was discovered that they had been interviewed by a foreign, *Christian* news agency, they could be imprisoned, or worse. However, when we proposed the veil for one of the women—I'll call her Joy—she objected. "This is what I escaped. It's what I'm resisting. Why should I put it on again?" We obliged. Instead, we videotaped her shadow on the wall.

Iran forbids dancing . . . everywhere. In fact, we were told that even during a wedding, police may raid the ceremony to make sure no one is dancing. Men and women are also forbidden to meet in public without permission. Lucy and Edmund told us that if they appeared together in public, they'd have to explain that some family member sanctioned their rendezvous. Otherwise, fines, reprimands, or even jail could follow.

More stories continue. They tell us a street vendor, taxi driver, or just any passerby might be an undercover policeman or woman. You never know. They say dogs are forbidden in public; they can be shot. The police prohibit drinking, yet drug addiction is epidemic. "In fact, the U.N. drug office estimates 2.2 percent of the Iranian population are addicts."[4]

They laugh when they tell us there are even police for window mannequins. If a store owner fails to properly veil his mannequin, the owner can be fined, his shop closed, and his mannequin removed. If they go to church three times, they may be arrested. Marriage to a Christian is strictly forbidden.

Many of their young people especially hate this paranoid regime. Many hate Islam.

During our conversation, at the end of the table Lucy picked up her empty teacup and turned it upside down. She said, "This is Iran. The living conditions are horrible." They all agreed. "Bad is becoming even worse. Even some young girls engage in prostitution to survive."

During our time together, I looked around the table, heard the laughter, saw their smiles, and thought what delightful, life-loving people, yet they live in one of the most repressive nations on earth. They hunger and thirst for freedom and righteousness.

Someone recalled the summer of 2009. At that time, Iranians went to the polls to elect a new president. They voted overwhelmingly for a reformer named Mousavi. Despite the results, the regime asserted Mahmoud Ahmadinejad won. In what became known as the "Green Revolution," millions of Iranians—including some of those around our dinner table—took to the streets. But the police, the Iranian Revolutionary Guard, and the infamous Basij—a brutal paramilitary group—met them with batons, pepper spray, sticks, and guns. They closed Tehran University, blocked web sites, cell phones, text messages, and banned rallies.

Not only that, they shot and killed one protestor, Neda Agha-Soltan. As she bled to death, the grisly scene was caught on camera and spread on YouTube. Her murder became the bloody symbol of their revolt. Many others died. The police arrested thousands, and infamous prisons like Kahrizak and Evin swelled with the incarcerated.

The dissidents waited for those in the free world—especially the U.S.—to speak up and speak out on their behalf. They waited and hoped for help, but "it didn't come." With dessert—cookies and watermelon—now on the table, our friends continued their grim recital. "Many Iranians are searching for life and peace." Behind the veil of Iran, men and women are longing to be free. I listened and pondered that our government's foreign policy had very likely emboldened their masters and made the liberty they pine for even more elusive.

# MORE THAN DREAMS

The next night we returned, this time to record their testimonies on camera for a CBN news story. We interviewed Lucy, Susan, Joy, and Edmund. Peter, the quietest of the group, says his wife Joy will do the talking for the both of them.

*Lucy was the first to speak:*

"I had a dream. The dream was 27 years ago when I was pregnant. I was having a hard life with my family and my husband. I was very, very sad. Suddenly, one of the nights when I was in my bed, I dreamed, and the Light was speaking as I'm speaking to you now. It was speaking to me, and calling my name, and saying, 'Come to Me. I will save you and I will rescue you.' But I didn't understand, actually, how this could be. Others in the dream said, 'Come with us. Please do not hesitate. Come to us and we will rescue you.'

"I believed in the dream, but I didn't surrender my whole life to the Source of the light, which was Christ. Actually, I didn't dare to talk about the dream or even about Jesus with my family because I was in a very extreme sort of family. I got a copy of the Bible, and I started to read it. I told my father-in-law about the dream. He also believed in Jesus. He loved the Christians. He loved the Gospel and read the Gospel every day, but he didn't tell others that he is a believer. 'Do not talk about this (dream) anywhere because they might kill you,' he said to me. 'You're putting your life at risk.'

"This year, about seven months ago, we made our own decision to follow Jesus with all our hearts. When we came here, they gave us an explanation about the life of Christ and the Kingdom of God according to the Gospel. Here we realized that the dream that I dreamed was Jesus. He is calling us to give us salvation and to give us rest, to give us life."[5]

*I asked what dangers she will face when she goes back.*

"If people knew about my faith, I would be rejected. This is a kind of social persecution. But if the government knew about my faith, I would be executed or hung on the street at once."[6]

*Susan told her story next:*

"When I first started to read the Gospel, a power came out through the Bible to my heart. It was just like a small rock in the middle of a sea, yes, of the sea. A power came into my life, and I feel that I'm not the same person. I'm about to be reborn, coming out from something very dead, very bad.

"Something that is unique happened to me. . . . I didn't know what, actually, but it was a very unique power. One of the nights when I went to my bed, I saw Jesus. He was talking to me in Heaven about the Kingdom of God. When I saw Jesus, He pointed to me. Later, He told me that I had to read the Gospel in order to strengthen my faith and be able to share my faith with my friends. It was midnight.

"I woke up and I called my brother. I told him I had a dream, and Jesus was talking to me about Heaven. 'What shall I do?' And he said. 'You have to keep silent, be careful about the dream. Do not talk to people until you get the Gospel and you start to read the Bible. Then, when you mature or God matures you in your faith, you can share your faith with other people.'[7]

*She then described Jesus.*

"I didn't see actually His face, but I saw His form, you know. He was a King and His kingdom ... or His kingship rule was over the whole universe, and everybody was bowing down to Him. He was talking about His kingdom and I was one of those who stood before Him."[8]

*I asked how she felt when she saw Jesus.*

"I actually cannot describe how with words. I feel that it was a kind of fire or flames coming up (in my being)."[9]

*"And how do you feel now that you believe in Jesus?" I asked.*

"I feel I have a very huge, big treasure. As much as I'm giving away, more comes back to me. You know, Iran is a very dangerous place. If you don't think just like the others or the majority, you're considered a rebel. So that means you will choose your fate or your death by your own hand. When I'm going back, the people might get surprised about what they hear from me about my faith. But concerning the government, I would be considered as a convert, so they might attack me on the street. This is a possible scenario for me when I go back if they can prove that I've converted to Christianity."[10]

*After refusing the veil, Joy shared this testimony.*

"There's a big library in my city. I went there looking for the Bible. I will never forget the day that I found the Bible on one of the shelves of the library. It was a small Bible written in Farsi. I didn't feel comfortable to take that Holy Book back home and show it to my entire family. They were forcing me to pray Islamic prayers five times a day and fast and practice Sharia, the Islamic law. So it was not easy for me to take the Bible home and show them.

"But I took it home anyway and hid it in a very private place. Every day, I took it out and read a passage in the Bible and put it back into its hiding place. For the first time, I saw both the Old Testament and New Testament in the Bible. I didn't understand what that meant. I didn't fully understand. When I was reading the Bible, I couldn't ask others to give an explanation about the passages that I'm reading. But then I went to university. During the studying at the university, I met an Armenian girl. She was very pretty, and I asked her so many questions concerning Christianity, the religion of Christianity, the faith of Christianity. How do they live? How do they worship? Many things like that about Christian life. She answered my questions, and that introduction caused me to make my own decision."[11]

*After Joy's decision, life changed.*

"You know the faithful Christ brought me many blessings. I cannot describe how faithful Jesus is in some words. But things which I cannot say in some words have happened to me.

Whenever I'm praying, and I'm lifting up my feelings in my heart to God, I do believe, and I feel the hand of God touching my heart and shaking my soul."[12]

*Like Lucy and Susan, Joy asked for prayer:*

"Pray for the people, the persecuted people. Right now I can lift up my prayers, but you can do also with many people. You can pray for their salvation . . . wherever they live . . . and asking God's face to shine on them. So please pray for our people and the location that I cannot mention."[13]

*Edmund, a single man, then told his story:*

"As anybody else in Iran, I grew up in a Muslim family. They were extremely religious. I was obligated to practice Islam and do what Islam said like praying and fasting and reading the Quran; doing everything Islam required. But my heart actually was not comfortable with it. That's why later, I hated Islam and I hated God and I hated everything else. I left everything behind. I didn't believe in religion.

"But in my heart, I couldn't believe that there was no God. I kept looking for God or for an answer to my questions. This is why I started to look for God in other religions like Buddhism and Judaism and the others. But I also found the need of my spirit was not satisfied through those religions. Two friends shared the Gospel with me, but I refused to accept it. I looked at God as a dictator, and I didn't accept what they said. But I kept asking Him to show Himself to me in order to believe Him."[14]

*One night Edmund went to sleep and had a dream about Jesus:*

"In that dream, He appeared in the sky above Iran. He was shining, and His brightness was very strong. When He shined on the people of Iran, I saw black wolves in the hearts of everybody. I even saw the black wolves in me. Later, He turned and looked at me in this vision in my heart. He gave me the strength and power to capture the black wolves in my heart and take them out and kill them. In the dream, I still remember some marks on His face and that He was wearing a crown, a king's crown, on His head. Very strong brightness came out of each part of His body, and many people were bowing down before Him."[15]

*The dream became a turning point.*

"I still live on the memory of that dream. It's still alive in me, and it's with me every day. I remember in my mind the things that I saw in Heaven. He's shown me many different things since I believed in Jesus. I didn't know how to reach out to the heart of the people and share about Him. . . . I was here with some friends of mine, and when we went back home, one of our friends betrayed us. He told the government about our visit (outside of Iran), and when I went back to Iran, the police started looking for me. I ran away, came here, and now I cannot go back to my country."[16]

*I asked him if others are coming to Jesus inside Iran.*

"Yes, many people are coming to Christ through a dream. You cannot imagine how Jesus is appearing to them. I experienced with my own eyes that everybody is looking for a home, looking for the truth. You know the experience that the Iranian people are passing through right now is very difficult. The only One who can change that situation is Christ Himself. So please pray and ask the others to pray for the people of Iran to experience the power of the Resurrection."[17]

During these interviews, I felt a heavy responsibility. Their identity rests in our hands. When we broadcast their stories, there's no room for error. I remember the story of one Chinese believer trying to escape his homeland. He came to an airport and felt the Holy Spirit telling him not to speak. Only later did he discover that Chinese security had installed a voice recognition system. If he had spoken, he might have been recognized. I wondered what photo, voice, or other security systems Iran uses to track down Christians.

I asked myself, *Does the veil hide enough? Can they identify my sisters by seeing just their eyes? Do we need to blur those as well?* We have since taken that precaution. These kinds of interviews feel like walking a high wire act without a net, except I'm not the one walking the tight rope. They are. No room for error. Error could mean death by hanging.

## AN EMPTY DAMASCUS CEMETERY

We met in a park next to King David Street. The walls of the Old City and the Tower of David stood sentry in the distance, marked by the warm Jerusalem summer sun. My good friend Tom Doyle exclaimed, "If you watch the news, you'd think everyone is getting creamed out there and that everyone is leaving! Far from it! The Southern Baptists are saying the fastest-growing church per capita now is in the Middle East."[18]

I admire the invaluable work Doyle does to chronicle how Jesus is moving in the Middle East. His book *Dreams and Visions: Is Jesus Shaking the Muslim World?* records stories just like Lucy, Susan, Joy, and Edmund. It's a powerful tome of how Jesus Himself is appearing to Muslims in dreams and visions, a profound chapter in the story of today's Middle East. In fact, you can't understand what's happening in the Middle East without knowing about this unprecedented movement.

I interviewed Doyle for a segment of *Jerusalem Dateline*. We stood in the relative safety of Jerusalem, less than two hundred miles away from the ancient city of Damascus. The Apostle Paul traveled there two thousand years ago and had his "Damascus road" experience. Now the city lay on the fault line between the deadly regime of President Bashar Assad and the bloodthirsty Islamist armies of ISIS and Al Nusra. It's one of the most dangerous cities in the world. Yet a number of believers in the city have counted the cost and made their choice. It's one of many heroic stories Doyle has recorded in his latest book, *Killing Christians: Living the Faith Where It's Not Safe to Believe*.

Doyle told us about some men who followed in Paul's footsteps nearly two thousand years after his dramatic conversion. These men, too, faced a life-and-death decision. "In Syria, there's a group of believers—ten of them, with Farid as their leader—who plant churches in the underground. It was getting so dangerous in Syria, with the war just dragging on into the fourth year with no signs of letting up. So Farid decided to give all the leaders a chance to leave the country. There might be a day when they can't get out, and they're all young and have families.

"So they had a prayer meeting, and he asked them to fast and pray for a week to see if the Lord wanted them to leave or to stay in Syria. He would certainly understand if they needed to leave. But they should come back with their decision. And so the team fasted and prayed for a week.

"A week later, Farid walked downstairs into the basement of this house in Damascus, thinking, *I wonder if anyone's even going to be there. I mean, why would they stay?* But when he opened the door, Chris, there were not two or five or ten people, there were actually twenty-five leaders there! The ten had gone out and recruited fifteen more. They said, 'We're ready to stay.' We're ready to suffer. We're ready to die here in Syria for Jesus.' And to seal this commitment, they went out and bought a plot of land so they can bury each other when they die as martyrs for Christ.

"When we get communications from them, it's so sobering. They'll talk about what the Lord is doing. 'Jesus is on the move.' 'He's winning hearts.' 'He's showing His love in Syria.' 'And the graveyard is still empty.'"[19]

When I heard Doyle's story, I didn't know what to say. During an interview, I am listening, but I am also mentally preparing my next question. His story, though, left me stunned. When I heard those words—"they went out and bought a plot of land so they can bury each other when they die as martyrs for Christ"—I got a knot in my throat. It took my breath away. They were willing "to give the last full measure of devotion." Jesus said it best: *"Greater love hath no man than he lay down his life for his brothers."* These men in Damascus, as well as other men and women throughout the Middle East, are living out their faith with Heaven-sent bravery. They're following in the footsteps of the heroes and heroines listed in Hebrews 11, of whom it was said: *"The world is not worthy."*

In his book, Doyle included a somber, yet uplifting personal message from Farid: "I think what followers of Christ in Syria fear most are the crucifixions. It's a horrifying prospect. Death on a cross is gruesome, and on top of that, crowds mock and torture the believers leading up to actually nailing them onto crosses. Some who face this are new in the faith, and I don't blame them for being frightened. But it would be an honor to die for Jesus in this way. Just think: The Lamb of God went to the cross in Jerusalem only two hundred miles from Damascus.

"Now, two thousand years later, the prospect hangs over our heads as a real possibility just like it did for Jesus and His followers in the first century. But regardless of which of us ends up literally crucified for Christ, the question is: Have we not died already? Paul, who was converted right here in Syria, proclaimed, 'I am crucified with Christ.' . . . Although Paul once sacrificed Christians, he met Jesus, gave up all his 'rights,' and made himself a living sacrifice. Once you live like this, you grasp the most profound fulfillment possible in life.

"Pray for us in Syria, but please do not feel bad for us. We have never been more free. And even though we're willing to die, our graveyard is still empty."[20]

I realize I have a lot to learn from my Syrian brothers.

## NEWS FROM A KURDISTAN ROOFTOP

About five hundred miles away from Farid in Damascus, another Christian worker labors in one of the many Middle Eastern spiritual fields. His plot sits about an hour's drive from the front line of ISIS. He's one of a growing movement in the region, those who are plowing deep spiritual furrows of intercession. For the past several years, prayer pioneers have planted these "lighthouses" of prayer throughout the region and in some of the most unlikely places.

We climbed several flights of stairs to the rooftop of a building under construction. It's scheduled to be their new home soon. With a setting sun behind us, a panoramic view all around us, and an open heaven above us, we began our interview with Fabian, the co-leader of the Mesopotamia House of Prayer. I asked him how the prayer movement is going after ISIS plowed their way into northern Iraq.

"We are actually seeing momentum building in the area of worship and prayer. Actually, since ISIS started coming into Iraq in June of last year. We know the plan of the enemy—besides killing and destroying lives—is to push salt and light out so that God's purposes will not be fulfilled. God, of course, has a plan and during that time is when God started to move on my heart to believe Him for a prayer movement. Same time the director of (another) house of prayer had a vision of the altar of worship and prayer starting to rise out of the Kurdish region of Iraq and other things, like a reservoir being prepared to hold the waters that were going to be poured out. And shortly after that, in September, we had fifty hours of continuous worship and prayer. God's presence during those prayer meetings came in very powerful ways. People were born again in the prayer meetings. People got physically healed. Believers were telling me, 'We don't want this to stop.'

"And since that time, we've had teams coming to join us in worship and prayer. Training locals to serve in the house of prayer and to lead in singing—the Iraqis have written new songs—so we've been seeing an increase in the presence of God in the prayer meetings. It's been wonderful! Just as He has spoken . . . yes, we are seeing the altar of worship and prayer rise from this land. And people are truly standing in the gap.

"More than anything, what means a lot to us is building a habitation for His presence. And that's the culture that's being cultivated among believers. That we don't pray and worship just because all this is happening around us. We do this because we love Him. And we want God to build a resting place where His presence can remain and where His church can grow and multiply and prepare for His return."[21]

Fabian sees new relationships being forged in the midst of this great Middle Eastern crucible.

"People falling in love with Jesus. Others opening up to the Gospel for the first time. So besides the darkness coming in and trying to get the salt and light out and taking lives, bringing so much pain and suffering, we're also seeing the rise of the presence of God, worship, prayer, people experiencing Jesus. And people coming to know Him and follow Him—even from a Muslim background."[22]

## A LION AND A KIDDIE POOL

After our interviews with Lucy, Susan, Joy, and Edmund, they are ready for the highlight of their visit, water baptism. They've been born again. Now they want to take the next step in their new life of faith. Earlier, the children filled their kiddie pool with water. The pool is blue, about two feet high, ten or twelve feet long and wide. Big enough.

Under a warm Middle Eastern sky, one leader explains baptism and why one should get baptized. "First of all," he says, "Jesus told us to do it. Second, the Bible says that when we're baptized, our old life is buried and we're raised up in the newness of Christ. We celebrate the death of our old life and welcome our new life. The angels in Heaven are watching and rejoicing."

By this time, Joy is already crying. She pours out her grateful heart, "What a beautiful life!"

She's the most vocal of the group and can't wait any longer. She wants to go first. Another leader and her husband Peter perform her baptism. They baptize her in the name of the Father, Son, and Holy Spirit and then plunge her beneath the water. She comes up, flings her arms into the air, and begins to weep. She falls into the arms of Peter and sobs, then yells, "Congratulations to me! Happy my new birthday!" Her English is awkward and her theology amiss, but her heart is overflowing. Everyone applauds.

Peter goes next. He says he was baptized as a child, but he insists, "I want to do this."

Mother and daughter—Lucy and Susan—follow. Both are deeply moved. Both are crying. The joy on their faces reflects the Scripture in 1 Peter 1:8: *"Though you have not seen Him, you love Him. And even though you do not see Him now, you believe in Him and are filled with inexpressible and glorious joy"* (NIV).

They shout "Hallelujah!" Wet and jubilant, they begin to sing. Their song wafts up in both English and Farsi, an exclamation point to this profound experience.

"This is a miracle," Joy declares and tells me that she had a dream the night before of this very scene. Under this Middle Eastern canopy of stars, in a blue kiddie pool, and in a typical neighborhood, the Bible marks these events as eternal works. For this husband and wife, mother and daughter, and single man, it's a spiritual demarcation, a plumb line in the spirit for these new believers sealing their faith in the waters of baptism.

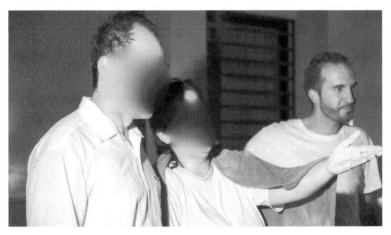

The scene reminds me of the Book of Acts, the book in the Bible that records the acts of the Apostles after Jesus ascended into Heaven. One verse sticks out: "He (Paul) went over the region of Galatia and Phrygia, strengthening all the disciples" (Acts 18:23). Within a couple of days, most of the five will return to Iran. They could be discovered, imprisoned, tortured, and even killed. Yet these Iranian believers—Lucy, Susan, Joy, Peter, and Edmund— now carry with them a deeper faith, a higher calling, and a more firm foundation from their Bible study, fellowship, and baptisms.

Profound geo-political movements are rearranging the chess board of the Middle East. Great nations vie for power. Major leaders make bold political and military moves. Yet around a dinner table or in a kiddie pool, you can see, hear, and witness the hidden history of the work of the Holy Spirit, changing hearts and transforming lives. This, too, is the story of the current crisis in the Middle East.

Aslan is on the move!

CBN News Story: "Supernatural Dreams Open Doors for Jesus in Iran"

Jerusalem Dateline Interview with author Tom Doyle.

# The Iranian Nuclear Deal

*"So I believe if this deal goes forward, we are at risk of entering a second nuclear age, and the loss of life will be not in the tens, not in the thousands, not even in the hundreds of thousands but in the millions."*

~ U.S. Senator Tom Cotton, R-AR[1]

JULY 14, 2015.

Early Tuesday morning, I came into the office and turned on the news. I wanted to get an update on the latest negotiations over **Iran's nuclear program** taking place in Vienna, Austria. The P5+1 (United States, Russia, China, Great Britain, France, and Germany) and the European Union had met for seventeen days of negotiations with the Islamic Republic of Iran. The fortnight and three days in Vienna became just the latest venue for this nuclear diplomacy that sojourned from Geneva, Lausanne, Muscat in Oman to New York City and back to Austria's capital. They'd extended the talks several times, and I expected one more postponement. But this time, the BBC, French 24, and Fox News all blared the news: They had reached an agreement! These negotiations represented the culmination of nearly two years of direct talks with a history going back more than a decade of on-and-off talks over the future and fate of one of the world's thorniest issues, **Iran's nuclear program**. While Iran insisted its nuclear program was peaceful, the world remained skeptical. This agreement aimed to ease global concerns, especially the worries of the Jewish State, the nation Iran promised one day to "wipe off the map."[2] It's a threat mulled by Iranian leaders at least since December 2001 when then President Rafsanjani said, "If one day, the Islamic world is also equipped with (nuclear) weapons like those that Israel now possesses, then the imperialists' strategy will reach a standstill because the use of even one nuclear bomb inside Israel will destroy everything. However, it will only harm the Islamic world."[3]

When I heard the news, I knew this was historic. Sitting there in my office, I really didn't think it would happen. The sides seemed too far apart and what had been leaked by then seemed a bad deal—even for the Obama Administration. However, the bad deal was now a "done deal." U.S. Secretary of State John Kerry trumpeted the breakthrough in Vienna: "This is the good deal that we sought."[4] He praised U.S. President Obama "who had the courage to launch this process, believe in it, support it, encourage it, when many thought the objective was impossible, and who led the way from start to finish."[5] President Obama for his part raced to the White House podium for a rare 7 a.m. announcement and proclaimed: "Today after two years of negotiation, the United States together with the international community has achieved something that decades of animosity had not: a comprehensive, long-term deal with Iran that will prevent it from obtaining a nuclear weapon."[6] With Vice President Joe Biden at his side, he added, "This deal is not built on trust. It's built on verification."[7]

Nearly six thousand miles away from the White House and just up the street from our Jerusalem bureau, Israeli Prime Minister Benjamin Netanyahu tweeted: "When willing to make a deal at any cost, this is the result. From early reports, we can see that this deal is a historic mistake."[8] Nearly another thousand miles further east, Iranian President Rouhani tweeted his own reaction from Tehran: "Shows constructive engagement works. With this unnecessary crisis resolved, new horizons emerge with a focus on shared challenges."[9]

Throughout the region, pro-Iranian newspapers and leaders reveled in the announcement. The pro-Hezbollah Lebanese daily *Al-Akhbar* celebrated 'the surrender of the West.'"[10] Mohammad Ra'd, the Hezbollah head in the Lebanese parliament, boasted: "Iran has started a new page (in the history) of the world . . . the world now recognizes a force (i.e., Iran) . . . that during 11 years of negotiations, not just over the past two, succeeded in humiliating the world's ruling powers."[11] Ibrahim al-Amin wrote: "The agreement between Iran and the superpowers was actually an American surrender to Iran . . . what Iran has achieved vis-à-vis the West puts us back at square one, where we must raise our voices and shout at the top of our lungs a single slogan: 'Death to America.'"[12]

The P5+1 called the agreement the Joint Comprehensive Plan of Action (JCPOA). I knew I needed to read for myself what was in the deal. After all, it represented perhaps the most important diplomatic agreement of our generation, a potential diplomatic Waterloo. The stakes have seldom been higher. One of the leading state sponsors of terrorism in the world—even according to the U.S.'s own Department of State—could be on its way to getting a nuclear bomb. Israeli officials warned the size of Iran's existing nuclear infrastructure meant it wasn't preparing to make one bomb or several, but a nuclear arsenal. They knew Israel's fate hung in the balance. Yet, they consistently warned that Iran was not just an Israeli dilemma, but a global one.

I printed a copy from the Internet and began poring over the nearly 150-page document. First, it stated what the world wanted to hear: "Iran reaffirms that under no circumstances will Iran ever seek, develop or acquire any nuclear weapons."[13] Then it declared what Iran wanted to know: "The JCPOA will produce the comprehensive lifting of all UN Security Council sanctions as well as multilateral and national sanctions related to Iran's nuclear program, including steps on access in areas of trade, technology, and energy."[14]

The good news? The agreement did set limits on certain parts of Iran's nuclear program. For example, it reduced Iran's stockpile of enriched uranium. It limited Iran's Arak heavy water plant. It restricted their research and development. It allowed some inspections of Iran's nuclear sites.

On its website, the White House boasted the "good news:"

• For the first decade, Iran will only be allowed to use its first-generation IR-1 centrifuges for enrichment purposes.

• For a decade, Iran will only be able to operate 5000 centrifuges at Natanz.

• International inspectors will have access to Iran's entire nuclear supply chain.[15]

But for all the White House optimism, the agreement contained a number of glaring flaws, that many called the "bad news."

• On page 34, it states: "Requests for access . . . will not be aimed at interfering with Iranian military or other national security activities."[16] That means inspectors would be barred from Iranian military sites. The International Atomic Energy Agency (IAEA) suspected for years that one of those sites, Parchin, was a prime location for nuclear experiments. They concluded: "Such experiments would be strong indicators of possible nuclear weapon development".[17]

• After the agreement, Senator Tom Cotton (R-AR) and Representative Mike Pompeo (R-KS) uncovered a separate secret agreement between the IAEA and Iran concerning Parchin. The one-page document revealed a stunning diplomatic capitulation. Iran would provide photos, videos, and environmental samples from Parchin to the IAEA without physically allowing IAEA inspectors on site. They added a humiliating gesture since they would only allow a public visit of the IAEA's Director General "as a courtesy by Iran."[18] Senator Cotton compared the agreement to an NFL player taking his own drug tests and phoning in the results to Commissioner Roger Goodell.

• In addition, on page 35, in case "of activities inconsistent with the JCPOA,"[19] it could take a total of 24 days before a suspicious site could be inspected. Comedian Jackie Mason quipped that New York City restaurants had more stringent inspections than the JCPOA: "You can surprise any restaurant without notice that you can walk in and inspect them … So we are protected in this city from a bad tuna fish. We're not protected from a bomb, but we're protected from a bad quality of tuna fish."[20]

• Under the heading "Nuclear Security," the agreement commits the P5+1 to protect Iran's nuclear facilities while seeming to limit Israel's ability to damage those nuclear sites. It pledged, "Co-operation through training and workshops to strengthen Iran's ability to protect against, and respond to nuclear security threats, **including sabotage**, as well as enable effective and sustainable nuclear security and physical protections systems."[21] For years, the main nation accused of sabotage against Iran's nuclear facilities has been Israel. It begs the question: **Does the deal put the U.S. in the position of protecting Iran from Israel?**

• Another aspect of the negotiations involved the breadth of the sanctions relief. For years, nearly every sector of Iran's economy labored under the burden of sanctions because of the danger of its nuclear program. The JCOPA contained a massive "get out of jail card." The deal freed nearly every one of those sectors including airlines, shipping, and petrochemicals. In fact, the bulk of the JCOPA (nearly 50 pages in my copy) listed dozens of Iranian companies no longer under sanctions.

• What's more, the sanctions relief meant the Iranian government would receive a boon of between $50 to $150 billion dollars. For the leading sponsor of terror in the world, it was a bonanza. Some called it a "jihadist stimulus plan." Israel and other nations in the Middle East braced for the day when this spigot of funds would enable Iran to fuel their conflicts throughout the region from Yemen to Syria and then around the world.

In our Washington, D.C. Bureau, I interviewed Clare Lopez, a former CIA operative and now Vice President of the Center for Security Policy. She brought a wealth of insight about the issue to our conversation. For one, she cautioned that the JCPOA didn't address Iran's covert nuclear program, uncovered for the first time in 2002. She said, "The real program moved underground and to this day remains a large part of the covert or clandestine nuclear program, and the proof of that is that every so often another site will be revealed."[22]

Dore Gold, the Director General of Israel's Foreign Ministry, confirmed this analysis when he told us at a Jerusalem press conference: "There's this other universe called 'undeclared sites,' and it is the undeclared sites to which is applied that principle of 24-day notice . . . this is a tremendous concern in Israel . . . to my mind, the real Achilles heel in this agreement are the undeclared sites from which I believe breakout will occur."[23] Back in D.C., Lopez added a sobering fact. Since World War II, no Western intelligence agency ever knew a country got to the nuclear breakout stage before they actually did. That list—more than seventy years long—included the Russians, the Chinese, Pakistanis, Indians, South Africans, and North Koreans. How Western intelligence agencies would know about Iran's covert nuclear program remains an open and vexing question.

The combination of Iran's covert program, sanctions relief, the sunset clause where many nuclear restrictions would be lifted in 10, 15 or 25 years, the failure to inspect sensitive military sites, the failure to include ballistic missiles as part of the agreement—all these and more prompted Middle East analyst Daniel Pipes to conclude: "The annals of diplomacy have never witnessed a comparable capitulation by great powers to an isolated, weak state."[24]

## NUCLEAR TRIP WIRES

After the P5+1 signed the JCOPA with Iran, the U.S. Congress began a 60-day review of the agreement. During that window, we talked to Senator Tom Cotton, the Republican Senator from Arkansas. He stood as one of the deal's fiercest critics and came to Israel to confer with Israeli leaders, including Prime Minister Benjamin Netanyahu, about the accord. We met Cotton in the gardens of the famous King David Hotel in Jerusalem. A Harvard grad, war veteran, and legislator, he believed the deal carried catastrophic consequences for the Middle East. He explained why, as a U.S. Senator, he was so passionate about the pact and what the American people needed to know about Iran.

"This is a time of unprecedented turmoil. Again, you have Iranian-backed proxies—whether they are militias, or state actors, or terrorist groups—that are largely in control of large swaths of Iraq, Syria, Lebanon, Yemen and that are going to continue to aggressively destabilize the region because Iran is going to get tens of billions of dollars to support them. Because Iran is going to get more conventional weapons and ultimately Iran is going to get nuclear weapons. That is all going to happen in almost the first day of this deal. They're going to get the money immediately. Very soon, they'll be getting more conventional weapons. And the nuclear umbrella they'll be developing will continue to deter—oftentimes effectively push back against—Iran's actions in the region. That's why it's so important to stand up to them now before they get stronger, before they realize that they can confront the U.S. and our allies throughout the region."[25]

While we relaxed in a serene setting on a warm Jerusalem afternoon, because of the deal, the Senator saw nuclear war on the Middle Eastern horizon.

"I'm afraid that if this deal goes forward, it won't just be Iran that becomes a threshold nuclear state; it will be other countries throughout the Middle East like say Saudi Arabia, the United Arab Emirates, or Turkey. And all of a sudden, you'll have the world's most volatile region crisscrossed with nuclear trip wires that could be used at a moment's notice. Because none of these countries will have enough of a nuclear arsenal to adequately insure that they have a second strike capability. Meaning they'll likely take first strike preemptive action if their nuclear arms are threatened. Many of these capitals don't have routine communications with each other, further heightening the risk of that kind of nuclear strike. So I believe that if this deal goes forward, we are at risk of entering a second nuclear age, and the loss of life will be counted not in the tens, not in the thousands, not even in the hundreds of thousands, but in the millions, and that loss of life could include U.S. life because Iran is also developing a ballistic missile program, and they also have terrorist groups that have shown they're willing to kill Americans."[26]

With the escalating tensions in the Middle East between Shiite Iran and Sunni Saudi Arabia, Cotton's warning takes on a new urgency.

A few months after we met with Cotton, we sat down with a former member of the legislative body on the other side of Washington's Capitol Hill, former Congresswoman Michele Bachmann. No longer a legislator, she spent months traveling around America, warning of the consequences of the Iranian nuclear deal, an agreement that grieved her. She explained, "My heart was burdened about the Iran agreement . . . so I've been trying to provide context to people to understand what this will mean, not only for the United States but also for the Jewish state of Israel."[27]

She continued, "The problem is that Iran will have nuclear bombs. They will have them legitimately, you might say, through the agreement. But as we know, they've cheated on every agreement they've ever had, so they'll either have them legitimately or illegitimately. The problem is that Iran has made their goal a hundred percent clear. Every day, they tweet out and they speak out, 'Death to Israel! Death to the United States!' They mean it. And so now imagine a trillion-dollar terror state because they'll be enriched by this agreement. And not only will they be very rich terrorists, but they will have nuclear bombs and their intention is to use them to annihilate both Israel and the United States. That is not a good plan."[28]

Bachmann then made a profound historical observation: "With the signing of this contract, the world has passed from one era of history to another." She cited two pivotal dates.

"The two significant dates in America's national security history are July 20 and September 30, 2015. The first, July 20, is the date that our nation, the United States, led the significant nations of the world to essentially pass Iran's death warrant against Israel. That death warrant is Iran achieving nuclear weapons. The United States of America was the lead nation to pass this agreement. The agreement went through the United Nations Security

Council on July 20th. That was the day the door slammed against the Jewish state led by America—that's the death warrant. That was unthinkable. . . .

"The second date is September 30, 2015. On September 30, we saw a new coalition come together, with Russia and Iran working together with Iran's proxies, which are Hezbollah, Hamas, and the rest. And they came together in Syria. Iran and Russia—they're the new big dog in the Middle East. The United States influence has receded because the United States, in my opinion, has turned its back—not the people of the United States—but our government has turned its back on the Jewish state of Israel. And now Russia and Iran have immediately come into that vacuum to fill it. This is a very bad move. Before 1943, the world was essentially dominated by the United Kingdom, the Brits if you will. And that period of time was called *Pax Britannica*, where Britain kept order in the world because they were the dominant world power. In about 1943, the baton, so to speak, handed peacefully from Britain to the United States. We were the dominant world power when Israel became an independent state in May of 1948. We brilliantly—through a Democratic President Harry Truman—recognized the sovereignty of Israel in May of '48. We have continually been for Israel. And I believe what happened on September 30 is that America, which had essentially controlled the global order, dropped the baton. And I think Russia and Iran have lifted themselves up to take that power. That is not good to have a Russian-Iranian Pax because there won't be any peace under Russia and Iran, there'll be war."[29]

Many others shared Bachmann's prediction. In September 2015, two hundred retired generals and admirals appealed to Congress to reject the nuclear deal. They added ominously, "In our professional opinion, far from being an alternative to war, the Joint Comprehensive Plan of Action makes it likely that the war the Iranian regime has waged against us since 1979 will continue, with far higher risks to our national security interests."[30]

Israeli Prime Minister Benjamin Netanyahu concurred: "They say that this agreement makes war more distant. This is not true; this agreement brings war closer. First, because Iran will receive hundreds of billions of dollars, and it is already openly declaring that it will use this money to finance and arm its terrorist movements and its aggression in the region and around the world. Second, there will be a nuclear arms race in the Middle East."[31]

## ISRAEL ON THE FRONT LINE

For Israel, it was *"Alea iacta est."* In Latin that means "The die is cast." The phrase is attributed to Julius Caesar when he crossed the Rubicon River in northern Italy. He came with his army to challenge Pompey and march on Rome. He knew, however, that according to Roman protocol, no general could cross the Rubicon without giving up command of his troops. Once the waters of the river lay behind Caesar and his forces, he couldn't turn back.[32] With this nuclear agreement with Iran, the world crossed its own Rubicon and Israel faced the consequences. The Jewish state now confronted its number-one foe but now with enriched coffers, poised on the edge of nuclear capability, along with an unrepentant agenda.

With the proverbial ink drying on the agreement, within days, Iran's leaders continued their denunciations against Israel. Iran's Supreme ruler Khamenei said, "We will take measures to support all those who fight against Israel."[33] Their Foreign Minister Zarif, who just negotiated the deal, told Hezbollah chief Hassan Nasrallah: "The nuclear agreement has created an historic opportunity to stand against the Zionist entity."[34] The Parliament Speaker for International Affairs Hossein Sheikholeslam said, "Our positions against the usurper Zionist regime have not changed at all; Israel should be annihilated and this is our ultimate slogan."[35] Khamenei added a chilling video where he warned the U.S.: "We neither welcome nor begin any war. They must know that should any war break out, the one who will emerge humiliated out of it will be (the) invading and criminal America."[36]

After the deal, we went to the streets of Jerusalem to hear what Israelis thought. One lamented, "It's a bad deal because sooner or later, it's going to reach us." Another warned, "The world doesn't realize that the Islamic people, they want to take over the world." As if to complement that sentiment, another chimed, "Iran keeps saying that Israel and the States and Europe have to be destroyed and everything has to be Islamic."[37]

Following the compact, one poll discovered 47 percent—nearly half—of Israelis would back a unilateral military strike against Iran's nuclear facilities.[38] The deal raised a question asked for years in the Middle East: Would Israel hit Iran and destroy or at least damage nuclear sites like Natanz, Isfahan, and Fordow? The Hebrew language *Walla!* (one of the most popular web sites in the country) reported that IDF Chief of Staff Gadi Eizenkot appointed Deputy Chief of Staff Maj. Gen. Yair Golan "to explore military options for Israel's protection from Iran. The appointment of such a senior officer indicates Israel's concern that the impending nuclear deal with Iran would significantly change the situation in the region and would likely necessitate a military response."[39]

The IDF asked the government for a bigger military budget to deal with Iran, its number-one mission. "Iran will be a central challenge for the IDF during this time. It will be a mission for Military Intelligence . . . to focus on Iranian (nuclear) efforts and (the regional) influence. Iran will continue to be the IDF's first mission, as it has been defined since 2006."[40]

Reports also surfaced that Israel had come perilously close to launching a strike against Iran at least three times between 2010 and 2012. The bombshell revelations came in recordings by former Defense Minister Ehud Barak, released by Israel's Channel 2. Barak recorded those interviews with two authors who wrote an upcoming biography on Barak's life. He said attack plans were "drawn up and approved by him and Prime Minister Benjamin Netanyahu . . . [but] according to Barak, when the plan went before the so-called 'forum of eight' ministers" two of them "melted."[41] The plan melted along with those ministers, since they needed a majority in agreement to take it to the full cabinet. He also revealed that Israel nearly launched another attack in 2012. "There was a major problem, however," he told his interviewers.

"We had scheduled a major joint military drill with the United States, and the Israeli government did not want to embarrass Washington by launching an attack against Iran just as it was set to engage in military exercises, since that would give the appearance that the Americans were involved."[42]

But 2012 is ancient history now. The dynamics have changed since both the signing of the JCPOA and the major involvement of Russia in the Middle East with its Iranian military alliance. Will Israel attack under these new conditions? Will they risk the wrath of the world after it stamped its imprimatur on the nuclear deal? Will Russia's presence change Israel's military calculus? Whatever the answers to those questions, one unnamed IDF officer said a Persian Empire rising from the East does not bode well for Israel.

"I think that history proves that large empires coming from the East never bring good tidings to the Jewish people. What we are witnessing now is the return of the Persian Empire. The nuclear agreement between Iran and the West freezes Iran's nuclear program for a decade or more, but allows Iran to become an empire and increase its activities and influence throughout the Middle East. From our perspective, this is bad news indeed. The Iranian adversary does not resemble any foe we have yet faced, on any scale of magnitude. The Persian civilization is much more impressive, developed, and powerful than what we have today among the Arab countries. All this should worry us a lot."[43]

Another watershed moment for the JCOPA came on January 16, 2016. The P5+1 called it Implementation Day when Iran satisfied its initial commitments to the International Atomic Energy Agency. The IAEA approved the deal after Iran shipped 98 percent of its nuclear fuel to Russia, dismantled twelve thousand centrifuges and deactivated a nuclear reactor.[44] In return; the P5+1 thawed from 50 to 100 billion dollars in frozen assets to Iran. Following the sanctions relief, U.S. Secretary of State John Kerry admitted, "I think that some of it will end up in the hands of the IRGC (Iranian Revolutionary Guard Corps) or other entities, some of which are labeled terrorists. You know, to some degree

I'm not going to sit here and tell you that every component of that can be prevented."[45] Critics of the deal felt it was a stunning admission the sanctions windfall would be a boon to designated terrorist groups. It also marked the end of American and European trade restrictions. Iran entered the world economy, began to trade its massive oil reserves and ended years of isolation.[46] It began the dawn of a new era in the region.

After this agreement and an emboldened Iran, the world is sailing into uncharted Middle Eastern waters with unseen and potentially catastrophic consequences. Many see the world at a hinge of history, a pivotal 1939 moment when the world has appeased the Nazi Germany of our time. During a similar situation in 1939, then British Prime Minister Chamberlain negotiated with Hitler, returned to Britain with his Munich Pact, and declared "peace for our time." But Hitler laid a trap for the naïve leader, and war lay in wait mere months away. Chamberlain's capitulation was one more concession by the West to the Chancellor of Germany. Given the apparent appeasement of the Joint Comprehensive Plan of Action in 2015, it reminded me of what Winston Churchill said of Chamberlain when he returned from Munich: "You were given the choice between war and dishonor. You chose dishonor and you will have war."[47]

CBN News Story: "Iran Deal: Advent of Second Nuclear Age?"

# The Russians Are Coming! The Russians Are Coming!

*"We are watching a catastrophic capitulation by the American government in the Middle East. It was bedrock U.S. foreign policy for six, seven decades to keep the Russians out of the Middle East. And yet President Obama and his administration have surrendered, surrendered."*

~ Joel Rosenberg, Author and Middle East Expert[1]

I remember walking down the hall at Shoemaker Elementary school in Lynn, Massachusetts. On the way from Mrs. Peters' first-grade class to Mrs. O'Brien's second grade, windows lined the upper part of the wall. Our teachers instructed us to stay away from those windows in case of a nuclear attack. For an eight-year-old boy, those orders made quite an impression. Ubiquitous "Fallout Shelter" signs added an exclamation point to the danger. We learned that if the blast didn't kill you, the radioactive fallout might. The year was 1961 and the Cold War burned hot. The possibility of a nuclear attack from the dreaded Soviet Union pervaded my young school life.

At home, the question floated around the dinner table: Would we build a nuclear bomb shelter? Are the neighbors building one? Every so often, sonic booms shook our house on Standish Road. After those booms, we and the neighbors went outside to see what happened. Up and down the street, our block buzzed with speculation. Even though we never saw the planes, it seemed clear to everyone—U.S. fighter jets were training. Next door to Lynn in the small town of Nahant, right on the Atlantic Ocean—even if it was a "secret"—we all knew Minute Man missiles in concrete-hardened silos guarded our Eastern seaboard from the Soviet menace. My generation grew up under the shadow of nuclear annihilation. Thankfully, it was only a drill.

During that Cold War, the Soviet Union and the United States of America squared off as the world's superpowers. Moscow—the bastion of Communism—and Washington—the center of the free world—stood as the epicenters in a bi-polar globe. They both possessed enormous nuclear arsenals. The idea of "M.A.D." or "Mutually Assured Destruction" kept both Russia and the U.S. at bay from any nuclear confrontation. After all, nuclear war meant extermination for both nations. The world held its collective breath during an age where one miscalculation could lead to "the unthinkable."

Into this tense, sometimes paranoid world, Hollywood produced a comedy that briefly broke the Cold War ice. The 1966 movie, "The Russians are Coming; the Russians are Coming!" portrayed a Russian sub that ran aground off the coast of Cape Cod. The captain sent out a landing party in order to get his vessel off the sand bar. Russian Lieutenant Rozanov, played by Alan Arkin, meets up with vacationing playwright Walt Whittaker, played by Carl Reiner. In one scene, Rozanov tells Whittaker he needs a boat and, if he doesn't get it, the consequences will threaten the whole world:

WALT WHITTAKER: Look, can I give you some advice? You'll never make it down to the harbor. Why don't you give yourselves up? Either way, you'll kill somebody or you'll get killed.

LIEUTENANT ROZANOV: What's your name?

WALT WHITTAKER: Whittaker, Walt

LIEUTENANT ROZANOV: Remark to this, Whittaker, Walt. We must have boat. Even now may be too late. This is your island. I make it your responsibility you help us get boat quickly; otherwise, there is World War III, and everybody is blaming YOU![2]

For the first time in a long time, Americans laughed at themselves and the enigmatic Russians. Comic relief came just a few years after one of the most dangerous moments of the atomic age. During the Cuban Missile Crisis (October 14-28, 1962), the Soviet Union and the United States stepped to the brink of the nuclear abyss. Yet with the fall of the Soviet Union in the late 80s and early 90s, the Russian bear went into hibernation. No longer a bi-polar world, the U.S. reigned supreme as the world's number-one superpower. However, nearly a quarter of a century later, the Russian bear has awakened from its slumber. Russia and the United States are facing off again. This time, though, it's not a comedy off the coast of New England, but a real-life drama in the Middle East with global implications.

## "WE REQUEST YOUR PEOPLE LEAVE!"

September 30, 2015, marked a turning point in that relationship. A three-star Russian General marched into the U.S. Embassy in Baghdad and delivered an ultimatum, in diplomatic terms called a "demarche." Webster defines a demarche as "a course of action; a diplomatic or political initiative or maneuver."[3] In layman's terms, think of this one as a diplomatic and military slap in the face. His condition: "We request your people leave." He asked the U.S. to remove their aircraft from Syrian air space around Homs within the hour. After that, Russian warplanes would begin their bombing campaign against ISIS targets.[4] It was like Lieutenant Rozanov telling Whitaker, Walt to get that boat.

As promised, within the hour, Russian bombs began falling. In a brilliant tactical move, Russia draped its military intervention inside Syria under the guise of joining the U.S.-led coalition to "degrade and ultimately destroy ISIL."[5] Russia even invited the U.S. to join Russian efforts to defeat their "common" enemy. But most Middle East observers saw through that veneer. The Russian military buildup begun weeks before had rested on the goal to protect the regime of Syrian President Bashar Assad, not to hit ISIS. It was a ruse. Vladimir Putin sent his military to preserve Syria, his client state in the region, or what was left of it after years of civil war.

The strikes themselves represented the opening bell in Russia's first major foreign military engagement since 1980, their ill-fated venture into Afghanistan. While it remains to be seen how this endeavor will turn out, it marked a historic shift in the Fertile Crescent. The gambit overturned a pillar of U.S. foreign policy in the Middle East. Both Democrat and Republican Presidents had blocked Russian influence in the region for decades. Yet this time the U.S. Pentagon, State Department, and White House all seemed unable to keep up with Putin's moves. At least one analyst compared the geo-political gamesmanship to Putin's chess and Obama's checkers. Putin confronted Obama; created a new reality in the Middle East. It looked like checkmate.

Conservative commentator Charles Krauthammer described the geo-political reversal this way: "… what's unprecedented is the utter passivity of the United States. The real story this week is what happened at the U.N., where Putin essentially stepped in and took over Syria. He's now the leader. And we conceded essentially that Assad will stay under the protection of the Russians."[6] Krauthammer concluded, "The irony is that the Russians aren't in there to fight ISIS. The Russians are in there to support Assad, establish their dominance in the region to bring in Iran and to establish military facilities. They have no interest in fighting Assad."[7]

Given the Obama administration's aversion to military confrontation, most expected little more than talk. Secretary of State John Kerry summoned his Russian counterpart Sergey Lavrov to "de-conflict" so they could keep Russian and U.S. warplanes from shooting each other over the now crowded Syrian skies. Yet because of their unwillingness to project U.S. power, the administration created a vacuum in the region. Russia filled that vacuum, grasped for dominance in the region, and re-shuffled the Middle East chessboard.

It marked a sea change in American foreign policy. Former U.S. Ambassador to the U.N. John Bolton called watching power pass in the Mideast from the U.S.'s weak hand to Russia's increasingly strong one "a fire bell in the night." He called it a "devastating concession" and added an ominous warning: "We haven't seen the last of this."[8]

It was a "game changer." Now the Russians—not the United States—sat ensconced as the region's main power broker. The vaunted "leading from behind" strategy of the Obama Administration led to a situation with major and long-lasting consequences for U.S. prestige in the region and the world. It led me to pen the following blog about the new gunslinger in the Wild West of the Middle East:

## THERE'S A NEW SHERIFF IN TOWN

In the past few weeks, Russian leader Vladimir Putin strode into the Middle East. Within days, it was clear "there's a new sheriff in town." He announced to the townsfolk he'd come in to get rid of the town bully, ISIS. He asked others to join him, especially the former sheriff, U.S. President Barack Obama. He'd been sheriff a while but for more than a year, everybody in town knew when dealing with the town bully, he just did enough to get by.

It got so bad, the outlaws didn't even look up when the sheriff came into the town bar. They just mumbled something about "red lines," stayed saddled up to the bar, and kept drinking.

What he didn't say was that he'd also come to save another town bully, Syrian President Bashar Assad. That became obvious the first time he fired a shot. He didn't fire at ISIS but the guys attacking his friend Assad. This new sheriff took care of his friends, even if they were bullies.

The old sheriff insisted he wouldn't take on the new gunslinger: "We're not going to make Syria into a proxy war between the United States and Russia. This is not some superpower chessboard contest. And anybody who frames it in that way isn't paying very close attention to what's been happening on the chessboard."[9] Except this new sheriff—like many Russians—was paying attention and playing chess. In fact, he played with some of the most sophisticated pieces of chess the world has to offer, like advanced

T-90 tanks, Sukhoi Su-24 and Su-25 jets, "Smerch" multiple launch rocket systems, and even Kalibr ship-launched cruise missiles.[10]

That's the way he played his match.

Some asked why not let Putin come in and take over. After all, let Russian "conscripts" or "volunteers" do the dirty work. When it's all over, the U.S. can come in and pick up the pieces. Well, it turns out there may not be pieces to "pick up." Those pieces—the country formerly known as Syria—may well be under the control of the new sheriff. From the way he "cleaned up" Crimea and parts of that town up north called Ukraine, everybody knew he didn't take kindly to giving up parts of towns he's already given to his deputies.

Back south in Syria, Putin's posse included some mean desperadoes. Nasty hoodlums like Hezbollah. They just happen to have more than 100,000 rockets and missiles aimed at Israel, one of the good guys in the neighborhood. The Israelis have spent years keeping advanced weapons out of their nemesis' hands. Any advanced weapons sent by Iran via Syria found themselves the brunt of Israel's punishing air assaults. Now, they might have to think twice if the new sheriff sends any of his advanced weapons to Hezbollah. Israel doesn't want a war, but this puts them into a very difficult situation, especially when villainous deputies like Ayatollah Khamenei keep bad-mouthing Israel and saying the Jewish state should be wiped off the map. Kind of makes them immune to retaliation when the new sheriff is standing alongside those ayatollahs.

Lots of confusion in town now. Who flies where? Who's shooting who? In the skies, all of a sudden it's become a dangerous place to fly.

The townsfolk know this new sheriff plays by different rules than the former sheriff. After all, one time he came into a town called Grozny in a place called Chechnya and leveled it. The UN called it "the most destroyed city on earth."[11] They warn he may say he wears a white hat, but he's ruthless. In Syria, he took a weak poker hand into the saloon and played it forcefully. Some people call the new sheriff "muscular"; the former sheriff, "feckless." Even if he says this is not some geo-political chess game, it doesn't make it so. Some folks say his inaction puts our main ally Israel in peril and our traditional allies in jeopardy. Right now, it looks like a Shiite crescent is forming throughout the town with a Russian sheriff.

Putin is putting much more on the line than the former sheriff who won't come out of his office much these days. He prefers to keep saying the new sheriff won't succeed, while his own posse including Jordan, Saudi Arabia and Egypt are getting fidgety. He hasn't turned in his badge yet, but everybody in town knows who's in charge. He keeps talking like it matters, but he doesn't seem to know he's getting run out of town. Too bad it's one of the most important towns in the world.

News is that once this new sheriff comes in, it's hard to get him out. Just ask the folks in Crimea. Nobody knows where he'll stop, but rumors around town say the folks up north in Estonia are getting nervous.

## A NEW POSSE IN THE MIDDLE EAST

The new sheriff saddled up with his posse—Syria, Iraq, Iran and Hezbollah—and agreed to a new intelligence-sharing agreement. Dubbed the P4+1, they formed a "counter-terrorism alliance."[12] That Iran, the leading state sponsor of terror, Bashar Assad's regime that killed more than a quarter of a million of their own people, and Hezbollah that has 100,000 missiles aimed at Israel formed a "counter-terrorism alliance" is one of the many oxymorons in the modern Middle East. The pro-Hezbollah Beruit daily *Al-Akhbar* described the "counter-terrorism alliance" between Russia, Iran, Syria, Iraq and Hezbollah as "the most important in the region and the world for many years."[13]

Other described it differently.

After Putin's move, I sat down in our CBN News Washington bureau with Middle East expert Retired Colonel Steven Bucci from the Heritage Foundation. His expertise rests on a lifetime of experience. He served as Defense Secretary Donald Rumsfeld's military attaché in the Pentagon, led deployments to east Africa,

Asia and the Persian Gulf as a commander of Special Forces, and served as a deputy assistant secretary of defense for homeland defense.[14] I asked him to describe the new relationship between Russia, Iran, Hezbollah and Syria.

He warned it was, "probably one of the most divisive and dangerous developments in the Middle East in decades. They have very similar interests, particularly with regard to Syria and with regard to America's role in the Middle East, and it runs the risk of setting up a situation that's very much akin to Europe right before WWI where you had these power blocks setting up, leading towards a potential conflict that gets kicked off by a very small event. In Europe before WWI, it was the killing of Archduke Ferdinand in Sarajevo, in Bosnia, Herzegovina. Something like that can happen here, and the entire Sunni and Shia worlds could be in armed conflict."[15]

In fact, with the new Middle East chessboard, Bucci's former colleagues in the Pentagon began to consider what was once "unthinkable": a war with Russia. According to the *Military Times*, "Russia's increasingly aggressive posture has sparked a sweeping review among U.S. defense strategists of America's military policies and contingency plans in the event of a conflict with the former Soviet state. Indeed, the Pentagon's senior leaders are asking questions that have been set aside for more than 20 years:

*"How much are the Russians truly capable of?"*
*"Where precisely might a conflict with Russia occur?"*
*"What would a war with Russia look like today?"*[16]

Thousands of miles away from the Pentagon, others pondered similar questions. After Russia's foray, I met with Middle East expert and best-selling author Joel Rosenberg on the Southern Steps of the Temple Mount. He came to speak to a visiting Christian tour group. After his message, we set up for an interview. I wanted to get his perspective on this profound new shift in the region. While we stood in Jerusalem—a place he calls the "epicenter"—just a few miles north of where we stood, the region had shifted dramatically. His words pounded home the gravity of the moment: "It's hard to overstate how significant this is. We are watching a catastrophic capitulation by the American government in the Middle East. It was bedrock U.S. foreign policy for six, seven decades to keep the Russians out of the Middle East. And yet President Obama and his administration have surrendered . . . surrendered! We have withdrawn, we have surrendered."[17]

He warned Putin fits the mold of past Russian rulers. "We have ceded the playing field to Vladimir Putin, who is a czar rising. He's an imperialist. He's dangerous. And the fact that he is operating with abandon—with complete freedom militarily just a few miles north of Israel—is stunning and incredibly dangerous."[18]

Those dangers may be just beginning. Just after interviewing Rosenberg, I met retired General William "Jerry" Boykin who came on the same tour. It was a unique opportunity to get the views of a man who spent 36 years during his military career analyzing threats to the U.S. As he looks at the rearranged Middle East chessboard, he sees a hidden agenda in Putin's end game. "Putin is there to stay. Putin needs to hold on to his naval base at Tartus. That's the first thing. But the second thing is Putin's ultimate objectives extend far beyond just that naval base at Tartus or even holding up Bashir Al-Assad. It includes dominating that part of the world. If I was a Saudi king or if I was one of the emirs of the emirates there I would be very concerned about whether I'm next, because if Putin can, for example, cut a pipeline out of Iran across Iraq, across Syria, across the northern part of Lebanon out to the Mediterranean to supply oil to the Middle East. If he could build that pipeline, he would dominate global oil prices and he would have the Europeans in the palm of his hand. NATO would fracture; the Europeans would never do anything to cut off their own energy supplies."[19]

## THE BEAR IN ISRAEL'S BACKYARD

Yet Russia not only poses a danger to NATO and Europe but a risk to Israel "just a few miles north." Israeli Prime Minister Benjamin Netanyahu knows those risks. Days after Putin's move into Syria, he flew to Moscow and paid an emergency visit. We accompanied Netanyahu on a previous trip to the Kremlin in November 2013. At that time, he lobbied Putin not to sign an interim nuclear agreement with Iran. He failed in that bid, but watching the two leaders together during their press conference, I sensed a mutual respect. Still Netanyahu brought a number of high-stakes concerns to the Kremlin table in 2015.

First of all, Netanyahu's worries include the possibility of advanced Russian weapons getting into the hands of Israel's arch nemesis on its northern border, Hezbollah. For years, Israel has attacked weapons shipments to Hezbollah from Iran via Syria. One of Israel's "red lines" was to keep advanced weapons out of the hands of Iran's proxy—weapons that would alter the strategic balance of power. I asked Colonel Bucci if he envisioned a scenario where Israel would need to strike a Russian weapons shipment to Hezbollah. His answer was troubling. "Very likely scenario, not just potential. With Russia in Syria and Hezbollah in Syria all over the place helping Assad, it would be very easy for them to transfer weapons outside the sight and range of Israel's normal response. It won't be as clumsy as just a convoy riding down the road next to the border and "Israel says, 'There it is; I'm going to hit it." And Israel would have to think twice about hitting Russian targets there because then they're not only fighting the Muslim world, now they're even fighting Russia to take them on as well. And Russia right now, the nationalism that's there. I can see Putin trying to get a lot of points off of smacking Israel if they do something like that."[20]

General Boykin believed that's exactly why Netanyahu flew to Moscow. "I really do believe that is just a practical issue of him being able to say to Putin, 'If we see anything that threatens Israel, if we see weapons or caches that are intended for southern Lebanon and Hezbollah, we're going to preempt. Now we need to work out a way to de-conflict because we're going to preempt them.'"[21]

The need for preemption may already be upon the Jewish State. Retired Israeli General Yaakov Amidror revealed, "Russian weapons, Moscow's most advanced, are already in Hezbollah's possession."[22] Amidror believes it's happened with a wink and a nod: "Russia sold its advanced weapons to the Syrians and the Syrians transferred them to Hezbollah. The Russians know that's what happens ... these are first-class weapons, such as Kornet and surface-to-air missiles, perhaps even Onyx missiles that are now in Hezbollah's possession."[23] Those Onyx missiles represent a serious challenge to Israel's safety. IDF officials "estimate that the Onyx can hit Israel's gas rigs and that their range covers a radius which includes Israel's two main ports in Haifa and Ashdod. The ports would be paralyzed in the event of being hit by such a missile."[24]

Yet Israel also needs to preempt Hezbollah's and Iran's goals in other areas: to prevent them from building a forward military base inside Syria next to Israel's Golan Heights. Another high-stakes issue Netanyahu likely put on that Kremlin table was to find out how Putin would react if Israel ever felt it needed to strike Iran's nuclear facilities.

## ECHOES OF EZEKIEL

Boykin not only gave his military views but also the point of view shared by many Christians around the world. When they saw Russia enter Syria, they heard the echoes from Ezekiel. He said, "Biblically and prophetically Russia is positioned for the events of Ezekiel 38 and 39. They're positioned, prophecy is happening right now." The Hebrew prophet Ezekiel wrote those chapters more than 2500 years ago. Here are some of those Scriptures:

"Now the word of the Lord came to me, saying, 'Son of man, set your face against Gog, of the land of Magog, the prince of Rosh, Meshech, and Tubal, and prophesy against him, and say, 'Thus says the Lord God: Behold, I am against you, O Gog, the prince of Rosh, Meshech, and Tubal. I will turn you around, put hooks into your jaws, and lead you out, with all your army, horses, and horsemen, all splendidly clothed, a great company with bucklers and shields, all of them handling swords. Persia, Ethiopia, and Libya are with them, all of them with shield and helmet; Gomer and all its troops; the house of Togarmah from the far north and all its troops—many people are with you ..." (Ezekiel 38: 1-6).

"Therefore, son of man, prophesy and say to Gog, 'Thus says the Lord God: "On that day when My people Israel dwell safely, will you not know it? Then you will come from your place out of the far north, you and many peoples with you, all of them riding on horses, a great company and a mighty army. You will come up against My people Israel like a cloud, to cover the land. It will be in the latter days that I will bring you against My land, so that the nations may know Me, when I am hallowed in you, O Gog, before their eyes" (Ezekiel 38:14-17).

Those Scriptures resonate with Joel Rosenberg. He's written and taught extensively on the book of Ezekiel. He believes Putin's moves raises profound prophetic questions: "From my perspective, the first question you have to ask is: Are we watching the preparations for the war of Gog and Magog? When you look at the prophecies of Ezekiel 38 and 39 and if you conclude, as I have, that there's historical, 'the conclusion' leads you to that Magog is Russia, then you are looking for an evil leader emerging in Magog, in Russia. Who will form a military alliance with Iran and a group of other countries that will come against Israel in the last days from the north? Now in the 2500 years since Ezekiel wrote that prophecy Russian and Iran never had a military alliance where they were never even friends. The last time Russia ever took military operations of this magnitude in the Middle East was to invade Iran at the end of World War II. So, we've never seen this before.… Suddenly Russia and Iran are operating in a military alliance in combat just north of the northern mountains of Israel. That has never happened in human history and it ought to draw our attention back to those Scriptures."[25]

He says it's time to ask some serious questions.

"Now does that mean the prophecies of Gog and Magog will happen soon or even in our lifetime? No. This could be decades or theoretically centuries off. However, when you actually have Russia and Iran fighting on the same side just miles north of the mountains of Israel, it does give you pause. It should cause evangelical Christians to ask, 'What is happening?' 'Why is our President allowing this to happen?' And 'what are the Biblical implications?' And I think it's an incredibly dangerous situation for the United States; it's an incredibly dangerous situation for Israel. And I would note, Chris, that the first leader to jump on a plane on a plane and meet with Vladimir Putin was Israeli Prime Minister Benjamin Netanyahu. That tells you how dangerous the Israelis see the introduction of Russian military operations just north of their border."[26]

It's safe to say those Russian military operations just north of Israel's borders trumpet a new reality in the Middle East, not only are "the Russians coming" …the Russians are here.

CBN News Interview with Joel Rosenberg: "Where are we on the End Times Timetable?"

CBN News Interview with Steven Bucci: "Jerusalem Dateline."

# Middle East Game of Thrones

*"Speaking in the military garrison town of Rawalpindi, Pakistani Army Chief Gen. Raheel Sharif said that any Iranian threat to Saudi Arabia's territorial integrity will 'wipe Iran off the map'."*

~ Caroline Glick, "In Pakistan they Trust," *The Jerusalem Post*[1]

Our CBN News crew walked into the storied lobby of the King David Hotel and into the echoes of Israel's history. Israel's first Prime Minister, Ben Gurion, met many of his contemporaries there. Paul Newman and Eva Marie Saint filmed a famous scene from the 1960 movie, *Exodus*, on its terrace. The world's rich and famous made the King David their destination. Movie stars like Sophia Loren and world leaders as Winston Churchill both graced its halls. The hotel embedded their autographs in the floor of the main hall, much like the Walk of Stars in Hollywood.

We, however, had come to address more contemporary issues in a press conference with the new Director General of Israel's Foreign Ministry, Dore Gold. We turned right, down the hall, over the autographs of the great and mighty, and took the stairs to the Jaffa Hall. The Foreign Press Association (FPA) arranged the conference. Bloomberg News showed up. So did the Associated Press. The *New York Times* reporter sat down as well as a cross section of the foreign media from around the world. I sat in the front row beside a reporter from Media Line.

Gold brought an impressive résumé to the event. He served as Israel's Ambassador to the United Nations and advised both former Israeli Prime Minister Ariel Sharon and current Prime Minister Benjamin Netanyahu. For years, he headed the Jerusalem Center for Public Affairs, one of Israel's prestigious think tanks. A veteran of negotiations for the Jewish state, he'd taken this latest position at a pivotal stage in Israel's diplomatic history. Shifting alliances in the region distinguished this phase. It resembled an episode from the popular HBO series "Game of Thrones." In that series, a number of families with Machiavellian ambitions vie for control over the mythical land of Westeros. The ultimate question is: Who will sit on the "Iron Throne" and rule over all? The series sizzles with political intrigue, thirst for power, and treachery. It's also dark with anti-Christian themes, paganism, and pornography. Yet, the singular goal of those families—who will sit on the "Iron Throne"?—parallels the Middle East of today. Great powers contend over who will dominate the most pivotal land on earth. Yet, in this real life drama, multitudes are at risk and the destiny of nations lie in the balance.

## THE ENEMY OF MY ENEMY

Gold made headlines weeks earlier when he took part in an unprecedented diplomatic meeting. At the time, the United States and five other world powers debated the future of Iran's nuclear program in Lausanne, Switzerland. Over four thousand miles away in Washington, Gold met face to face with a retired Major General from Saudi Arabia, Anwar Majed Eshki, at the Council of Foreign Relations. Their parley marked another "game changer" in the Middle East. It's hard to overestimate the significance of this ground-breaking meeting. Since the establishment of the State of Israel in 1948, Saudi Arabia and Israel have been bitter enemies. Now, the representatives of their respective countries appeared together—in public—with the same message: stop Iran from trying to take over the Middle East. As an exclamation point to their discussion, Gold and Eshki added they'd already had five previous secret rendezvous.

Former Israeli Ambassador to the U.S. Congress Yoram Ettinger told CBN News the meaning of the meeting: "The Saudis and the Israelis are very, very concerned about President Obama's preoccupation with Lausanne, which conflicts dramatically with the reality in the Persian Gulf. In fact, the Iranians are trying to topple every single pro-American Arab regime."[2] He said the meeting sent a clear message to the White House—the Saudis and Israelis are on the same Iranian page. "The Saudi message is basically President Obama, listen to Prime Minister Netanyahu. . . . They totally disagree with the very naïve misrepresentation of Iran by President Obama. As far as the Saudis are concerned, the Israelis constitute the most effective life insurance which they now have in the face of Iran."[3]

The meeting heralded one more sign of an historic geo-political change taking place in the Middle East. While Saudi Arabia—a major Sunni power—and Israel have been enemies for decades, they both see Shiite Iran's nuclear program as a threat to their very existence. Huge differences remain between these two historic foes, but their alliance seems a classic example of the Middle East maxim, "The enemy of my enemy is my friend."

Given Gold's earlier meeting in Washington with his Saudi counterpart, I came to the press conference with one pressing question. After his opening remarks, I raised my hand and asked, "Can you describe the growing relationship between Israel and some of the other Sunni Arab countries in the Middle East?"

Gold, a master communicator and seasoned diplomat, carefully crafted his words. He wouldn't divulge anything more than necessary, but ever so slightly pulled back the curtain to one of today's most intriguing relationships in the Middle East:

"Well, you know, many times when you give a speech these days from Israel and you start talking about ISIS and Iran, it all looks pretty depressing. But there is a silver lining in Israel's regional situation. And that is that the threats emerging have created a growing . . . how do I put this? . . . a **similar perception** on the part of Israel and many of its Sunni Arab partners about **the real challenges** in the Middle East. And it's necessary that we communicate how we see the region and what can be done. Many times, parts of our problem in the Israeli sector of the Middle East overlap with **other countries' challenges**."[4]

Gold's diplomatic speak of "similar perceptions," "real challenges" and "other countries' challenges" meant Israel and Saudi Arabia see Iran as their common enemy. He went on to identify another of their common enemies—Hezbollah—fighting on a faraway battlefield.

"All of us observed, for example, that the Iranians were deploying Hezbollah in Yemen. And all of a sudden, an issue that Israel had to deal with for many years (on its northern border) is now positioning itself on the Saudi Arabian border. And what are the Iranians putting in Yemen? Ballistic missiles that have struck Saudi territory. So there is a **great convergence**."[5]

Gold listed more "convergence of interests" but then adroitly drew back the curtain on this largely covert liaison:

"What we actually decide to do about it—well, that remains in confidential channels. But the fact that when I met General Anwar Eski, I was operating in the context as the president of the Jerusalem Center for Public Affairs. And the fact that the head of an Israeli think tank to meet the head of a Saudi think tank and present their conclusions in Washington D.C. is part of the new world we're getting into."[6]

Then Gold closed the curtain on this "new world": "What happens on the official level, I'd rather not expand on."[7]

Behind closed curtains, Middle East countries are dealing with the shifting of the regional geo-political tectonic plates. Those new alliances are part of a dizzying realignment throughout the region. The old order is passing away and in its place a new order is rising. One regional analyst sees the nations scrambling. "In this fractious landscape, powerful regional states are seeking to gain advantage, extend their own power, and diminish that of their rivals."[8] A top IDF officer—who remained anonymous—explained the hazards of trying to keep their balance in this new world order: "Today, you frequently find yourself caught in the same boat as your sworn enemies; interests cross, but they also conflict. There is no beginning and no end to it."[9]

Weeks after the Gold press conference, I met with retired U.S. General William "Jerry" Boykin in Jerusalem. I asked what he made of this bewildering new Middle East. He listed the region's major competitors. "Right now, we have Russia that has come into Syria to prop up Bashir Al-Assad at a time when the United States has made it very clear that our intention is to depose Al-Assad. And then you have ISIS taking over major sectors of Iraq with every intention—in fact, *announced* intentions—of taking over the Middle East first and then extending that into the rest of the world. And then you have the Iranians that are about to get a nuclear weapon. As 15 percent of the Islamic world, the Shia will suddenly be sitting on a nuclear weapon that will give them greater influence among those nations in the Persian Gulf in the Middle East, so I think it's a time of total confusion."[10]

He warned that this time of confusion was also an hour for Americans to stay alert: "I think it's a time of very incredible uncertainty and a time when Americans need to be paying attention to what's going on there. And also paying attention to what our own politicians and our own leaders are saying about what's going on there, because it will be a good indication as to what America is going to do with regards to the events unfolding there."[11]

## SUNNI/SHIITE SHOWDOWN

By far, the major rivalry casting a giant shadow on this confused Middle East is the Sunni/Shiite divide. For a non-Muslim, it's hard to understand the depths of this great gulf. I received some understanding into this rupture when I listened to Mohammad, a Jordanian tour guide I've used several times when visiting the Hashemite Kingdom. My daughter Grace and I had just finished a day of touring Petra, the ancient capital of the Nabateans. As we drove away from the fabled city, I asked about the Sunni/Shiite rift in the Muslim world. Instantly, Mohammad's emotions rose along with his voice. He passionately explained how

Shiites had corrupted the teachings of the Prophet; they stood as apostates. It wasn't just his words but his animated response and obvious hatred for Shiites that spoke far more than his explanation. This dynamic is one of the most potent powder kegs in today's Middle East.

This Sunni/Shiite division has percolated in the region for years. Yet when Saudi Arabia executed Sheik Nimr, a top Shiite cleric in early 2016, it began to boil. One Israeli expert called it "a declaration of war" by the House of Saud.[12] After the execution, Iran allowed a mob to ransack the Saudis' embassy in Tehran. Saudi Arabia then cut diplomatic relations with the Islamic Republic. In the midst of the diplomatic furor, we interviewed Israel's former Mossad Station Chief in Tehran. During the 1979 Islamic Revolution, he'd helped many Jews escape from the tyrannical anti-Semitic regime. He told us in order to understand the crisis, you need to consider the impact of the nuclear deal with Iran. He said when the U.S. signed the deal, the Saudis felt betrayed. He added, "Not only Saudi Arabia—all the Arab Sunni states. They feel that they were betrayed by America. Everybody knows for sure the Iranians are pushing decisively to reach nuclear power. There is no doubt about it."[13]

Tsafrir says a nuclear Iran terrifies the Saudis. "In my opinion, they are praying at nights to God that America and or Israel will do the job for them to hit the nuclear projects in Iran."[14] Tsafrir and other experts don't expect a direct war between the two powers but rather an escalation of their proxy wars in Syria, Iraq and Yemen. "It will get worse," Michael Barak of the International Institute for Counter-Terrorism told us.[15]

The war of words got worse when predominately Sunni Pakistan entered the Middle East quarrel. "Speaking in the military garrison town of Rawalpindi, Pakistani Army Chief Gen. Raheel Sharif said that any Iranian threat to Saudi Arabia's territorial integrity will 'wipe Iran off the map'."[16] *Jerusalem Post* Managing Editor Caroline Glick wrote an op-ed called "In Pakistan they Trust'." She concluded since Saudi Arabia doesn't trust the Obama Administration, they've turned to Pakistan and its nuclear umbrella for protection. She added ominously, "It would be foolish to view Sharif's nuclear threat as mere bluster."[17]

Then just days later, a group affiliated with Iran's Revolutionary Guard produced an animated film that simulated a rocket attack on Saudi Arabia from their allies in Yemen. The video revealed the GPS coordinates of Saudi Arabia's main oil facility at the Ghawar Oil Field and showed missiles devastating the Saudi Aramco facility with the entire area ablaze. It also simulated attacks on Saudi Arabia's capital, Riyadh, which it called the Freemason Tower. Then missiles struck the Saudis' main air base and crippled its anti-missile system.[18] While just a video, it portrayed the apocalyptic hope one day of some Shiite Iranians.

This blood feud between Sunnis and Shiites goes back more than 1300 years. After their prophet Mohammad died, a great debate arose within the Islamic community over who would succeed Mohammad. Sunnis believed the successor should come from the Islamic community, while Shiites believed he should come from the descendants of Mohammad. Both claimed to be the rightful heirs of Islam. The enmity began and rages to this day. While these experts don't see a direct confrontation now, the Saudi/Iran feud has the potential of sparking a greater Middle East war. Israel's former Mossad chief sees Iran as the real danger in the region. "The head of the serpent lies in Tehran. This is the major threat on peace, on the world, on the Middle East, on the Iranian people."[19]

Israel now found itself in the middle of two Middle East giants.

"We are in a battle of titans between the Shiite and Sunni axis. . . . This is an historic event, the biggest saga of our generation. In this equation, it's impossible to determine who is the good part or the bad part. We have to be wary of everyone."[20]

Back in Washington D.C., retired Colonel Steven Bucci agreed Israel had to be wary of everyone and told me Israel could get caught up in a future Shiite-Sunni war. "It's incredible because you would think okay; it's a Sunni-Shia war, Muslims fighting Muslims. That won't affect Israel. But I can't believe that if that size of a conflict started, at least some of these countries would not take advantage of it and use it as an excuse to attack Israel. And Israel is very capable, very tough, very determined. But that's a lot of adversaries to fight at the same time."[21] He also saw the potential for a wider Middle-East war. "I do and it concerns me a great deal. It should concern Israel, it should concern Jordan. These other countries that are our best friends in the region, people with good intentions for the region, and they're the ones who are now at risk."[22]

For now, this Sunni-Shiite competition flares up in various places throughout the Middle East. Proxies for Iran and Saudi Arabia battle over strategic points on the Middle East map from Syria to the Arabian Peninsula. Gold identified one of those campaigns with implications for the region and beyond.

"Let's look at the naval choke point known as Bab-el Mandeb (or Mandab Strait) which, as you know, is at the bottom of the Red Sea and connects Yemen with the Horn of Africa. Now the Iranians exercise a great deal of authority over the Strait of Hormuz, the exit point from the Persian Gulf to the Indian Ocean. But now through the Houthis, they are building a potential to take eventual control of the area of Bab-el Mandeb through which oil tankers travel to go up to the Suez Canal and to European markets. This is a global issue. But which countries are affected by an Iranian takeover of Bab-el Mandeb? Whose freedom of navigation could be compromised in the future? First and foremost, Israel, Egypt and Saudi Arabia, so there is a **convergence of interests** on the part of Israel and several Middle Eastern states."[23]

## THE RUSSIAN SURPRISE

Just as this embryonic "convergence of interests" between Israel and Sunni powers began forming, a new and unexpected player stepped into the Middle East game of thrones—the Russian bear. When the U.S. and those five other world powers completed their negotiations in Vienna and signed a nuclear deal with Iran, the Middle East map changed again. Few saw it coming. "It is not for nothing that the Russian deployment was put in play only after Iran signed a nuclear agreement with the West, which lent the Islamic republic the international legitimacy it craves. . . . This move represents a de facto regional alliance between Tehran and Moscow, even if neither of them has declared as much publicly. . . . Moscow's regional involvement spells a potential change in the balance of power on the ground."[24]

The balance of power changed when the West vacillated and Putin did not. He may not be a match for the West, but he began to flex Russia's military muscles. For example, he unveiled a new multi-billion-dollar command and control center in Moscow "designed to be a new nerve center for the Russian military that will coordinate military action around the world, including ballistic missile launches and strategic nuclear deployments. . . . It was finished in 2014 and is part of a massive, decade-long modernization of Russia's army, which has cost hundreds of billions of dollars."[25]

Russia also revealed it possessed "a global strike capability that before, only the United States possessed" when it "apparently deployed for the first time a new, radar-evading cruise missile . . . the Kh-101 long-range cruise missile."[26] On the nuclear front line, Putin instructed his Defense Ministry that "new weapons should go to 'all parts' of the nuclear triad of air, sea, and land forces."[27] This move among many others revived chilling Cold War tensions with the U.S. and NATO. It led "Marine General Joseph Dunford, chairman of the Joint Chiefs of Staff, to call [Russia] the country the most pressing threat to U.S. national security."[28]

But for all this military bluster, others suggest Russia's military rests on a feeble and shrinking economy. Reuters reported: "Buffeted by Western sanctions imposed over the Ukraine crisis, falling oil prices and a weakening ruble, Russia's economy is forecast to shrink by around 4 percent this year, its sharpest contraction since the global financial crisis."[29] Others warn Russia's incursion into Syria could "morph into a contemporary version of Afghanistan, where so much Soviet blood was shed that the country was forced to slink away. A very highly placed Israeli officer told *Al-Monitor* on condition of anonymity, only a short time after the start of Russia's involvement in Syria that "Syria can become Russia's Vietnam."[30]

While history will show how Russia's foray pans out, in this Middle East game of thrones, other nations jockeyed for position and power, some with historic ramifications. For example, hours after the International Atomic Energy Agency gave Shiite Iran the green light for its nuclear program, two Sunni powers made a dramatic move. They "announced that Turkey is setting up a permanent military base in the Persian Gulf emirate **for the first time since the fall of the Ottoman Empire a century ago.** Their announcement indicates that the informal partnership between Turkey and Qatar on the one side, and Hamas, the Muslim Brotherhood, and Islamic State on the other hand, which first came to the fore last year during Operation Protective Edge, is now becoming a more formal alliance."[31]

As all the other nations in this Middle East "game of thrones," Turkey pursues its own national interests. For example, it wages a war against its Kurdish population to quash any attempt by them to break away and form an independent state. Also despite vehement denials, Turkey is accused of aiding and abetting ISIS. They're blamed for allowing fighters access to and from the Islamic State through its border and it's been charged with buying oil on the black market from ISIS.

Another major player in this game of thrones—ISIS— is expected by many analysts to survive for a while. After all, it's been said, those who have the power to defeat ISIS don't have the will, and those who have the will don't have the power. But Daniel Pipes, the President of the Middle East Forum posits a contrarian view. He cites two main reasons. First, he says ISIS is "not exactly the equivalent of Nazi Germany. It's a little bug that the powers could quash at will if they put their minds to it. It survives only because no one really takes it seriously enough to fight with ground troops, the only gauge of an intention to prevail."[32]

"On the second . . . ISIS has made enemies of nearly everyone. Recent days alone have seen attacks on three powerful states: Turkey (the bombing in Ankara), Russia (the airliner over Sinai), and France (the attacks in Paris). This is not a path for survival. Friendless and despised, its every success shortens its life." Pipes believes ISIS will disappear and the world can "focus on the real 'unprecedented threat to international peace and security,' namely nuclear weapons in the hands of Iran's apocalyptic leadership."[33]

Until that day though, ISIS remains a major player in this Middle East "game of thrones."

While a great deal of attention rivets on ISIS, the greater player in the region, as Pipes noted, remains Iran. Middle East expert Jonathan Spyer observed that "Perhaps the single best organized and most aggressive alliance active currently in the Middle East is the bloc of states and movements gathered around the Islamic Republic of Iran."[34] Many Israelis agree. "When I compare the Sunni radical axis with the Shiite one, it's clear to me who's most dangerous. With all due respect to Islamic State achievements, the Sunni threat is along the lines of 'more of the same.' It's something we are familiar with. But the Shiite axis, on the other hand, is based on Iran. We are talking about a regional power that dominates 25 percent of the world's natural gas reserves and 11 percent of its petroleum reserves. It has tremendous human capital, high capabilities in science, technology, infrastructure, operational abilities, and cyber developments. Iran, Iraq, Syria, Hezbollah and now also Russia are closing ranks against the Sunni axis—including, to our stupefaction, even an international coalition headed by the United States—and this should worry us. Do we want Iran sitting on our doorstep? Do we want Iran, a country that de facto rules Iraq, Syria, and Lebanon and enjoys Russian backup—to win in this confrontation? A country that maintains its standing as a nuclear-threshold state?"[35]

The major battleground in this "game of thrones" is Syria. Since the start of its civil war in 2011, war has torn its soil and its soul. It's nearly disappeared as a country and stands as the nadir of human tragedy in this Middle East "game of thrones." The UN lamented, "Civilians are suffering the unimaginable, as the world stands witness. Without stronger efforts to bring parties to the peace table, ready to compromise, current trends suggest that the Syrian conflict—and the killing and destruction it wreaks—will carry on for the foreseeable future,"[36] The statistics are mind-numbing: More than 250,000 killed, over 4 million refugees, and 7.6 million "internally displaced."[37] They represent a lost generation of Syrians. Few knew when it started that it would go so long or cost so much. Europe paid its own price of not intervening when the biggest exodus since World War II ended up on its shores. The continent will reap yet untold and unseen consequences. While peace talks may offer a reprieve from the deadly war, Syria will never be the same again.

## ISRAEL AND THE GAME OF THRONES

The demise of Syria as we knew it, the Russian intervention, and its de facto alliance with the Islamic Republic of Iran represented an unforeseen change in Israel's national security calculus. For example, Israeli radar operators watch Russian jets fly not just in northeastern Syria but along Israel's northern border. In fact, some have violated Israeli air space. "All of this means that the IDF's Northern Command, Military Intelligence, and IAF must quietly recalibrate their preparations on this highly tense front."[38] The stakes are high, where "accidental run-ins with the Russian Air Force, which, without sufficient caution, could entail grave and even global unintended consequences."[39]

When Russia deployed S-400 anti-aircraft batteries inside Syria, it added to the potential danger. Their range "covers the entire region, meaning that any Israeli aircraft taking off there can be detected and shot down by Russian crews."[40] Israel found itself deeper inside the new Middle East game of thrones. Complicating Israel's situation even further, Russia is now allied with Iran, Israel's lethal nemesis. While it daily curses Israel and pledges to destroy the Jewish State, Russia's alliance gives it legitimacy inside Syria.

Joel Rosenberg believes Russia doesn't fully comprehend the nature of the Islamic Republic of Iran:

"I don't believe that Russian leaders, Putin namely, understand the apocalyptic eschatology for end-time's theology of Iran's leaders. I believe that Putin is a Czar, he's an imperialist. He sees an opportunity. President Obama cutting and running, surrendering, capitulating from the Middle East, he sees an opportunity to move. So I believe for Putin, this is a power play for him. But he doesn't understand who he's working with. Iran's leaders are apocalyptically motivated. They have an end-times theology. And that is so different to how Putin sees the world. But the danger is that Putin could get hooked into an attack or a threat against Israel that he doesn't initially plan. Because he doesn't know who his partners are. In fact, most people in Washington and the world don't understand that the leaders of Iran are driven; they're motivated by an apocalyptic version of Shia Islamic eschatology. And if you don't understand the genocidal nature of this eschatology, then it's hard to be worried about it. Putin's not worried about it. President Obama's not worried about it. I'm worried about it and I believe Netanyahu is as well."[41]

## THE LAST MOVE

Many share Rosenberg's concerns about today's Middle East, this "game of thrones" with its competing kingdoms. Putin throws his military weight around. The U.S. shrinks from its historic dominant position. Iran stands poised to increase its role as the leading state sponsor of terror in the world. ISIS boasts its murderous reign over its portion of the Levant. Turkey forms its own duplicitous alliances. The Kurds steer their people through waters dominated by larger and more powerful ships of state. Two kingdoms—ISIS and Iran—feed on global, apocalyptic ambitions. Into this labyrinth, Israel relies on its best statecraft to navigate through a new and more dangerous Fertile Crescent.

But the dream of a king more than 2500 years ago reveals who has the last move in the Middle East "game of thrones." Nebuchadnezzar, the king of Babylon, summoned his wise men to interpret a dream so troubling "his sleep left him" (Daniel 2:1). But the king would not tell them the dream. This unprecedented request stunned his wise men. They replied, "There is not a man on earth who can tell the king's matter; therefore no king, lord, or ruler has ever asked such things of any magician, astrologer, or Chaldean" (v. 10). The king persisted and decreed if they didn't tell him both the dream and its interpretation, he'd kill them all.

The decree also applied to a Hebrew wise man named Daniel. Before the executions proceeded, Daniel asked the king for a reprieve and more time. The king granted his request. Then Daniel went before the King of Heaven "that they might seek mercies from the God of heaven concerning this secret, so that Daniel and his companions might not perish with the rest of the wise men of Babylon. Then the secret was revealed to Daniel in a night vision. So Daniel blessed the God of heaven" (vv. 18-19).

Daniel went back to the king and declared, "There is a God in heaven who reveals secrets, and He has made known to King Nebuchadnezzar what will be in the latter days" (v. 28). Daniel proceeded to tell the king his dream of a great image: "This image's head was of fine gold, its chest and arms of silver, its belly and thighs of bronze, its legs of iron, its feet partly of iron and partly of clay. You watched while a stone was cut out without hands, which struck the image on its feet of iron and clay, and broke them in pieces. Then the iron, the clay, the bronze, the silver, and the gold were crushed together, and became like chaff from the summer threshing floors; the wind carried them away so that no trace of them was found. And the stone that struck the image became a great mountain and filled the whole earth" (vv. 32-35).

Daniel explained that the image represented great kingdoms that shall rise and fall. But at the end, one kingdom—"this great mountain"—shall arise that will rule them all. "And in the days of these kings the God of Heaven will set up a kingdom which shall never be destroyed; and the kingdom shall not be left to other people; it shall break in pieces and consume all these kingdoms, and it shall stand forever" (v. 44).

This kingdom contains no "Iron Throne" like the mythical "Game of Thrones." Instead, in the Book of Revelation, the Apostle John describes a "white throne" in the center of this Kingdom, a new King and a new age. "Then I saw a great white throne and

Him who sat on it, from whose face the earth and the heaven fled away" (Revelation 20:11). "Then He who sat on the throne said, 'Behold, I make all things new.' And He said to me, 'Write, for these words are true and faithful'" (21:5). "And there shall be no more curse; but the throne of God and of the Lamb shall be in it, and His servants shall serve Him" (22:3).

After Russia expends its energy, when Iran is vanquished, and ISIS cannot be found, there will come a Kingdom and a King who will rule over all. Despite the dark days in the earth today, there is another day dawning for the earth and its peoples. The Bible says it will be a day when "the earth will be filled with the knowledge of the Lord as the waters cover the sea" (Habakkuk 2:14). Jesus said in the last days, "nation would rise against nation and kingdom against kingdom" (Matthew 24:7). But He added that these would be just the "beginning of the birth pangs" (v. 8 NIV). Those birth pangs represent the dawn of a new age, the birth of a new kingdom and its coming King. It's why so many cry, "Even so, come, Lord Jesus!" (Revelation 22:20).

The last move in the "game of thrones" will be reserved for the King.

# Apocalyptic Islam

*"We are waiting for you in Dabiq."*

~ Islamic State Fighter[1]

The capture of a small town in northern Syria by ISIS in August of 2014 may sound insignificant compared to the Iranian nuclear deal or Russia's major incursion into the Middle East. But in the eschatology of the Islamic State, it marked a milestone. The town is called Dabiq and, according to Sunni theology, it's a pivotal venue at the end of the age. ISIS followers believe it will be the scene of a great end-time battle. The belief springs from a prophecy found in the Hadith, the sayings attributed to Mohammad.

The prophecy states:

> The (last) Hour will not come until the Romans would land at al-Amaq or in Dabiq. An army of the best of the people of the earth at that time will come from Medina against them. When they arrange themselves in ranks, the Romans will say: Do not stand between us and those (Muslims) who took prisoners from amongst us. Let us fight with them.' Then Muslims will say, 'Nay, by Allah, how can we withdraw between you and our brothers. They will then fight and a third (part) of the army will run away, whom Allah will never forgive. A third (part of the army), which will be constituted of excellent martyrs in the eye of Allah, will be killed and the third who will never be put to trial will win and they will be conquerors of Constantinople.[2]

This prophecy holds a central part in the world view of ISIS. For example, they named their monthly magazine *Dabiq*. "The editors, calling themselves the '*Dabiq* team,' explain why they adopted the name for their magazine: 'The area will play a historical role in the battles leading up to the conquests of Constantinople, then Rome.'"[3] Every issue of *Dabiq* includes a quote from Mus'ab al-Zarqawi, who founded Al Qaeda Iraq, the forerunner of ISIS. He claimed, "The spark has been lit here in Iraq, and its heat will continue to intensify—by Allah's permission—until it burns the crusader armies in Dabiq."[4]

According to the prophecy: "An infidel horde flying 80 banners meets a Muslim army"[5] in Dabiq. Ironically, today ISIS fighters rejoice when the coalition of nations fighting the Islamic State expands. As this "infidel horde" grows closer to 80 nations, ISIS believes the prophecy is closer to being fulfilled.

Welcome to the world of apocalyptic Islam.

## END OF THE WORLD

Ryan Mauro of the Clarion Project explained this growing phenomenon: "One of the interesting developments I've seen, particularly with ISIS and other jihadists, is how much they're wrapping themselves in end-time theology. When a jihadist says something like, 'We're going to break the cross,' or 'America, we condemn you for being the protector of the cross,' they're referencing an end-time prophecy. They believe Jesus comes back, helps their Islamic messiah (the Mahdi) defeat Christianity, the Jews, and the rest of the world. Then they believe Jesus bans Christianity. So, there's much more to it whenever you hear a jihadist say, 'Oh, we're going to break the cross.' That's not just a threat to the United States and to Christianity. They're saying that they're creating the conditions for their version of Jesus (far different from the Bible's version) to show up and help them conquer the world."[6]

ISIS fighters and followers see themselves as those called to conquer the world. In his groundbreaking article in the *Atlantic*—"ISIS: What They Want"—contributing editor Graeme Wood revealed: "The Islamic State is no mere collection of psychopaths, it is a religious group with carefully considered beliefs; among them that it is a key agent of the coming apocalypse ... it considers itself a harbinger of—and headline player in—the imminent end of the world."[7] Wood noted that the establishment of their caliphate in the summer of 2014 gave ISIS credence in this Sunni apocalyptic scenario and set it apart from other Sunni groups like Al Qaeda.

Yet Shiite Iran believes, too, that they're "a headline player in the imminent end of the world." What makes the beliefs of both Iran and ISIS so toxic is the idea they can hasten the return of the Islamic messiah through violence and weapons of mass destruction. It's why a nuclear Iran poses such a global threat. For example, "[During a 2014 conference in Tehran,] Ayatollah Hassan Mamduhi, a member of the Assembly of (Clerical) Experts, offered an enigmatic quotation from the late Ayatollah Aziz-Allah Khoshwaqt to the effect that **the Hidden Imam would conclude his Grand Occultation only when his 'sword' was ready. 'The Return of the Mahdi is conditional on what our nuclear scientists are doing,' Mamduhi said, without elaborating. The Tehran media, however, claimed that 'The Sword of the Imam' in the modern world could only mean a nuclear arsenal.**"[8] Given these beliefs, some wonder if U.S. Secretary of State John Kerry and other world diplomats understood these end-time beliefs when they negotiated a deal some expect will all but guarantee Iran gets a nuclear arsenal.

Whether it's Sunni ISIS or Shiite Iran, both openly boast about their beliefs. Iranian leaders made the following pronouncements:

• "The caravan of humanity from the day of creation has been moving . . . to the time of The Coming of Imam Mahdi. The awaiting for The Coming [of the Mahdi] is a hopeful and powerful wait, providing the biggest opening for the Islamic society."(Iran's Supreme Leader Ayatollah Khamenei, 2014.)[9]

• "The Iranian nation and the Islamic Revolution have a pivotal role in preparing the ground for the coming of the Hidden Imam. . . . We must rapidly develop Iran in order to create the [right] conditions for his coming, and we must also help the rest of the world's nations [to prepare for his return], in order to precipitate this great event. . . . The responsibility that currently rests on Iran's [shoulders] is very heavy; it is the kind of mission [with which] the divine prophets [were entrusted]. It does not permit us to rest or slumber even for a moment. Have you ever seen a prophet take a rest from the fulfillment of his mission?" Iranian president Mahmoud Ahmadinejad, August 29, 2007.[10]

• "[The] battle [to establish the Mahdi's kingdom] will only end when the [Islamic] society can get rid of the oppressors' front, **with America at the head of it.**" Iran's Supreme Leader Ayatollah Khamenei, 2014.[11]

## "THE GRAND BATTLE"

While Iran sets its sights on America—what it calls the "Great Satan"—ISIS looks to Rome and beyond:

• "We will conquer your Rome, break your crosses, and enslave your women, by the permission of Allah, the Exalted. This is his promise to us; he is glorified and he does not fail in his promise. If we do not reach that time, then our children and grandchildren will reach it, and they will sell your sons as slaves at the slave market." Official ISIS spokesman, *Dabiq*, Issue #4.[12]

• "God has chosen us! We have the Truth! You're either with us or you're a traitor. . . . Only those who fight with the Mahdi will enter paradise." Unidentified ISIS fighter in Syria.[13]

• "If you think all these mujahidin came from across the world to fight Assad, you're mistaken. They are all here as promised by the Prophet. This is the war he promised—it is the Grand Battle." Unidentified Sunni fighter in Syria.[14]

In this "Grand Battle," ISIS and Iran share common traits, but major differences mark their eschatology. They also employ distinct strategies: "The leaders of ISIS are focused on developing the territorial, financial, and administrative infrastructure required to build the caliphate. The leaders of Iran are focused on developing the scientific, technological, and financial capacities they need to build a nuclear bomb. The leaders of

ISIS believe in committing genocide now, and for them simple swords and AK-47s suffice. The leaders of Iran are preparing to commit genocide later and so are investing enormous sums of time and money on their nuclear program."[15]

Both represent profound threats to the world!

The Islamic State has its sights set on Rome, what they consider the center of Christendom. They laid out their agenda in a publication called *Black Flags from Rome*. Robert Spencer, author of *The Complete Infidel's Guide to ISIS*, told CBN News correspondent Dale Hurd: "Rome is one of its primary goals and is in its timetable. It has a timetable where in 10 years, by the year 2025, it hopes to bring about Armageddon, the final struggle between good and evil or between the Muslims and the non-Muslims. And one of the chief stepping stones to that Armageddon battle is the conquest of Rome, which they think they're going to be able to do within the next five years, by 2020."[16]

Some scoff at the idea of ISIS conquering one of Europe's largest cities. But ISIS is not anticipating a frontal assault, and they've already begun to implement one of their strategies. That includes infiltrating the flood of refugees—nearly a million strong—during the summer of 2015. Spencer explains, "They're not talking about doing it by conventional armies; they're talking about doing (it) by overwhelming these lands with sympathizers from within, and an influx of people from outside. And that's something we see happening right now in Europe. And so it's not that far outside of the realm of possibility that they could at least make these attempts."[17] Those sympathizers include non-Muslims, sleeper cells, and Muslims serving in European armies.

At the end, ISIS anticipates a bloodthirsty climax at the Vatican. "The main event, as they see it, will be the beheading of the Pope in St. Peter's Square, broadcast and live-streamed to a horrified international audience."[18] Spencer said a member of ISIS recently boasted, "'Once we take Rome, we are going to carry out mass beheadings in St. Peter's Square. . . . And so this is the plan, to convert St Peter's Square into a huge site of executions to people judged to be enemies of Allah, chief among them the Pope, in order to cow and frighten the rest of the world into submitting to their rule. . . . They think that the conquest of Rome will be the complete sign of Islam's superiority over Christianity and defeat of Christianity. Once Rome is conquered, in this view within the next five years, then Israel will follow shortly after. They also believe that during this time period, they're also going to conquer Saudi Arabia and Iran."[19]

## "HIJACKED MESSIAH"

On the Shiite side of the end-times' ledger, those who believe in the Mahdi or Twelfth Imam are sometimes called "Twelvers." But where did this belief of the Mahdi come from? Ron Cantrell, author of *The Mahdi: Hijacked Messiah*, told me the Mahdi descended from the Islam's Prophet Mohammad himself, but vanished in the middle of the ninth century. Now more than eleven hundred years later, Shiites anxiously expect the Twelfth Imam to come back at the end of the age.

Cantrell explained the Mahdi comes "with a promise that he would return and he would bring Islam to its total fruition as the world's last standing religion. The Mahdi is a personage that is expected to come on the scene by Islam as a messiah figure. He is slotted to come in the end of time according to their writings, very much like how we think of the return of Jesus, although there are some staggering differences between our Messiah and the Islamic expected messiah."[20]

In Shiite eschatology, chaos precedes the return of the Mahdi and the end of the age. This is an apocalyptic time marked by wars, plagues, and famines, followed by the Day of Judgment. Cantrell says, "This is an important situation that we are heading into with the nation of Iran. Chaos and worldwide turmoil is a prerequisite for the coming of the Mahdi."[21] When you mix this messianic theology with nuclear weapons, Iran's current foreign policy becomes a toxic brew with regional and global ramifications. If Iran gets the bomb, it would change the face of the Middle East.

This belief in the return of the Mahdi spreads throughout the Islamic world. A 2012 Pew Research poll discovered a huge number of Sunni and Shiite Muslims believe Islam's Mahdi will return "in their lifetime." In the research 83 percent in Afghanistan, 72 percent in Iraq, 67 percent in Tunisia, and 62 percent in Malaysia anticipate his appearance. While the percentage in other countries like Indonesia—23 percent—is far less, the percentages worldwide translate to more than 600 million Muslims who expect Islam's messiah in their lifetime. Sunnis and Shiites both agree the earth will eventually become an Islamic world."[22]

Given these two competing end-time visions, author Lela Gilbert of *Saturday People, Sunday People* asked the question: "Which Islamists, in the long run, pose the greatest threat? The calculating Iranian mullahs with their nuclear ambitions and aggressive exportation of the Islamic Revolution, or the Islamic State's insatiable jihadis with their land-grabs, bloodlust, and swelling numbers of fresh recruits?"[23] She posed this question to her colleague, Hillel Fradkin, at the Hudson Institute and also what he thought lay ahead for the Middle East. He replied, "What lies ahead in the short term is, indeed, an ongoing struggle between the radical Sunni Islam of ISIS and the radical Shiite Islam of the Islamic Republic of Iran. Each aims at and embodies a vision of a radical and redemptive 'Islamic State.' The two versions contradict one another, so there can be no peace between them. But they also feed off one another. Iran is already the more successful of the two. It has transformed what was formerly a loose alliance called the 'Shiite Crescent' into a 'Shiite Empire,' which it now proudly and loudly proclaims while consolidating control over Baghdad, Beirut, Damascus, and Sana."[24]

Regardless of who dominates the Middle East, some warn we need to take both of these apocalyptic visions seriously. The rise of an apocalyptic Nazi Germany offers a sobering history lesson of what happens when the world ignores fanatic beliefs. Wood reminds us that, like Hitler, these end-time beliefs run deep. "That the Islamic State holds the imminent fulfillment of prophecy as a matter of dogma at least tells us the mettle of our opponent. It is ready to cheer its own near-obliteration, and to remain confident, even when surrounded, that it will receive divine succor if it stays true to the Prophetic model. Ideological tools may convince some potential converts that the group's message is false, and military tools can limit its horrors. But for an organization as impervious to persuasion as the Islamic State, few measures short of these will matter, and the war may be a long one, even if it doesn't last until the end of time."[25]

# Ten Things You Need to Know about the Middle East

*"The Middle East is coming to a neighborhood near you and the United States will remain connected both strategically and financially to the Middle East. So there's no detaching."*

~ Michael Oren, Former Israeli Ambassador to the United States[1]

Understanding the Middle East can be daunting. The news emitted from the region often seems like a blur to many Westerners: one more terror attack, another suicide bombing; an odd assortment of religious sects—the Sunnis, the Shiites; unfamiliar names and places, and an alien history. It's tempting to divorce ourselves from the region. But as former Israeli Ambassador to the U.S. Michael Oren warns, we do so at our peril. We need to know more, not less, about the region.

My own education began in earnest in August of 2000. My wife, Elizabeth, and our three children—Philip, Kathleen, and Grace—disembarked in Israel, straight into the heart of the Second Intifada which started five weeks later. For the next three and a half years, we lived through a torrent of suicide bombs, shootings, and various terror attacks. During this baptism of fire, we prayed and lived out the meaning of Psalm 91 that says, "He that dwells in the secret place of the Most High shall abide in the shadow of the Almighty" (v.1).

In the midst of trying to keep my family together, survive the intifada, and keep up my reporting, I also entered into a steep learning curve. Surrounded by an emotionally charged conflict, beset by passions on all sides and a dizzying array of "narratives," I struggled to keep up. Overwhelmed would be a fair description.

Since those tumultuous days, I've watched the Middle East evolve and witnessed my own understanding find footing on more solid ground. The opportunity to be an eyewitness on the ground proved invaluable. For example, in 2005, we reported the gut-wrenching Israeli "disengagement" from the Gaza Strip that led to the 2007 takeover by Hamas. In 2006, we reported from Israel's northern border when it fought its longest war at that time with Hezbollah. I remember the many sirens announcing another Katyusha rocket attack from the front-line town of Metula. In 2008-09, 2012, and 2014, we went to the front lines down south to the three wars Israel would fight with Hamas.

We watched Israel's Iron Dome knock Hamas rockets from the sky. In 2011, I reported in the middle of a riot from Cairo's Tahrir Square during the heat of the Arab Spring. That historic phenomenon re-shuffled the Middle East. Egypt tottered. Libya fell. Civil war tore Syria apart while millions fled. We're still living with the momentous effects of that geo-political earthquake. In 2014, we raced to Iraq when ISIS devoured so much of that nation-state. They erased the Sykes-Picot line that divided the Middle East nearly one hundred years earlier. We went to the front lines with the Kurdish military just half a mile from ISIS. We met face to face with Christians who had come face to face with ISIS and were given four choices, including conversion to Islam or death.

Once again, the region reels in the throes of cataclysmic change. Russia bullied itself into Syria's civil war and the middle of the Middle East maelstrom. They struck an alliance with Hezbollah in Lebanon, Assad in Syria, the Baghdad government of Iraq, and the Ayatollahs in Tehran. Iran itself sat on the cusp of developing nuclear weapons after an improbable agreement with the West. Turkey confronted an emboldened Russia, while Israel devised a precarious course through uncharted and turbulent geo-political waters. The region started drifting when the Obama Administration pulled up the anchor of Pax Americana. Now no one knows in which direction the region is drifting. Christian persecution reached historic levels while millions of Middle Eastern Muslims migrated to Europe in the biggest population shift since World War II. With all of these changes, many hear the echoes of 1914 growing louder, and some wonder if we're on the brink of another world war.

How do we understand all these pivotal changes? Through the years, I've found 1 Chronicles 12:32 a great rudder in turbulent times. It says "the Sons of Issachar," one of Israel's ancient tribes, "had understanding of the times, to know what Israel ought to do." It's an incentive that we too can "understand the times" in which we live. Despite the powerful experiences I've had for more than fifteen years, I remain a student of the Middle East. Much of my continuing education comes from the opportunity to interview many experts of the region. During the last several months, I've had the privilege of interviewing a number of people on the diplomatic, military, and spiritual front lines. In that quest to help you also understand, I've asked many of these experts the following question: What do people in the West and especially the U.S. need to know about the Middle East?

Here are ten of those experts whose insight I value. I expect they'll contribute to your understanding about the most volatile region on the globe.

## MICHAEL OREN, FORMER ISRAELI AMBASSADOR TO THE UNITED STATES

I first met Michael Oren when he served as a scholar and historian at the Shalem Center in Jerusalem. We interviewed him several times through the years, and I've esteemed his keen grasp of current events through history's prism. He's written heralded works such as *Six Days of War: June 1967 and the Making of the Modern Middle East; Power, Faith, and Fantasy: America in the Middle East, 1776 to the Present;* and *Ally, My Journey across the American-Israeli Divide*. When called upon, he's also served as a spokesman for the Israeli Defense Forces. I remember vividly arranging a satellite live shot with Michael on the front lines of the 2008 war with Hamas on the Gaza border. With the threat of Hamas missiles raining down on us, we established a satellite connection. He stood, helmet in hand, vested in body armor and armed with a cogent defense of Israel's actions where he presented Israel's case to the world.

Later, he would labor on another front line—the halls of power in Washington D.C. From 2009-2013, Michael served as the Israeli Ambassador to the United States. I wonder which front line Oren thought the more dangerous. Now he serves as a Knesset member of Israel's parliament. He understands both the West and the Middle East like few people today. He's not only studied it as an historian, but has also played a key role in its recent history. Yet, even now, he can't tell you what's coming. In his new, but tiny Knesset office, I sat down with Oren. He believes the Middle East is in a transformational and unpredictable era.

> There are events like this that happen about every century. In 1798, Napoleon invaded Egypt and introduced the European West to the Middle East and it was a profound upheaval. One hundred years later, the Ottoman Empire collapsed and that was a profound upheaval. The map that we lived with for the next hundred years was drawn by the French and the British. And now that map has unraveled and now we are going through another massive upheaval. And nobody knows how it's going to turn out. If anybody tells you – I'm an historian. I have enough problems predicting the past. Anybody who tells you they know what's going to happen in the Middle East in the next two months, two weeks, two hours, Chris, don't believe them. Because I don't.[2]

As I quoted Oren earlier, he believes the West—specifically the U.S.—cannot escape the magnetic pull of the Middle East.

> What they need to know is this: it's not necessarily about the West. It's about tensions and problems and insecurities within the societies themselves. The state system as devised by the

Europeans, they're arbitrary borders that didn't take into consideration ethnic and religious differences. It's not adaptable; it's not sustainable in an area of the world where people don't necessarily organize themselves along nation state lines. If anybody in the United States thinks that they can turn their back on the Middle East and walk away, then they're kidding themselves. The Middle East is not like Vietnam, where you can pull your troops out and go home and be pretty confident that the Viet Cong are not going to follow you to wherever you're going—Chicago or Florida. The Middle East is going to come after you. **The Middle East is coming to a neighborhood near you, and the United States will remain connected both strategically and financially to the Middle East. So there's no detaching.** If the United States wants to be a player in this region, a player diplomatically, it has to be a player militarily as well. So you need two things. You need leverage, and leverage you get by devoting assets. Whether it's sending a battleship, an aircraft carrier off the shores of Syria and showing your strength. And you need to give your partners a sense of credibility.[3]

## U.S. SENATOR TOM COTTON

We set up for a three-camera interview in the gardens behind the King David Hotel and waited. We expected U.S. Senator Tom Cotton from Arkansas. He'd arrived in Jerusalem to meet with Israeli leaders and discuss the proposed nuclear agreement with Iran. Israel has sat on the front lines of Iran's venom for years. Now this tiny nation potentially stands face to face with its nuclear ire. Their ubiquitous cries of "Death to Israel," mixed with a nuclear weapon, meant a life-or-death threat to the Jewish State. The freshman senator from Arkansas ranked as one of the most outspoken opponents of the deal in the U.S. Congress. Even at 38, he brought a wealth of real-life experience to his critique. A veteran of tours of duty in Iraq and Afghanistan, he led a 41-man air assault infantry platoon and won a Bronze Star.[4] When he won election to the U.S. Senate as its youngest member, Politico named him the Senator "most likely to succeed."[5] With a CNN crew waiting in line for their own interview, we sat down with Cotton, fresh from a meeting with Israeli Prime Minister Benjamin Netanyahu.

First, he explained why the U.S. relationship with Israel is so important to America and its people.

> What they need to know about what's happening in Israel in particular is that Israel remains the beacon of constitutional democracy, individual liberty, and free market economics in the Middle East. The United States and Israel have had an alliance going back to the very beginning of their declaration as a sovereign state. And that is based secondarily on the United States Congress and our support for the State of Israel, but primarily on the American people and their support for the State of Israel. And that's because the American people realize that we share the same values and same interests as the Jewish people here in the State of Israel and that we need to stand steadfast with Israel and support them in a very volatile region.[6]

As I cited Cotton earlier, he illustrated why he believes the Middle East is entering one of the most dangerous times in history, especially in light of the Iranian nuclear deal.

> More generally in the Middle East, what the American people need to know is that this is a time of unprecedented turmoil. Again, you have Iranian-backed proxies, whether they are militias, or state actors, or terrorist groups that are largely in control of large swaths of Iraq, Syria, Lebanon, Yemen and that are going to continue to aggressively destabilize the region because Iran is going to get tens of billions of dollars to support them; because Iran is also going to get more conventional weapons and, ultimately, nuclear weapons. That is going to happen on almost the first day of this deal. They're going to get the money immediately, so very soon, they'll be getting the conventional weapons. And the nuclear umbrella they'll be developing will continue to deter, oftentimes effectively push back against Iran's actions in the region. That's why it's so important to stand up to them now before they get stronger, before they realize that they can confront the U.S. and our allies throughout the region.[7]

## U.S. GENERAL JAY GARNER (RET.)

I first met retired U.S. General Jay Garner in Erbil, Kurd-istan. A mutual friend arranged an introduction, reminding me that that few people understand the Kurds like the General. His ca-reer and the history of the Kurdish people intersected several times in the past quarter of a century. In 1991, he played a part in Op-eration Provide Comfort. That operation intervened after Saddam Hussein attacked the Kurds following the first Gulf War. As so many times in their past, they fled to the mountains for refuge. Garner, along with other U.S. personnel, came to their rescue in an operation that "saved countless lives."[8]

Later, in 2003, Garner led the Office for Reconstruction and Humanitarian Assistance after Saddam Hussein fell. Through-out the years, he's maintained a close relationship with the Kurds and remains a champion of their cause. Now in 2015, once again, he came to visit the Kurdish leaders he holds in high esteem.

When I asked him about what people need to know about the Middle East, he painted a bleak picture of a fractured region:

> The Middle East is beginning to break apart. It's beginning to be subverted by terrorist elements like Al Qaeda or like Al Qaeda in the Sinai Peninsula. There's no coherent U.S. policy for how you deal with the Middle East. We don't recognize the realities in the Middle East, especially in Syria and Iraq, and we're running the gamut of nuclear proliferation. And we need to have a policy, with the resources behind the policy to correct that.[9]

The General surprised me when he suddenly connected the geo-political dots of today with the writings of Ezekiel the prophet about twenty-five hundred years ago. I followed up then with this question: "In what way do you see biblical prophecy like Ezekiel 38 and 39 unfolding?"

> Well, what I think you see right now, you see for the first time since the early '50s; there seems to be a crack in the solidarity between the United States and Israel. And I think that gives a lot of impetus to those enemies of Israel that they're not as well-shielded or protected by the United States. So you have

that scenario developing. And then you have now the emergence of the Russians into Syria, which is also joined with the Iranians in Syria—you have that scenario unfolding. Now that's the birthing of that. But somewhere along the line, you could stop that if you had the correct policy and took the right recourse. . . . I think the worst thing you can have is nuclear proliferation in the Middle East. And if you have that and we don't guarantee the survival of Israel, you're probably looking at Ezekiel 38 and 39, and it's not a good picture.[10]

## U.S. GENERAL "JERRY" BOYKIN (RET.)

Another U.S. General, William "Jerry" Boykin is a warrior, a patriot, and a deeply committed Christian. Boykin served as Commander of U.S. Army Special Forces and was chosen as a founding member of the Army's elite Delta Force. His thirty-six-year Army career included a tour with the CIA and four years as Deputy Under-Secretary of Defense for Intelligence. He also came face to face with radical Islam in the battle over Mogadishu, Somalia, a conflict dramatized in the movie *Black Hawk Down*. He summed up his view of the battle we face with radical Islam today in the last page of his book *Never Surrender: A Soldier's Journey to the Crossroads of Faith and Freedom*:

> But we are not the bad guys. Our motto is life and liberty. The jihadist's motto is "convert or die." And no matter how much the PC crowd would like to deny it, the inalienable right to liberty that America is fighting for is part of the Judeo-Christian heritage that is the bedrock of our nation. . . . That's why America's cause is just. That's why we're the good guy. **And that's why we will never surrender.**[11]

Boykin now serves as the Executive Vice President of the Family Research Council. When he joined the organization, he told reporters, "It's no longer about me. It's about my grandchildren. Is it going to be our generation that gives our future away? Or is it going to be our generation that preserves it."[12] We interviewed Boykin on the southern steps of the Temple Mount, a fitting setting for his reply to what's going on in the Middle East.

"If you want to know about the region, look to the Bible—and Israel," he said.

> At the end of the day, you can think it's about oil, you can think it's about a caliphate. It's about Israel. It's about the prophecies associated with the nation of Israel, if you go back and read prophets like Daniel and Isaiah and Ezekiel and you bring it all together. Read the books by Joel Rosenberg, our dear friend, who I think articulately, explains in his books (how prophecy is unfolding). But you got to look at what he writes as well as what the prophets wrote, and you got to say, *Wow! I see that happening right now! Oh, wow! That's already happened!*
>
> Right here, we're standing at the Temple Mount today. Go back and listen to the audio of the Commander of the 55th Airborne Brigade when he came in and took this Temple Mount right here. On the 7th of June 1967, he said, 'The Temple Mount is under our control, do you understand?' He began to weep as he said, "The Temple Mount is under our control. . . ." His voice broke and then the shofar sounded and then the people began to cheer. That's because they knew that that was biblical prophecy, and as Bible-believing Christians, we need to get beyond this idea that today's Israel is insignificant spiritually or scripturally or biblically because, in fact, it is (significant).[13]

## ROBERT SPENCER: JIHAD WATCH

As director of www.jihadwatch.org, Robert Spencer tracks the advance of Islamic jihad on the home front and in far-away lands. He's written more than a dozen books on the subject. His latest, *The Complete Infidel's Guide to ISIS*, provides invaluable insight into the latest mutation of radical jihad in our time. Despite his scholarship and breadth of knowledge, he's also considered politically incorrect. He once led seminars on Islam and jihad "for the FBI, the United States Central Command, United States Army Command and General Staff College, the U.S. Army's Asymmetric Warfare Group, the Joint Terrorism Task Force (JTTF), and the U.S. intelligence community."[14] However in

October 2011, "Muslim Brotherhood-linked groups wrote to Homeland Security Advisor (and current CIA director) John Brennan, demanding that Spencer be removed as a trainer for teaching JTTF agents about the belief system of Islamic jihadists; Brennan immediately complied."[15] He's also unwelcome in the United Kingdom "for the crime of pointing out that Islam has doctrines of violence against unbelievers."[16] The U.S. Conference of Catholic Bishops has also boycotted Spencer "for refusing to adhere to their 'Islam is a Religion of Peace' line." In addition, a senior member of al-Qaeda "invited (Spencer) by name to convert."[17]

When Spencer came to CBN to talk about his latest book, I had the opportunity to interview him for our weekly program, "Jerusalem Dateline." We talked about the book, the goals of ISIS, and also "what people in the West need to know about the Middle East." Here's his reply:

> They need to know that groups like ISIS are not some twisted, hi-jacked version of Islam that is a terror group abhorred and rejected by most Muslims. They need to know that the Islamic State is making recruits among peaceful Muslims and winning broad support among peaceful Muslims by virtue of justifying and explaining their actions with reference to Islamic texts and teachings, the Quran and the Sunna, the example of Mohammad. And that means that this is an appeal far broader than just the Islamic state itself. And we need to address that if we're ever going to come up with any effective means to counter it. But we also have to remember that this is a spiritual battle, that this is a concentratedly evil force. That they say, 'We will win because we love death more than you love life.' And we know that the Author of life will never allow death to conquer life. And so ultimately, the Islamic State will not prevail.[18]

## BARONESS CAROLINE COX OF QUEENSBURY

In the fall of 2015, I visited my daughter in London during her internship with a fashion company. One priority on my trip included introducing her to a woman I consider one of the heroines of our time, Baroness Caroline Cox. I had met the Baroness years before and admired her tireless work on behalf of persecuted Christians. I called her office and she graciously agreed to meet. On a typical cold, rainy, and raw London evening, she picked us up at one of the city's subway stations and drove us to a quaint Italian restaurant. The owners knew the Baroness, but like everyone she meets, she wanted them—and us—to simply call her "Caroline."

"Caroline" came to dinner with a rich, storied past of reaching out in Christian love to people suffering under the heel of tyranny. Just after being appointed a member of the House of Lords (how she got her title), she "set off in a 32-ton truck for Communist Poland, Romania, and the Soviet Union, to bring medical supplies behind the Iron Curtain."[19] When it was politically incorrect, she "called openly for Soviet regime change from the House of Lords at the height of the Cold War." Then she made at least 60 trips to Armenia when the Armenians "were being relentlessly attacked in their villages by violent Islamists from Azerbaijan, and no one in the world seemed to care."[20] Later, she "brought news of the carnage to the West"[21] of the genocide in Darfur. "Caroline carried the shining courage of Sudanese Christians before her as she made repeated, dangerous trips back to Sudan."[22] Through all those dangerous trips and "dark moments of fear she recalled words she learned as a child, and was encouraged: 'Have I not commanded thee? Be strong and of a good courage; be not afraid, neither be thou dismayed: for the Lord they God is with thee whithersoever thou goest'" (Joshua 1:9).[23]

After we finished dinner and she drove us back to the train station, I asked this winner of the Wilberforce Award, "which recognizes 'an individual who has made a difference in the face of formidable societal problems and injustices'"[24] what people need to know about the Middle East and England. This woman who has stood up to totalitarianism warned of an ominous and dangerous threat to the Middle East and our way of life in Western countries like Great Britain. This menace not only endangers us but our future generations.

Some of what's happening in the Middle East and England are all part of the same current situation with regard to the growth of a political and strategic Islam that is working in many ways to achieve its domination. In the Middle East, of course, it's using all the tactics of real terror and perpetrating atrocities which I would call definitely evil. In the West, it's more subtle but there are many ways in which political Islam is advancing legally through the development of Sharia courts. In this country and elsewhere politically, financially with the development of Sharia finance compliance in many of the major, major banks and financial institutions. Culturally, Saudi Arabia's massive investment, particularly in the schools, universities ... I think that we need to really seek the wisdom and discernment how to use our own values, in my case Christian values of love and justice. But try to reach a situation whereby we can protect our political, cultural, and spiritual heritage. And in the meantime, with that growth of this form of Islam, many Muslims are also suffering. Particularly Muslim women are suffering from the edicts of Sharia law. If a man can say divorce three times, the woman is divorced. Polygamy is rife where there's a lot of violence which can be condoned under chastisement. And I think we need to pray for wisdom and discernment and take whatever action is necessary **to ensure that we pass on our heritage of freedom and justice and, as a Christian, our freedom of the Gospel of love undiminished to our children and to our grandchildren.**[25]

## TONY PERKINS: PRESIDENT, FAMILY RESEARCH COUNCIL

Tony Perkins fights for the family. He serves as president of the pro-family organization, Family Research Council (FRC). I first met Tony at a gas station in Jerusalem. I had just pulled in to fill up our van at the Yellow Gas Station on King David Street. When I went in to pay, I saw Tony standing in line. He had obviously just finished an early-morning jog and had come in for a snack. I recognized him and knew I'd seen him on TV. But I couldn't place his name. Regardless, I introduced myself and we struck up a conversation.

From that initial meeting several years ago, I've had the opportunity of seeing Tony a number of times and have had the privilege of being interviewed on his "Washington Watch" radio show. He also lives on the front lines of the culture wars in the U.S. In 2013, a lone gunman strode into his Washington offices with a plan "to kill as many people as possible."[26] Miraculously, their security guard wrestled the gunman down before he could hatch his deadly plot. The shooter targeted the FRC because of its pro-marriage views.

In the fall of 2015, Tony brought a tour group to Jerusalem and asked me to speak to the people about what's happening in the Middle East. Afterwards, I got to turn the tables, interview Tony, and ask him what he thinks is going on in the Middle East, what people need to know about the region. He brought up one of the most under-reported and yet important issues of the day—Christian persecution.

> I think primarily we need to see that the persecution of Christians in the Middle East is unprecedented. And we get these news flashes and it gets our attention and in this 24–hour news cycle, we move on to another tragedy—a flood or a hurricane, an earthquake. And we lose sight of the fact that there are literally hundreds of thousands of Christians who have been displaced. This is unprecedented; it's historical what we see happening in the Middle East. And the fact that Christians are laying down their lives for their stand for Jesus Christ, refusing to renounce their faith in Him. And that should be such a sobering but challenging message for Americans—that this time when we see increasing hostility toward our faith in America at the hands of our own government, we shouldn't shrink back. We shouldn't deny our faith in Jesus Christ, but we, too, should live boldly so that we exercise our rights and freedoms and advocate for those that are losing theirs.[27]

Being both an advocate and activist, Perkins added steps to address this crisis:

> Number one; there are a number of relief organizations that can give immediate aid in times of crisis. You know, Samari-

tan's Purse, the Voice of the Martyrs, and so many others that are working on the ground to meet the physical need because, quite frankly, the United States is not doing a whole lot from the reports I've gotten. That's one. But two, we need to advocate that America would be a greater voice. This administration has lost its voice when it comes to the persecution, not just of Christians but of other religious minorities—the Yazidis and others who have been persecuted for their faith, literally slaughtered. This administration can't find its way to speak out on their behalf. So we need to put pressure on our elected officials to speak out for that. And pound the UN, who is always eager to take up a cause that means nothing. They should take up this cause. And then we need to strengthen our relationship with Israel because it is the only place in the Middle East where Muslims, Christians, and people of no faith can coexist peacefully and exercise their freedoms. They have freedoms, they have rights, and they can exercise them. This is an example of what the Middle East could look like. And we certainly should stand by Israel and support them as they try to do the right thing in a very, very difficult neighborhood.[28]

As a Christian, Perkins added evangelism and courage as the order of the day for the Church.

We need to be praying for the Gospel of Jesus Christ to go forth. This is such an unprecedented time of trouble, tribulation where people are looking for the answers and—guess what! We have them! There's no reason for us to be discouraged, disappointed, afraid, fearful. This is a time to be bold, to be courageous and speak without compromise. This is not a time to fear. This is a time to live with no fear.[29]

## TOM DOYLE: AUTHOR, *KILLING CHRISTIANS*

I consider it an honor to call Tom Doyle a friend. The son of a FBI agent, this former pastor and now author, Tom tracks the movement of the Holy Spirit in the Middle East and encourages a beleaguered Body of Christ. His landmark book, *Dreams and Visions: Is Jesus Awakening the Muslim World?* brought the largely untold story of Muslims coming to faith in Jesus Christ through supernatural dreams and visions to the world. His latest book, *Killing Christians: Living the Faith Where It's Not Safe to Believe*, chronicles the modern-day Book of Acts stories throughout the Middle East. As the book's cover testifies, "Doyle takes readers to the secret meetings, the torture rooms, the grim prisons, and even the executions that are the 'calling' of countless Muslims-turned-Christians."[30]

It tells the story of men like Shukri. ISIS tortured and killed this modern-day martyr after he passed out Bibles at the Great Mosque in Mosul. Doyle's stories evoke the same salute Hebrews 11 gave to those willing to give their "last full measure of devotion" to Jesus: "Others were tortured, not accepting deliverance, that they might obtain a better resurrection. Still others had trial of mockings and scourgings, yes, and of chains and imprisonment. They were stoned, they were sawn in two, were tempted; were slain with the sword. They wandered about in sheepskins and goatskins, being destitute, afflicted, tormented—of whom the world was not worthy" (Hebrews 11:35–38).

When we interviewed Tom, we stood outside a park overlooking Jerusalem's Jaffa Gate and the Old City walls built by Suleiman the Great. The original Christian martyr Stephen would have been stoned not far from where we stood. Now other Christians follow Stephen's footsteps in places like Damascus, Aleppo, and Mosul. I asked Doyle, "I see this book as sort of a bridge between what's happening to the believers here in the Middle East and believers in the West, especially the U.S. What do they need to know—those believers that are watching this or listening in the U.S?"[31]

Tom answered with a plea for Western believers to extend their hearts and prayers to their suffering, persecuted family in the Middle East:

> You know that's a really good point. We may not be called to suffer for Christ in the West, but Paul said, 'When one of us suffers, we all suffer.' And Jesus said, 'They're going to hate you because they hate me.' ***It's a war on Jesus, and we are Jesus'***

*body together, so we may not go through suffering, but we want to stand with those who are.* So we pray for them, we pray for them daily, we set our watches at 8:38 p.m. every night, and when it goes off, we pray for the believers here in prison, in danger, and under persecution. We want to show them that we stand with them even though life for us is vastly different here. We haven't forgotten them; they are family, but we're all a part of this together and we just want to join with them and stand with them in prayer in the midst of the difficulty.[32]

## JOEL ROSENBERG: BEST-SELLING AUTHOR

General "Jerry" Boykin recommended reading Joel Rosenberg to understand "the times." Millions more would endorse that charge. Rosenberg splashed onto the scene with his first best-selling book, *The Last Jihad*. His fictional account of a terror attack on the U.S. presaged the 9-11 attacks by months. His subsequent prescient series of books seems to telegraph what's coming to our world before it happens. He's brought millions of his readers an insight into the geo-political world married with biblical prophetic perspective.

We also talked with Rosenberg in Jerusalem, the place he likes to call the "epicenter of the epicenter." Rosenberg brings a unique balance to an understanding of the times we're in. He sees not only darkness, but Light. He quoted from Isaiah, who wrote these words not far from where Joel and I stood: "Arise, shine; For your light has come! And the glory of the Lord is risen upon you. For behold, the darkness shall cover the earth, and deep darkness the people; But the Lord will arise over you, and His glory will be seen upon you. The Gentiles shall come to your light, and kings to the brightness of your rising"[28] (Isaiah 60:1-3). He warned of great darkness coming to the Middle East, but exhorted it's time for the church to arise to its destiny.

At this moment, Christians around the West, Christians around the world, we need to understand that while our government or governments are not necessarily doing the right thing, we can't wait. We can't wait for our government to do the right thing. We as the church have commands from the King of kings and the Lord of lords. Jesus told us to preach the Gospel to all creation; to make disciples of all nations; to care for the poor, care for the suffering; to pray for and stand with those who are persecuted and in prison. And the church needs to mobilize to do these very things and not wait for Washington.[33]

## FABIAN, MESOPOTAMIA HOUSE OF PRAYER

First of all, his name really is Fabian. When we baby boomers from the States see that name, we often think of the 1960s crooner Fabian. This Fabian co-leads one of the many lighthouses of prayer rising up throughout the Middle East. He calls theirs the Mesopotamia House of Prayer. I first met Fabian in the summer of 2014 when ISIS rampaged throughout much of northern Iraq. Sitting in his prayer room at that time brought solace and comfort from the unspeakable horrors taking place just miles away. We visited Fabian again in 2015 where he continues to spiritually plow in one of the most difficult places in the world. His team encourages believers and reaches out to many people who have lost nearly everything. These refugees are now moored in refugee camps scattered throughout the area.

This time, we met Fabian on the roof of a building under construction near his house of prayer. With a panoramic view of the area, the setting sun in the distance, and an open sky above us, Fabian answered the question "What do people in the West need to know?" with a decidedly heavenly perspective. While most people have their eyes focused on earthly events, Fabian and a faithful host throughout the Middle East are fixed on things above. They're part of a movement of a growing crescendo of prayer rising in the region. They see a biblical narrative coursing through the crises of the region. They observe a zone filled with desperate hearts willing to listen to the Good News. They recognize trends beyond the 24/7 secular news cycle. These movements are seldom, if ever, covered by CNN, the BBC, or the *New York Times*. It's the knowledge that the Holy Spirit is at work, even in the darkest of places, and that at this time He's sending out a Macedonian call.

> They do need to know that God's Spirit is moving. We so easily look at the secular news and are impacted by what we see and hear. And the enemy is using that, and he tries to bring fear . . . even to keep away from places like this (Kurdistan). But what people need to hear is that God has bigger plans. We are not to be influenced by negative news, by what the devil is doing. We need to hear what God is doing. And believe His promises in the Scriptures.

> And yes, God is pouring out His Spirit and we know that it's going to happen more and more. That's why this is no time to fear; it's time to have courage, to have compassion and love. And go to places in the Middle East. Yes, places like Iraq and Syria because the harvest is very ripe and people are desperate. They've lost everything; they're in pain. They need help and they're ready to listen. People in the States need to know that. Yes, there are many bad people who want to kill and destroy, but there are so many more people who are desperate for answers in life. **And we as the light and salt, we need to be here "for such a time as this," to be His voice and His hands and bring the Gospel of the Kingdom to their lives.**[34]

Senator Tom Cotton story: "Iran Deal Advent 'Second Nuclear Age'?

# A Time for War

*"Arrived somewhere in North Africa. When this messed-up world settles down, I will be able to tell you in the fullest details the episodes of my travels."*

~ May 8, 1943—"Mitch" to his "Dearest A.J."[1]

They echoed whispers of love from an era gone by. Seventy-two handwritten letters, hidden in the closet, stuffed in a shoe box, and locked in her heart. They held the aroma of romance, the sounds of war, and the pain of separation. Who knew she'd kept these treasures after all these years?

Anne Jean "A.J." Mitchell slipped into eternity on March 28, 2002. Of all the earthly belongings left behind by this wife, mother, and grandmother, the most treasured were these letters.

Sylvester Chris Mitchell, lovingly known as Mitch, wrote them. He'd captured her heart more than sixty years before and had never let go. Three years earlier, she'd had to let him go. For the first time in fifty-three years, a heart attack separated them. Death became the final separation, but the war came first. These letters told that story.

As it had for millions of other young lovers, World War II tore A.J. and Mitch apart. The letters he wrote from the front lines latched their hearts together while the winds of war swept over the earth in the 1940s.

Mitch and A.J.—my Dad and Mom—lived through World War II, one of the most tumultuous periods in recent history. When this "messed-up world"—as Mitch called it—settled down, they raised four kids, including yours truly. If Mitch and A.J. were alive today, they'd see that the world is messed up again. Instead of the threat of global domination by Nazism, Islamism threatens the earth with world conquest. Its zeal threatens the same Western Civilization that Mitch and millions fought to preserve. Paris and San Bernardino are just the latest signs Western Civilization is once again at war and on the edge of the abyss.

Mitch and his generation—called by some "the great-est"—vanquished Nazism. It wasn't easy. On December 3, 1943, Mitch wrote from "somewhere in Italy:"

*Dear Anne,*

*. . . . It is now 7 o'clock and off in the distance the artillery can be heard. They are really laying it on. You get so accus-tomed to the noise that when it stops you feel a little uneasy. . . .Well, my sweet one, I will close until tomorrow.*

*All yours,*

*Mitch[2]*

Later on, January 9, 1944, he wrote a letter that any GI in Iraq or Afghanistan could have penned and began his new year with a prayer.

*Dear A.J.,*

*. . . I hope and pray that this mess will be over soon. I have seen all I want to see. The U.S. will really look good to me, so will you. Won't we do the rounds the day I get my feet on that precious soil? You know, dear, the people in the U.S. don't know how lucky they are.*

*Honey, I hope my letters don't sound or read depressing.*

*Hope all is well. I love you.*

*Love,*

*Mitch[3]*

Seven months later, Mitch both rejoiced and lamented:

*July 26, 1944*

*Dearest A.J.,*

*. . .It looks like this ---- war will be over soon, at least the end is in sight. The Germans still have a lot of fight left in them even though they know they lost the war. It looks like they are intent on making it a costly victory.*

*Darling, every day that passes is a day nearer to home and a day closer to you. Let's hope and pray that God will hasten the end.*

*Will write tomorrow.*

*All my love,*

*Mitch*[4]

Like soldiers from time immemorial, he shared the heartache of separation.

*Dearest A.J.,*

*Darling, I just received your Valentine, which I had been waiting for. It was very nice. This is Saturday night and always the loneliest night of the week for me. Oh! Darling, how I would love to be with you, to have you in my arms, to talk and talk. I wonder what you are doing tonight. I sit and brood over how we are cheated of so many precious moments on account of this terrible war. I am not complaining, darling. I also get a lot of enjoyment dreaming about you and the things we will do when I return.*

*War news is again looking good. Although the end is in sight, the war will be as hard or even harder than before. Everyone over here has given up predicting the date of its end, but hoping it will be over soon.*

*Will close, darling, hoping all is well with you, and that you are thinking of me tonight.*

*All my love for you,*

*Mitch*[5]

## MITCH'S WAR

The letters themselves became a chronicle of the war and a testament of their love. They began in North Africa, May 8, 1943. Mitch had just survived the gauntlet of the Atlantic, where German U-boats regularly sank Allied shipping. The successful Allied campaign to free North Africa from the grip of German and Italian troops had just ended, but Mitch's war had just begun.

The Army trained him for setting up field hospitals and treating the inevitable casualties of war. He landed in Sicily on

D-day and stayed with his unit until he contracted malaria. After his recuperation, he joined his unit "somewhere in Italy" and became part of the Fifth Army's advance up the Italian peninsula.

It was difficult. At the start of 1944, Mitch and the Fifth Army faced ferocious resistance from the German army. The combination of battle-hardened German soldiers, man-made defenses, and natural barriers made the Italian front one of the most formidable battlefields of World War II. The Allies faced German defensive lines called the Volturno, the Barbara, and the Gustav.

Mitch's 379th Medical Collecting Company followed the Fifth Army's advance. They trailed some of history's greatest war machines ever assembled to face off in mortal combat. The "379th" collected the human debris of war. Mitch often told A.J. he was "busy," but didn't explain. Often under fire, Mitch set up the field hospitals just behind the lines. He directed combat ambulances. He made triage calls on both litters and ambulances. This was sometimes a life-and-death decision of who needed medical attention immediately, who could wait, and who was beyond help. This was the kind of war Mitch lived through in 1944.

*Feb. 18, 1944*

*Dearest A.J.,*

*. . . I had a good time at the Officers' Rest Center, but it was impossible to rest when you knew you were on borrowed time and that in a few days you would be back "sweating them out" (waiting for the shells to come in).*[6]

By mid-1944, Mitch saw the fall of Rome and the steady, if costly, Allied advance up the Italian peninsula. He rejoiced in their victories. But a tenacious enemy and maddening war continued to keep Mitch away from his A.J. Throughout the summer and the long fall of 1944, Mitch slogged through the bitter Italian campaign. At 10 Bullard Street in Boston—the home front—A.J. fought lesser battles of limited rations and other deprivations for the war effort. But they both faced the timeless battle fought by lovers throughout the ages—uncertainty—born of time, distance, and doubt.

Through this "terrible war" as Mitch called it, their letters—and their faith—held them together. Battles fought for months from the next ridge to the next mountain to the next valley left the men and machines of the Fifth Army weary and exhausted. They still faced a highly skilled and stubborn foe. Yet as the winter of 1944 turned into the spring of 1945, the Fifth Army stood on the cusp of its final advance of the war. The North Apennines campaign pushed the Germans past the vaunted Gothic Line, and the Allies prepared for the campaign toward the Po Valley. By Valentine's Day 1945, the world may still have been at war, but spring and the scent of the war's end was in the air. Mitch hoped and prayed one day soon, he and A.J. would be together.

*Dearest A.J.,*

*. . . The war news is wonderful. It should be over soon.*[7]

In the spring of 1945, the Fifth Army amassed more than a quarter of a million men for its final push north. It was the beginning of the end. Mitch could feel it. He wrote about Hitler, something anyone could say about ISIS today.

*. . . Oh! Anne, I am praying for this war to end and to get home to you. The way it looks now, Hitler is going to fight until the last German. I can't understand how a few men can have such control over a country when the majority know that they are fighting for a lost cause. Such useless loss of life and limb. The Germans were supposed to be a smart race but . . . when they picked Hitler, that - - - - (fill in anything as long as it is real bad) is beyond me.*

*When you receive this letter we should be working real hard. Remember, my sweet, that I am always thinking of you and that you have all my love.*

*Yours,*

*Mitch*[8]

By April 1945, Mitch and the men of the Fifth Army were working "real hard." The final push of the war was underway. The combined might of the U.S. Fifth Army and British Eighth Army broke through the remaining German forces and poured into the Po Valley and up to the foothills of the Alps. Finally, on May 2, the war in Italy was officially over. Mitch witnessed the victory and the final defeat of their implacable foe. After the long Italian campaign, Mitch and the Fifth Army stood as victors, but at a great price.

By the cease-fire of May 2, the Fifth Army had been engaged in continuous combat for over 600 days, more than any other combat group during the war. They fought through rugged terrain, harsh, bitter weather, and a skillful and determined adversary. It was a dogged advance of hundreds of miles. Throughout the war, the Fifth Army suffered more than 100,000 casualties. Who knows how many Mitch's unit treated?

For his service, Mitch was awarded the Bronze Star.

Like millions of other soldiers, he faced the dangers and witnessed the horrors of war. His generation rose to the challenge of their age and defeated the tyranny threatening their world. But Mitch, like many veterans, seldom mentioned the war when he came back. There was a family to raise and a country to rebuild.

## HOME AT LAST

*Mr. and Mrs. Michael Joseph Manning*

*announce*

*the marriage of their daughter*

*Anne Jean*

*to*

*Lt. Sylvester Christopher Mitchell*

*Army of the United States*

*on Saturday, the seventeenth of November*

*nineteen hundred and forty-five*

*Saint Peter's Church*

*Dorchester, Massachusetts*

The war was over, but the romance went on. With Tom, his brother, as best man and Elly, her sister, as maid of honor, Mitch and A.J. were wed on November 17, 1945. Like many other young couples after the war, they lived in various places for a while, including the Hotel Edison in Lynn, Massachusetts, for six months. By the fall of the next year, they settled into their first new home, an apartment right on the border of Lynn and Swampscott, Mass. It looked out over the Atlantic, the same ocean that had kept them apart for three long years. But now they could walk its beaches and build the life they had longed for, hoped for, and prayed for. This new life deserved a good start and one last letter.

*Nov. 20, 1946*

*My darling Wife,*

*I thought it would be proper and nice for me to be the sender of the first letter to you in our new home.*

*What memories are running thru my mind . . . of the places where I used to be, and how far away you were when writing to you and how close you are now. This being my first letter to you since our marriage seems very strange esp. after leaving you this morning, in fact after just talking to you on the telephone about a chair for our home.*

*I wish so much for you and me. I hope that God will be good to us and protect and bless our home. I desire your happiness so much.*

*So, my darling, I wish you all the best in our new home.*

*Your loving Husband* [9]

God answered Mitch's prayer. He was good to them. He gave Mitch and A.J. four children and, later, seven grandchildren. They lived through the Cold War, survived the tumultuous '60s, endured financial setbacks, physical ailments, and met the challenges of raising four children in an ever-changing world. Through 53 years of marriage, two constants remained: their unshakable faith in God and the enduring love they shared. It's been years since they've been here. But when their children re-discovered these letters—this long-silent heritage came alive—they bore witness to the love that survived between Mitch and his "dearest" A.J.

More than seventy years later, the winds of war are sweeping the world once again. Perhaps the love of Mitch and A.J. displayed through their crucible can offer a lesson for today, a way to navigate these new turbulent waters of terror, chaos, and war. Today the enemy is different. There are no great battles with tanks, airplanes, and armies arrayed on the battlefield. The battle lines now are a café in Paris or a county office in San Bernardino. Terror is the order of the day. ISIS sends out fiendish commands, giving detailed instructions on how to attack Westerners: "Rig the roads with explosives for them. Attack their bases. Raid their homes. Cut off their heads. Do not let them feel secure. Hunt them wherever they may be. Turn their worldly life into fear and fire. Remove their families from their homes and thereafter blow up their homes."[10]

Fueled by Islamic State directives, rogue couples, small bands, or "lone wolves" can attack us on our home turf. It's like attacking A.J. on Bullard Street in Dorchester instead of Mitch on a ridge in Italy. Suddenly, ISIS isn't just "over there" but now "over here." Maybe terrorists are plotting next door. People go to work, thinking, *Could I be next? What if I go to the mall and something happens?*

Call it the "new normal" when someone doesn't "go postal" but "goes ISIS." Today's ubiquitous streams of communication—Facebook, Twitter, Instagram, and the 24/7 news cycle—amplify these attacks. Everybody knows.

For ISIS and other Islamic terror groups, it's all part of their strategy. To intimidate, sow fear, and bully a people . . . or a nation. It's psychological and spiritual warfare. It's by design. It's terror . . . it's fear . . . on the loose. As this Arab folk tale tells us, it can be deadly:

> *A wise old man, traveling on a desert road to Baghdad, met the figure of Pestilence hurrying ahead of him. 'Why are you in such a haste to reach Baghdad?' asked the old man. 'I am due to take 5,000 lives in the city,' Pestilence replied, before it went away.*
>
> *Later, on the return journey, they met again. 'You lied to me,' said the old man reproachfully. 'You said you would take 5,000 lives, but you took away 10,000 instead.'*
>
> *'I did not do it!' Pestilence swore. 'I took 5,000 and not one more. Fear killed the rest.'*[11]

## FACING AND FIGHTING FEAR

Yet the fear ISIS spreads is just one threat to the world's stability. With the Middle East in turmoil, radical Islam on the march, and a possible second Russian Cold War coming, the world seems just one economic shaking away from a crash, one wrong move from a wider Middle East war—or a world war. In the twenty-first century, the world is fragile, fearful, and dangerous.

In the midst of this, how do we gird our minds and hearts for even greater perilous times to come? What will we do if the stock markets rattle or the governments shudder? If we're heading into this "gathering storm," how should we then live? The book of Proverbs tells us to prepare: "A prudent man foresees evil and hides himself; the simple pass on and are punished" (27:12). Proverbs also says, "If you faint in the day of adversity, your strength is small" (24:10).

How then do we draw strength and hide ourselves, especially if we're in what the Bible calls the "end-times"? Two thousand years ago, the apostle Peter wrote that he was in the end-times. If two thousand years later, the "end-times" have become our times, are we ready? Jesus warned in those days: "For then there will be great tribulation, such as has not been since the beginning of the world until this time, no, nor ever shall be" (Matthew 24:21).

Even in the best of times, we all face personal trials that shake our world. What do we do when the doctor says, "Cancer," the boss says, "Laid off," the checkbook says, "Broke" or the child says, "Drugs"? These personal trials rock the foundations of our lives. Yet Jesus said we'd all face storms and showed us what to do: "Whoever comes to Me, and hears My sayings and does them, I will show you whom he is like: He is like a man building a house, who dug deep and laid the foundation on the rock. And when the flood arose, the stream beat vehemently against that house, and could not shake it, for it was founded on the rock. But he who heard and did nothing is like a man who built a house on the earth without a foundation, against which the stream beat vehemently; and immediately it fell. And the ruin of that house was great" (Luke 6:47–49).

## PREPARING FOR THE DAYS AHEAD

How do we build our house on the rock? Thankfully, the Bible provides a number of ways to prepare, to be strong, to be ready. Here's a list of ten exhortations from the Scriptures:

## 1. WATCH AND PRAY!

Jesus emphasized this many times:

"Watch therefore, for you do not know when the master of the house is coming—in the evening, at midnight, at the crowing of the rooster, or in the morning—lest, coming suddenly, he find you sleeping. And what I say to you, I say to all: Watch!" (Mark 13:35–37).

"Watch therefore, for you know neither the day nor the hour in which the Son of Man is coming" (Matthew 25:13).

Peter called prayer crucial for these times: "But the end of all things is at hand; therefore be serious and watchful in your prayers" (1 Peter 4:7).

## 2. DEVELOP INTIMACY WITH THE LORD!

If we are to weather the days ahead, we need to draw close to the Lord. The most intimate book in the Bible, the Song of Solomon, portrays His affection: "I am my beloved's and my beloved is mine" (6:3). "The voice of my beloved! Behold He comes leaping upon the mountains, skipping upon the hills. My beloved is like a gazelle or a young stag. Behold He stands behind our wall; He is looking through the windows, gazing through the lattice. My beloved spoke, and said to me: 'Rise up, my love, my fair one, and come away'" (2:8–10).

Do we know the voice of the Lord? Jesus said, "My sheep know My voice." Do we spend time with Him?

"Let us therefore come boldly to the throne of grace, that we may obtain mercy and find grace to help in time of need" (Hebrews 4:16).

## 3. HIDE THE WORD IN YOUR HEART.

Of all the books in your library, the Bible is the one that's alive.

"For the word of God is living and powerful, and sharper than any two-edged sword, piercing even to the division of soul and spirit, and of joints and marrow, and is a discerner of the thoughts and intents of the heart. And there is no creature hidden from His sight, but all things are naked and open to the eyes of Him to whom we must give account" (Hebrews 4:12–13).

"And do not be conformed to this world, but be transformed by the renewing of your mind, that you many prove what is that good and acceptable and perfect will of God" (Romans 12:2).

"Your Word I have hidden in my heart, that I might not sin against You" (Psalm 119:11).

## 4. LOOK UP!

"Now when these things begin to happen, look up and lift up your heads, because your redemption draws near" (Luke 21:28).

"Beloved, now we are children of God; and it has not yet been revealed what we shall be, but we know that when He is revealed, we shall be like Him, for we shall see Him as He is. And everyone who has this hope in Him purifies himself, just as He is pure" (1 John 3:2–3).

The anticipation of the coming of Jesus is one of the most powerful antidotes to the darkness of the current age. Cultivating this sense of expectancy is what author Joel Richardson, who has written extensively on the "end-times," believes our ultimate focus needs to be on the coming age. "It's easy in the end-times to think about the difficulties, to put all the emphasis on the difficulties; (but) our primary emphasis, our eyes of hope, our expectation, our longing needs to be on the Marriage Supper of the Lamb, the return of Jesus, the age to come, the beauty and the glories of the age to come . . . that's exactly what's going to get us through the days ahead."[12]

The Good News is that the Bible heralds a coming Kingdom and a King coming to Jerusalem, "the city of the Great King," where "the government will be upon His shoulders."

## 5. JOIN WITH BELIEVERS.

"And let us consider one another in order to stir up love and good works, not forsaking the assembling of ourselves together, as is the manner of some, but exhorting one another, and so much the more as you see the Day approaching" (Hebrews 10:24–25).

One of my favorite verses is Malachi 3:16. It says, "Then those who feared the Lord spoke to one another, and the Lord listened and heard them; so a book of remembrance was written before Him for those who fear the Lord and who meditate on His name. 'They shall be Mine,' says the Lord of Hosts, 'On the day that I make them My jewels. And I will spare them as a man spares his own son who serves him.'"

It's incredible to think that when believers get together, the Lord listens! Not only does He listen, He has a book of remembrance, a record of who we are and what was said. How about that for a Facebook page! The point is to get together with fellow believers. We'll need the strength and support that comes from close fellowship.

## 6. DRAW CLOSE TO FAMILY AND DEVELOP A SMALL, TRUSTED GROUP WITH WHOM YOU CAN PRAY.

Have a family meeting. Talk about the future and what your plans are as a family. Over the years, I've prayed with one or two trusted prayer partners. They have been invaluable help as we navigate life's trials, testing, and temptations.

Ecclesiastes says: "Two are better than one, because they have a good return for their work: If one falls down, his friend can help him up. But pity the man who falls and has no one to help him up! Also, if two lie down together, they will keep warm. But how can one keep warm alone? Though one may be overpowered, two can defend themselves. A cord of three strands is not quickly broken" (4:9–12 NIV).

## 7. GIVE AND PREPARE FOR OTHERS.

When rough times come, the tendency and temptation is to hoard and make sure just you and your family have enough. Certainly we need to provide for our families—it's our duty—but we also need to "prepare to share." Many grassroots efforts underway already take this attitude.

"But whoever has this world's goods, and sees his brother in need, and shuts up his heart from him, how does the love of God abide in Him? My little children, let us not love in word or in tongue, but in deed and in truth" (1 John 3:17–18).

"Give and it will be given to you: good measure, pressed down, shaken together, and running over will be put into your bosom. For with the same measure that you use, it will be measured back to you" (Luke 6:38).

## 8. INVEST IN ETERNITY.

Another way to prepare is to invest in eternity, redeem these days, and heed the exhortation of Jesus who said: "Do not lay up for yourselves treasures on earth, where moth and rust destroy and where thieves break in and steal; but lay up for yourselves treasures in heaven, where neither moth nor rust destroys and where thieves do not break in and steal. For where your treasure is, there your heart will be also" (Matthew 6:19–21).

Many can offer expertise in financial planning for this life—it's vital—but this kind of investing will pay dividends "out of this world" (an eternal perspective).

## 9. HOLINESS AND HUMOR.

One mighty weapon against fear is a well-developed sense of humor. It's been said, "He who laughs, lasts." The Bible says, "A merry heart does good, like medicine" (Proverbs 17:22).

"But as He who called you is holy, you also be holy in all your conduct, because it is written, 'Be holy, for I am holy'" (1 Peter 1:15–16).

"Pursue peace with all people, and holiness, without which no one will see the Lord" (Hebrews 12:14).

Peter says, "Therefore, since all these things will be dissolved, what manner of person ought you to be in holy conduct and godliness, looking for and hastening the coming of the day of God, because of which the heavens will be dissolved, being on fire, and the elements will melt with fervent heat" (2 Peter 3:11–12).

## 10. DEVELOP A KINGDOM PERSPECTIVE.

One of my favorite Bible verses sums it up for me. I can just imagine the scene. Paul is leaving the believers in Ephesus after being with them for three years, "not ceasing to warn everyone day and night with tears." He's about to sail away. The sailors grunt as they bring the last of the supplies onboard. The captain checks the wind and shouts the order to unfurl the sails. The believers gather around Paul. He's sad, but rises to the moment to exhort his beloved Ephesians one last time. Some softly weep. Others, clear-eyed, concentrate on these last words. Their mutual love fills the sea breeze. He tells them he will see them no more. Now he's on his way back to Jerusalem, "not knowing the things that will happen to me there, except that the Holy Spirit testifies in every city, saying that chains and tribulations await me" (Acts 20:22–23).

Yet, Paul's sight is set on eternity and his finish line.

"But none of these things move me; nor do I count my life dear to myself, so that I may finish my race with joy, and the ministry which I received from the Lord Jesus, to testify to the gospel of the grace of God" (Acts 20:24).

The lyrics to this song echo Paul's thoughts:

WHEN IT'S ALL BEEN SAID AND DONE
*Licensed by Capitol CMG Publishing:*

When it's all been said and done,
There is just one thing that matters.
Did I do my best to live for Truth?
Did I live my life for You?

When it's all been said and done,
All my treasures will mean nothing.
Only what I have done
For love's reward
Will stand the test of time.

Lord, Your mercy is so great
That You look beyond our weakness.
And find purest gold in miry clay
Turning sinners into saints.

I will always sing Your praise
Here on earth and in heaven after,
For You've joined me at my true home.
When it's all been said and done,
You're my life when life is gone.

When it's all been said and done,
There is just one thing that matters.
Did I do my best to live for Truth?
Did I live my life for You?
Lord, I'll live my life for You.[13]

The ultimate goal for many is not a PhD, an Oscar, a World Series ring, or to climb Mt. Everest. Their ultimate goal is to hear thirteen words: "Well done, good and faithful servant . . . Enter into the joy of your lord" (Matthew 25:21).

## PREPARING THE WAY

Those thirteen words envision a time called the Great Day of the Lord, a Day the prophet Daniel saw coming:

"I was watching in the night visions, and behold, One like the Son of Man, coming with the clouds of heaven! He came to the Ancient of Days, and they brought Him near before Him. Then to Him was given dominion and glory and a kingdom, that all peoples, nations, and languages should serve Him. His dominion is an everlasting dominion, which shall not pass away, And His kingdom the one which shall not be destroyed" (Daniel 7:13–14).

We do not know when His Kingdom will come, but it will come. The church has prayed "His Kingdom come" for two thousand years, ever since Jesus "taught us to pray" the Lord's Prayer. So how do we prepare for His Kingdom? We can take "this Gospel of the Kingdom" to the whole world and help fulfill His Great Commission: "Go therefore and make disciples of all the nations, baptizing them in the name of the Father and of the Son and of the Holy Spirit, teaching them to observe all things that I have commanded you; and lo, I am with you always, even to the end of the age" (Matthew 28:19–20).

## THE BEST IS YET TO COME

Whether we are preparing ourselves or preparing the way for others, we can take heart the Lord has saved the best for last. Jesus began His ministry at a wedding feast and turned the water into wine. John 2:9–10 records the result: "When the master of the feast had tasted the water that was made wine, and did not know where it came from (but the servants who had drawn the water knew), the master of the feast called the bridegroom. And he said to him, 'Every man at the beginning sets out the good wine, and when the guests have well drunk, then the inferior. You have kept the good wine until now.'"

I believe the Lord is saving the best "until now."

Pastor and author Don Finto of Caleb Company (https://calebcompany.org/web/) echoed those thoughts in his new book *Prepare! For the End-Time Harvest*: "The darkest time in all of history as well as the most brilliant for the people of God lie before us. It is the exciting possibilities of this next season that compelled me to write this book."[14]

Isaiah depicted a similar theme: "Arise, shine; for your light has come! And the glory of the Lord is risen upon you. For behold, the darkness shall cover the earth, and deep darkness the people; But the Lord will arise over you, and His glory will be seen upon you" (60:1–2).

Our age encompasses two voices. Radical Islam is like the wolf in the story of the three pigs. He bellowed, "I'll huff and I'll puff and I'll blow your house down!" Yet another sound comes from the roar of the Lion of the Tribe of Judah! Finto says the hour demands a generation of Joshuas and Calebs, men who during their biblical history gave a good report and did not believe the bluster of the giants of their day. "The church is reliving the days of the giants. The circumstances around us are bewildering and foreboding. Two voices are dominant. One is the voice of fear that describes walled cities and giants. The other is the beckoning of God to a life of faith and victory over every enemy."[15]

While bad news fills the world—the rise of radical Islam, unprecedented persecution, and humanitarian crisis—the headlines of God's Word can dispel the fog of the world's headlines. The book of Revelation talks of a people who "overcame by the blood of the Lamb and the word of their testimony." Daniel says: "But the people who know their God shall be strong, and carry out great exploits" (11:32).

At a similar stage in recent history, England faced annihilation from Hitler's Nazi Germany. With the dark clouds overshadowing his nation, Winston Churchill stirred his countrymen to valor...and victory:

> The Battle of Britain is about to begin. Upon this battle depends the survival of Christian civilization; upon it depends our own British life, and the long continuity of our institutions and our Empire. The whole fury and might of the enemy must very soon be turned on us. Hitler knows that he will have to break us in this island or lose the war. If we can stand up to him, all Europe may be freed and the life of the world may move forward into broad, sunlit uplands. But if we fail, then the whole world, including the United States, including all that we have known and cared for, will sink into the abyss of a new dark age made more sinister, and perhaps more protracted, by the lights of perverted science. Let us therefore brace ourselves to our duties, and so bear ourselves that if the British Empire and its Commonwealth last for a thousand years, men will still say, this was their finest hour.[16]

Mitch and A.J. lived through that "finest hour." May it be said in a thousand years that this generation—like theirs—revealed our "finest."

# Epilogue: A Time for Peace

As the world today teeters on the brink of war, history will judge how our generation—like those of the "greatest generation" —will respond. Yet the Bible teaches that each one of us will have a judgment of our own. *"For we must all appear before the judgment seat of Christ, that each one may receive the things done in the body, according to what he has done, whether good or bad"* (2 Corinthians 5:10). This judgment can be a terrifying prospect while we wage our own personal battles. But in the midst of this life, God has made a way from our "time of war" to a "time of peace." Sin built a wall between us and our Creator. *"But your iniquities have separated you from your God; and your sins have hidden His face from you, So that He will not hear"* (Isaiah 59:2). Yet He bridged that separation through His Son. *"For the wages of sin is death, but the gift of God is eternal life in Christ Jesus our Lord"* (Romans 6:23). Peace comes by crossing that bridge: *"… and the peace of God, which surpasses all understanding, will guard your hearts and minds through Christ Jesus"* (Philippians 4:7). This is my story of how I found personal peace. It's a story replicated through the ages, across the world and to every tribe, tongue, people and nation. I hope it can be a way you, too, can find "a time for peace."

This reporter—a young Chris Mitchell with lots of questions and few answers—went to meet someone at McDonald's on May 8th, 1977, in Washington D.C. A pastor who knew us both recommended we meet. Over a Filet o' Fish sandwich, French fries and a vanilla shake, I probed this man just two years my senior with a number of questions. *What did it mean to be "born again?" How do you "invite" Jesus into your heart?* I had sojourned and searched in many places, but still found myself lost, dry, and thirsty in a spiritual desert. Several months earlier I stood in a grocery store, peering at an "Inspirational" book kiosk. I picked one off the rack called *Voices from the Edge of Eternity* http://

www.amazon.com/Voices-Edge-Eternity-Unlocking-Mystery/
dp/1557485488. It recounted the last few moments on earth of
famous people. Some experiences were heavenly; others, hellish.
Standing there in the store near the vegetable aisle, this book
pried my heart open. I knew this sin-sick soul wasn't ready for
the afterlife.

Back in McDonald's and long after the sandwich, fries and
shake were gone, my friend talked for nearly two hours. My questions answered, we went to the door, shook hands and left. But
not before I noticed the theme from *Jesus Christ Superstar*—then a
famous rock opera—playing over the sound system. It might not
have been meaningful to most, but under the circumstances, it
brought a twinkle inside. I walked down the street. My destination: a house on D Street on Capitol Hill I shared with several
others. Yet as I walked down the sidewalks, crossed the streets, and
traversed the avenues of downtown Washington—step by step—
something happened. The despair that shackled my heart for years
began to fall away; the clouds of gloom I had huddled under for
so long started to part. For the first time in a long time, my heart
began to unfurl and hear the sound of a new song. Looking back,
I know this was an epiphany, a transforming moment in time. The
Apostle Paul—a man who knew what a Damascus Road experience was all about—called it becoming a "new creation, the old has
passed away, the new has come."

By the time I arrived at D Street, I felt like a new person.
This newness hoisted the black ceiling of my life, and what was a
spiritual desert bloomed into a watered garden. I called my new-
found friend from McDonald's and accepted his invitation to go
to church the next Sunday. I went for the first time in years—not
because I had to, but because I wanted to. That day, I didn't find an
answer. I met a Person … who was the Answer.

From that day to this, Jesus has been a faithful Friend, a
trusted Savior. His promises have withstood the test of time, the
stress of trials and the cares of this life.

He promised to "never leave or forsake" me. He's kept His
word. Now I look forward to another destination, not D Street

nor this earthly Jerusalem but the Bible's promise of the New Jerusalem. This world is not my final destination, or home. Now my voice can join those other "voices on the edge of eternity" and tell that He promised He would prepare a home for me in His Kingdom "not of this world." Death itself has lost its sting and the grave its victory. His message is simple and His invitation open to all: *"For God so loved the world, that He gave His only begotten Son, that whosoever believes in Him shall not perish but have everlasting life"* (John 3:16). His Word is true, "for all who call upon the name of the Lord shall be saved" (Romans 10:13).

If you'd like to know more about this Savior who promised "life and life more abundantly," or if you simply need prayer, you can call someone who cares like my friend at McDonald's. At CBN's 24/7 Prayer Center you can call 1-800-759-0700 and talk with someone who cares. Join me and millions more who—as my friend says—are "enjoying the walk home."

## CBN NEWS AND JERUSALEM DATELINE:

When I wrote ISIS, Iran and Israel, I strove to keep the book as up to date as possible. Yet the Middle East – especially now – continues to go through historic changes. To keep up with the latest developments, you can log onto CBNNews.com and also log onto our weekly program *Jerusalem Dateline* or use this QR code. Thanks for reading and God bless you as you keep watching and praying.

# NOTES

CHAPTER ONE: A PERFECT STORM

1.   (Ret.) Gen. Yaakov Amidror, "Perfect Storm: Implications of Middle East Chaos," http://besacenter.org/policy-memorandum/perfect-storm-the-long-term-implications-of-middle-east-chaos, BESA: Begin-Sadat Center for Strategic Studies, July 5, 2015.

2.   Chris Mitchell, "Iran's Weapon Cache: 'Awake from Your Slumber'", http://www.cbn.com/cbnnews/insideisrael/2014/March/Irans-Weapon-Cache-Awake-from-Your-Slumber/, March 11, 2014.

3.   Ibid.

4.   Ibid.

5.   "PM Netanyahu's Remarks on the Iranian Weapons Ship", http://mfa.gov.il/MFA/PressRoom/2014/Pages/Seizure-of-an-Iranian-arms-ship-in-the-Red-Sea-5-Mar-2014.aspx, Prime Minister's Office, March 10, 2014.

6.   Chris Mitchell, "Iran's Weapon Cache: 'Awake from Your Slumber'", http://www.cbn.com/cbnnews/insideisrael/2014/March/Irans-Weapon-Cache-Awake-from-Your-Slumber/, March 11, 2014.

7.   "PM Netanyahu's Remarks on the Iranian Weapons Ship", http://mfa.gov.il/MFA/PressRoom/2014/Pages/Seizure-of-an-Iranian-arms-ship-in-the-Red-Sea-5-Mar-2014.aspx, Prime Minister's Office, March 10, 2014.

8.   Chris Mitchell, "Iran's Weapon Cache: 'Awake from Your Slumber'", http://www.cbn.com/cbnnews/insideisrael/2014/March/Irans-Weapon-Cache-Awake-from-Your-Slumber/, March 11, 2014.

9.   "PM Netanyahu's Remarks on the Iranian Weapons Ship", http://mfa.gov.il/MFA/PressRoom/2014/Pages/Seizure-of-an-Iranian-arms-ship-in-the-Red-Sea-5-Mar-2014.aspx, Prime Minister's Office, March 10, 2014.

10.  "Winston Churchill's Prewar Effort to Increase Military Spending," http://www.historynet.com/winston-churchills-prewar-effort-to-increase-military-spending.htm, HistoryNet, June 12, 2006.

11.  Yaakov Katz, "Security and Defense: The War between Wars," http://www.jpost.com/Features/Front-Lines/Security-and-Defense-The-war-between-wars, *Jerusalem Post*, May 10, 2012.

12.  (Ret.) Gen. Yaakov Amidror, "Perfect Storm: Implications of Middle East Chaos," http://besacenter.org/policy-memorandum/perfect-storm-the-long-term-implications-of-middle-east-chaos, BESA: Begin-Sadat Center for Strategic Studies, July 5, 2015.

13.  Chris Mitchell, "Turkey, Russia Headed for a Military Faceoff?"http://www1.cbn.com/cbnnews/insideisrael/2015/November/Turkey-Russia-Headed-for-a-Military-Face-Off/, *CBN News*, November 25, 2105.

14. "NATO meets as Russia confirms one of two pilots dead after jet shot down – as it happened," http://www.theguardian.com/world/live/2015/nov/24/russian-jet-downed-by-turkish-planes-near-syrian-border-live-updates, *The Guardian*, November 24, 2015.

15. "Iran: Saudis face 'divine revenge' for executing al-Nimr," http://www.bbc.com/news/world-middle-east-35216694, BBC News, January 3, 2106.

16. (Ret.) Gen. Yaakov Amidror, "Perfect Storm: Implications of Middle East Chaos," http://besacenter.org/policy-memorandum/perfect-storm-the-long-term-implications-of-middle-east-chaos, BESA: Begin-Sadat Center for Strategic Studies, July 5, 2015.

17. "Quick facts: What you need to know about the Syria crisis," https://www.mercycorps.org/articles/iraq-jordan-lebanon-syria-turkey/quick-facts-what-you-need-know-about-syria-crisis, MercyCorps, January 1, 2016.

18. Shaul Shay, "The Third Lebanon War Scenario," http://www.jpost.com/Arab-Israeli-Conflict/The-third-Lebanon-war-scenario-406193, *Jerusalem Post*, June 18, 2015.

19. Seth J. Frantzman, "Civil Duty: The Home Front Command is tasked with protecting and preparing civilians in Israel for war or for a natural disaster," http://www.jpost.com/Magazine/Civil-duty-413423, *Jerusalem Post Magazine*, August 28, 2015.

20. "IDF Plans for possible Syria Operation as Jihadist, Hezbollah threats Mount," http://www.timesofisrael.com/idf-plans-for-possible-syria-attack-after-recent-hezbollah-maneuvers, *The Times of Israel* Staff, August 17, 2015.

21. Scott Ross, "Rockets, Terror Tunnels 10 Years after Gaza Pullout," http://www.cbn.com/cbnnews/insideisrael/2015/August/Rockets-Terror-Tunnels-10-Years-after-Gaza-Pullout/, August 24, 2015.

22. Seth J. Frantzman, "Civil Duty: The Home Front Command is tasked with protecting and preparing civilians in Israel for war or for a natural disaster," http://www.jpost.com/Magazine/Civil-duty-413423, *Jerusalem Post Magazine*, August 28, 2015.

23. "Jordan's King Calls Fight against Islamic State 'A Third World War'," http://www.jpost.com/Middle-East/Jordans-king-calls-fight-against-ISIS-third-world-war-392645, *Jerusalem Post* Staff, March 2, 2105.

24. "Pope Francis warns on 'piecemeal World War III'," http://www.bbc.com/news/world-europe-29190890, BBC News, September 13, 2014.

25. Allen West, "What Turkey did this morning may have just sparked the next world war," http://www.allenbwest.com/2015/11/what-turkey-did-this-morning-may-just-have-started-world-war-iv/, www.allenwest.com, November 24, 2015.

26. Rush Limbaugh, "Turks Shoot down Archduke Ferdinand's Jet As Obama's Abandonment of Iraq Causes More Pain in the Mideast," http://www.rushlimbaugh.com/daily/2015/11/24/turks_shoot_down_archduke_ferdinand_s_jet_as_obama_s_abandonment_of_iraq_causes_more_pain_in_the_mideast, www.rushlimbaugh.com, November 24, 2015.

27. Roger Cohen, "World War III," http://www.nytimes.com/2015/11/27/opinion/world-war-iii.html?_r=0, *New York Times*, November 26, 2015.

28. *CBN News* Interview, Michael Oren, Jerusalem, November 2015.

CHAPTER TWO: ON THE FRONT LINES OF THE FREE WORLD

1. Chris Mitchell, "Mosul Dam a Ticking Bomb in Terrorist's Hands," http://www1.cbn.com/cbnnews/world/2014/August/Mosul-Dam-Ticking-Bomb-in-Terrorists-Hands, *CBN News*, September 8, 2014.

2. Chris Mitchell, "Kurdish Army Holding the Line against ISIS," http://www1.cbn.com/cbnnews/insideisrael/2015/October/Kurdish-Army-Holding-the-Line-against-ISIS, *CBN News*, November 12, 2015.

3. Ibid.

4. Ibid.

5. Ibid.

6. *CBN News* Interview, Major General Bahjat Arab, Kurdistan, September 2015.

7. Ibid.

8. Chris Mitchell, "Kurdish Army Holding the Line against ISIS," http://www1.cbn.com/cbnnews/insideisrael/2015/October/Kurdish-Army-Holding-the-Line-against-ISIS, *CBN News*, November 12, 2015.

9. *CBN News* Interview, Major General Bahjat Arab, Kurdistan, September 2015.

10. Mohammed Shareef, The United States, Iraq and the Kurds: Shock, Awe and Aftermath, https://books.google.co.il/books?id=0cYTAwAAQBA-J&pg=PA143&lpg=PA143&dq=kurds+algiers+accord&source=bl&ots=f-8nx0xd7BL&sig=GSlHGoWG0ylesL4S-uiD-rySPoU&hl=en&sa=X-&ved=0ahUKEwi_h8njx53KAhXFVhoKHciRBFAQ6AEINTAE#v=onepage&q=kurds%20algiers%20accord&f=false, London and New York, Routledge, 2014.

11. *CBN News* Interview, Major General Bahjat Arab, Kurdistan, September 2015

12. Ibid.

13. Ibid.

14. Chris Mitchell, "Kurdish Army Holding the Line against ISIS," http://www1.cbn.com/cbnnews/insideisrael/2015/October/Kurdish-Army-Holding-the-Line-against-ISIS, *CBN News*, November 12, 2015.

15. *CBN News* Interview, General Karzan, Kurdistan, September 2015.

16. Chris Mitchell, "Kurdish Army Holding the Line against ISIS," http://www1.cbn.com/cbnnews/insideisrael/2015/October/Kurdish-Army-Holding-the-Line-against-ISIS, *CBN News*, November 12, 2015.

17. Ibid.

18. Ibid.
19. Ibid.
20. Ibid.
21. Ibid.
22. Ibid.

CHAPTER THREE: BACK TO MAKHMUR

1. *CBN News* Interview, Erbil, Kurdistan, September 2015.

2. Chris Mitchell, "Military Experts: Want to defeat ISIS? Arm the Kurds," http://www1.cbn.com/cbnnews/insideisrael/2015/November/Military-Experts-Arm-the-Kurds/, *CBN News*, November 24, 2015.

3. Sofia Barbarani, "U.S. Colonel Richard "Dick" Naab: America has never had a clear policy towards Kurdistan," http://www.mesop.de/u-s-colonel-richard-naab-america-has-never-had-a-clear-policy-towards-kurdistan, BasNews, December 24, 2013.

4. Ibid.

5. Ibid.

6. Ibid.

7. *CBN News* Interview, (Ret.) Col. Richard Naab, Erbil, Kurdistan, September 2015.

8. Howard Altman, "To Defeat Islamic State, arm the Kurds, retired General says," http://www.tbo.com/list/military-news/altman/to-defeat-islamic-state-arm-the-kurds-retired-general-says-20150705, *Tampa Tribune*, July 5, 2015.

9. Chris Mitchell, "Military Experts: Want to defeat ISIS? Arm the Kurds," http://www1.cbn.com/cbnnews/insideisrael/2015/November/Military-Experts-Arm-the-Kurds/, *CBN News*, November 24, 2015.

10. *CBN News* Interview, (Ret.) General Jay Garner, Erbil, Kurdistan, September 2015.

11. Caroline Glick, "Israel's Great Opportunity," http://www.jpost.com/Opinion/Column-one-Israels-great-opportunity-406531, *Jerusalem Post*, June 19, 2015.

12. Con Coughlin, "US Blocks attempts by Arab allies to fly heavy weapons directly to Kurds to fight Islamic State," http://www.telegraph.co.uk/news/worldnews/islamic-state/11712237/US-blocks-attempts-by-Arab-allies-to-fly-heavy-weapons-directly-to-Kurds-to-fight-Islamic-State.html, *The Telegraph*, July 2, 2015.

13. Ibid.

14. Ibid.

15. *CBN News* Interview, (Ret.) General Jay Garner, Erbil, Kurdistan, September 2015.

16. *CBN News* Interview, (Ret.) Col. Richard Naab, Erbil, Kurdistan, September 2015.

17. Ibid.

18. *CBN News* Interview, (Ret.) General Jay Garner, Erbil, Kurdistan, September 2015.

CHAPTER FOUR: ISIS: INSIDE THE CALIPHATE

1. Ashley Collman, "How Homeland's Peter Quinn delivered prophetic speech on ISIS and America's 'strategy' in Syria six weeks ago," http://www.dailymail.co.uk/news/article-3320487/Homeland-s-Peter-Quinn-delivers-prescient-speech-ISIS-America-s-lack-strategy-Syria.html, Daily Mail Online.com, November 16, 2015.

2. Intelligence Briefing, Erbil, Kurdistan.

3. "Obama Secures Support to Press On with Iran Nuke Deal," http://www.jerusalemdateline.com/, *CBN News, Jerusalem Dateline*, September 4, 2015.

4. "Statement by the President on ISIL," https://www.whitehouse.gov/the-press-office/2014/09/10/statement-president-isil-1, The White House, September 10, 2014.

5. "Is ISIS Islamic? Brother Rachid clarifies for President Obama," https://www.youtube.com/watch?v=fjh24NG1jvc, You Tube, September 14, 2014.

6. Graeme Wood, "What ISIS Really Wants," http://www.theatlantic.com/magazine/archive/2015/03/what-isis-really-wants/384980/, *The Atlantic*, March 2015.

7. Ibid.

8. Ibid.

9. Erick Stakelbeck, "Nun: 'Islam is ISIS. Whoever Says Otherwise Is a Liar'," http://www.cbn.com/cbnnews/world/2015/may/nun-islam-is-isis-whoever-says-otherwise-is-a-liar, *CBN News*, January 3, 2016.

10. Ibid.

11. "A Message to the Mujahidin and the Muslim Ummah," http://www.gatestoneinstitute.org/documents/baghdadi-caliph.pdf.

12. Robert Spencer, *The Complete Infidel's Guide to ISIS*, Regnery, Washington D.C., 2015, pp. 167 and 168.

13. Ibid.

14. "Obama Secures Support to Press On with Iran Nuke Deal," http://www.jerusalemdateline.com/, *CBN News, Jerusalem Dateline*, September 4, 2015.

15. Bill Gertz, "DIA: Islamic State Spreading Beyond Syria and Iraq," http://freebeacon.com/national-security/dia-islamic-state-spreading-beyond-syria-and-iraq/, *Washington Free Beacon*, February 5, 2015.

16. "Christians Suspect Islamic State Influencing Muslims in Palestinian Territories, Israel," http://morningstarnews.org/2015/06/christians-suspect-islamic-state-influencing-muslims-in-palestinian-territories-israel/, *Morning Star News*, June 11, 2015.

17. Bruce Hoffman, "ISIS Is Winning," http://www.politico.com/magazine/story/2015/09/isil-is-winning-213136, Politico, September 10, 2015.

18. Hannah Fairfield, Tim Wallace and Derek Watkins, "How ISIS Expand," http://www.nytimes.com/interactive/2015/05/21/world/middleeast/how-isis-expands.html?_r=0, *New York Times*, May 21, 2015.

19. "Islamic State rakes in $1 million per day in extortion, taxation: Report," http://timesofindia.indiatimes.com/world/middle-east/Islamic-State-rakes-in-1-million-per-day-in-extortion-taxation-Report/articleshow/47355674.cms, May 20, 2015.

20. Sarah Almukhtar, "ISIS Finances Are Strong, " http://www.nytimes.com/interactive/2015/05/19/world/middleeast/isis-finances.html, *New York Times*, May 19, 2015.

21. "Antiquities scholar beheaded by IS in Palmyra, refused to say where treasures hidden," http://www.timesofisrael.com/syrian-antiquities-scholar-beheaded-by-is-in-ancient-palmyra/, *The Times of Israel*, August 19, 2015.

22. James M. Arlandson, "The sword of Jesus and the sword of Muhammad," http://www.answering-islam.org/Authors/Arlandson/sword2.htm, Answering Islam.

23. James M. Arlandson, "The Quran and the Sword," http://www.answering-islam.org/authors/arlandson/sword/05.html, Answering Islam.

24. "ISIS Tot Taught to Practice Killing by Beheading Teddy Bear," http://www.clarionproject.org/news/isis-tot-taught-practice-killing-beheading-teddy-bear#, The Clarion Project, August 25, 2015.

25. "ISIS enforces Ramadan fast by crucifying two children," http://www.jpost.com/Middle-East/ISIS-enforces-Ramadan-fast-by-crucifying-two-children-406876. The *Jerusalem Post*, June 23, 2015.

26. James M. Arlandson, "Crucifixion and mutilation? Just say NO to Islamic law!," http://www.answering-islam.org/Authors/Arlandson/crucify.htm, Answering Islam.

27. Sara A. Carter, "ISIS 'Mein Kampf' Blames Israel for Global Terrorism," http://www.israelnationalnews.com/News/News.aspx/199531#.VqKW-Z4df2Uk, *Israel National News*, August 8, 2015.

28. Ibid.

29. Ibid.

30. Ibid.

31. Todd Wood, "ISIS Planning 'nuclear tsunami," http://www.washingtontimes.com/news/2015/sep/28/l-todd-wood-isis-planning-nuclear-tsunami/, *Washington Times*, September 28, 2015.

32. Adam Withnall, "ISIS's dirty bomb: Jihadists have seized 'enough radioactive material to build their first WMD'," http://www.independent.co.uk/news/world/middle-east/isiss-dirty-bomb-jihadists-have-seized-enough-radioactive-material-to-build-their-first-wmd-10309220.html, *The Independent*, June 10, 2015.

33. Ashley Collman, "How Homeland's Peter Quinn delivered prophetic speech on ISIS and America's 'strategy' in Syria six weeks ago," http://www.dailymail.co.uk/news/article-3320487/Homeland-s-Peter-Quinn-delivers-prescient-speech-ISIS-America-s-lack-strategy-Syria.html, Daily Mail Online.com, November 16, 2015.

34. *CBN News* Interview, Bernard Lewis, Jerusalem.

CHAPTER FIVE: THE SIREN SONG OF ISIS

1. Chris Mitchell, "Father of Slain ISIS Teen: 'My Son Was No Spy," http://www1.cbn.com/cbnnews/insideisrael/2015/March/Father-of-Slain-ISIS-Teen-My-Son-Was-No-Spy/, *CBN News*, March 15, 2015.

2. Ibid.

3. Ibid.

4. Roi Kais, "ISIS video purportedly shows child executing 'Israeli Spy'," http://www.ynetnews.com/articles/0,7340,L-4635622,00.html, YNet News, March 10, 2015.

5. Stuart Winer and AP, "Islamic State releases execution video of 'Mossad Spy'," http://www.timesofisrael.com/islamic-state-releases-execution-video-of-mossad-spy/, *The Times of Israel*, March 10, 2015.

6. "Father of Palestinian killed in Syria says son duped into IS," http://www.ynetnews.com/articles/0,7340,L-4635964,00.html, AP, YNet News, March 11, 2015.

7. Tamar Pileggi, "Israeli Arab man said seeking to join IS with wife, 3 kids," http://www.timesofisrael.com/israeli-arab-man-said-seeking-to-join-is-with-wife-3-kids/, *The Times of Israel*, June 22, 2015.

8. "Global Terrorism Index 2015," http://economicsandpeace.org/reports/, Institute for Economics and Peace, p. 3.

9. Chris Mitchell, Interview with Robert Spencer, http://www1.cbn.com/video/jerusalem-dateline/2015/09/4/obama-secures-support-to-press-on-with-iran-nuke-deal-ndash-september-4-2015, *Jerusalem Dateline*, September 4, 2015.

10. Thomas Joscelyn, "Why Islamic State tells supporters to swear allegiance before dying," http://www.longwarjournal.org/archives/2015/12/why-the-islamic-state-tells-supporters-to-swear-allegiance-before-dying.php, *The Long War Journal*, December 4, 2015.

11. Dr. Sebastian Gorka, PhD, Katharine Gorka, "ISIS: The Threat to the United States," www.ThreatKnowledge.org, p. 4.

12. Susannah George, "US-led coalition: IS has lost 30 percent of ite territory," http://bigstory.ap.org/article/9eff6f351ea748f98d811d4e53f08a52/us-led-coalition-has-lost-30-percent-its-territory, Associated Press, January 5, 2016.

13. Jonathan Spyer, "ISIS is retreating – but ISIS isn't the main problem, " http://jonathanspyer.com/2016/01/20/isis-is-retreating-but-isis-isnt-the-main-problem/, PJ Media, January 20, 2016.

14. Jay Sekulow, *Rise of ISIS: A Threat We Can't Ignore*, Howard Books, New York, 2014, p. 109.

15. Richard Fausset, "Young Mississippi Couple Linked to ISIS, Perplexing All," http://www.nytimes.com/2015/08/15/us/disbelief-in-mississippi-at-how-far-isis-message-can-travel.html?_r=0, *New York Times*, August 14, 2015.

16. James Comey Transcript, Washington Post Video, https://www.washingtonpost.com/posttv/world/national-security/comey-extremists-exist-in-all-50-states/2015/02/25/8bb6a716-bcfd-11e4-9dfb-03366e719af8_video.html, February 25, 2015.

17. Ibid.

18. Ibid.

19. Dr. Sebastian Gorka, PhD, Katharine Gorka, "ISIS: The Threat to the United States," www.ThreatKnowledge.org, p. 1.

20. Ibid. p.8.

21. Chris Mitchell, Interview with Robert Spencer, http://www1.cbn.com/video/jerusalem-dateline/2015/09/4/obama-secures-support-to-press-on-with-iran-nuke-deal-ndash-september-4-2015, *Jerusalem Dateline*, September 4, 2015.

22. Dr. Sebastian Gorka, PhD, Katharine Gorka, "ISIS: The Threat to the United States," www.ThreatKnowledge.org, p. 11.

23. Caleb Weiss, "Islamic State Spokesman again threatens West in new speech," http://www.longwarjournal.org/archives/2014/09/islamic_state_spokesman_again.php *The Long War Journal*, September 21, 2014.

24. Ibid.

25. Chris Mitchell, "ISIS Underground Highway at America's Doorstep?" http://www1.cbn.com/cbnnews/insideisrael/2015/August/ISIS-Underground-Highway-at-Americas-Doorstep/, *CBN News*, August 24, 2015.

26. Ibid.

27. Ibid.

28. Ibid.

29. Ibid.

30. Ibid.

31. Ibid.

32. Ibid.

33. Ibid.

34. Ibid.

35. "To Kill and To Die In The name of Allah," http://www.answering-islam.org/NonMuslims/die_kill.htm, Answering Islam.

36. "The Holy War," http://answering-islam.org/Nehls/Ask/war.html, Answering Islam.

37. Dr. Sebastian Gorka, PhD, Katharine Gorka, "ISIS: The Threat to the United States," www.ThreatKnowledge.org, p. 17.

## CHAPTER SIX: ESCAPE FROM DARKNESS

1. Chris Mitchell, "Escaped Yazidis Share Chilling Tales of ISIS Captivity," http://www1.cbn.com/cbnnews/insideisrael/2015/November/Escaped-Yazidis-Tell-ISIS-Horror-Stories/, *CBN News*, November 29, 2015.

2. Chris Mitchell, "For Yazidis, Christians: 'They Cut Us Like Sheep," http://www1.cbn.com/cbnnews/world/2014/August/Fleeing-Yazidis-Face-Uncertain-Future, *CBN News*, September 8, 2014.

3. Ibid.

4. "UN Family Tent for Hot Climate," www.unhcr.org/53fc7df49.pdf.

5. Chris Mitchell, "Escaped Yazidis Share Chilling Tales of ISIS Captivity," http://www1.cbn.com/cbnnews/insideisrael/2015/November/Escaped-Yazidis-Tell-ISIS-Horror-Stories/, *CBN News*, November 29, 2015.

6. Ibid.

7. Ibid.

8. Ibid.

9. Ibid.

10. Robert Spencer, "Robert Spencer, PJ Media: Islamic texts justify sex slavery," http://www.jihadwatch.org/2015/08/robert-spencer-pj-media-islamic-texts-justify-sex-slavery, *Jihad Watch*, August 14, 2015.

11. Ibid.

12. *CBN News* Interview, "Nazda", Kankle UN Refugee Camp, Kurdistan, September 2015.

13. Ibid.

14. Ibid.

15. Chris Mitchell, "Escaped Yazidis Share Chilling Tales of ISIS Captivity," http://www1.cbn.com/cbnnews/insideisrael/2015/November/Escaped-Yazidis-Tell-ISIS-Horror-Stories/, *CBN News*, November 29, 2015.

16. Ibid.

17. Ibid.

18. Ibid.

19. Ibid.

20. *CBN News* Interview, "Mamo", Kurdistan, September 2015.

21. Chris Mitchell, "Escaped Yazidis Share Chilling Tales of ISIS Captivity," http://www1.cbn.com/cbnnews/insideisrael/2015/November/Escaped-Yazidis-Tell-ISIS-Horror-Stories/, *CBN News*, November 29, 2015.

22. Ibid.

23. Ibid.

24. *CBN News* Interview, Abdullah, Kurdistan.

25. Chris Mitchell, "Escaped Yazidis Share Chilling Tales of ISIS Captivity," http://www1.cbn.com/cbnnews/insideisrael/2015/November/Escaped-Yazidis-Tell-ISIS-Horror-Stories/, *CBN News*, November 29, 2015.

26. Ibid.

27. Ibid.

CHAPTER SEVEN: FOR WHOM THE BELL TOLLS

1. Chris Mitchell, "Iraqi Christians Flee ISIS, Find Refuge in Jordan," http://www1.cbn.com/cbnnews/insideisrael/2015/June/Iraqi-Christians-Flee-ISIS-Find-Refuge-in-Jordan/, *CBN News*, June 16, 2015.

2. Ibid.

3. Ibid.

4. Ibid.

5. Ibid.

6. Ibid.

7. Ibid.

8. Chris Mitchell, "Christian Refugees: 'Please Pray for Us,'" http://www1.cbn.com/cbnnews/world/2015/September/Christian-Refugees-Please-Pray-for-Us/, *CBN News*, October 12, 2015.

9. Ibid.

10. *CBN News* Interview, Sabah Jamil, Erbil, Kurdistan.

11. Chris Mitchell, "Christian Refugees: 'Please Pray for Us,'" http://www1.
cbn.com/cbnnews/world/2015/September/Christian-Refugees-Please-Pray-
for-Us/, *CBN News*, October 12, 2015.

12. Ibid

13. Ibid.

14. Ibid.

15. Ibid.

16. "Myriam's Story and Song," https://www.youtube.com/watch?v=_ige6CcX-
uMg, Sat 7, February 26, 2015.

17. Chris Mitchell, "Christian Refugees: 'Please Pray for Us,'" http://www1.
cbn.com/cbnnews/world/2015/September/Christian-Refugees-Please-Pray-
for-Us/, *CBN News*, October 12, 2015

18. John Donne, "No Man is an Island," https://web.cs.dal.ca/~johnston/poet-
ry/island.html.

## CHAPTER EIGHT: UNDER THE SHADOW OF ISLAM

1. Chris Mitchell, "Jewish Cartoonist Confronts 'Holocaust' of Mideast
Christians," http://www.cbn.com/cbnnews/insideisrael/2015/January/Jew-
ish-Cartoonist-Confronts-Holocuast-of-Mideast-Christians/, *CBN News*,
January 2, 2015.

2. Ibid.

3. Ibid.

4. Ibid.

5. Ibid.

6. Ibid.

7. Ibid.

8. Ibid.

9. Sharona Schwartz, "Read the Contract the Islamic State Group Is Forcing
Christians to Sign in Syria," http://www.theblaze.com/stories/2015/09/06/
heres-the-contract-the-islamic-state-group-is-forcing-christians-to-sign-in-
syria/, *The Blaze*, September 6, 2015.

10. Dr. Mordechai Kedar, "Op-Ed: Life in the Shadow of Islam," http://www.
israelnationalnews.com/Articles/Article.aspx/17533#.VqOJFIdf2Uk, *Israel
National News*, September 10, 2015.

11. Ibid.

12. "ISIS Video: Christians Forced to Pay Jizya Poll Tax in Syrian Town Qa-
ryatayn," http://www.memritv.org/clip_transcript/en/5093.htm, Clip No.
5-93,October 4, 2015.

13. Andre Mitchell, "Christians in Syria commanded by ISIS to stifle their
faith if they don't want to die," http://www.christiantoday.com/article/
christians.in.syria.commanded.by.isis.to.stifle.their.faith.if.they.dont.want.
to.die/64017.htm, *Christian Today*, September 6, 2015.

14. Nick Gutteridge, "ISIS dig up and desecrate saint's bones after bulldoz-
ing 1,600-year-old Christian church," http://www.express.co.uk/news/
world/599816/ISIS-Islamic-State-Mar-Elian-monastery-Homs-Syria-bull-
doze-saint, Express, August 21, 2015.

15. "IS turns Christian houses in Mosul into military headquarters and stores for weapons," *Mideast Christian News*, February 1, 2015.

16. "Islamic State turns churches in Mosul into abattoirs for slaughtering Eid al-Adha sacrifices," http://www.mcndirect.com/showsubject.aspx-?id=64498#.VqOTbodf2Uk, *Mideast Christian News*, September 25, 2015.

17. "Islamic State prepares curricula describing Christian as 'crusaders, infidels'," http://www.mcndirect.com/showsubject.aspx?id=64162#.VqOT3Ydf2Uk, *Mideast Christian News*, August 29, 2015.

18. George Thomas, "Islam's War on Christians: Worst Yet to Come?", http://www.cbn.com/cbnnews/world/2015/January/Sound-the-Alarm-Islam-Intensifies-War-on-Christians/, *CBN News*, January 1, 2015.

19. Robert Reilly, "Exterminating Christians in the Middle East," http://www.wsj.com/articles/exterminating-christians-in-the-middle-east-1440112782, *Wall Street Journal*, August 20, 2015.

20. "Pope Francis demands end of 'genocide' of Middle East Christian," http://www.jpost.com/Christian-News/Pope-Francis-demands-end-to-genocide-of-Middle-East-Christians-408585, The *Jerusalem Post*, July 10, 2015.

21. "H.Con.Res.75 – 114th Congress," https://www.congress.gov/bill/114th-congress/house-concurrent-resolution/75/text,

22. Lauretta Brown, "Bipartisan Resolution Introduced: Persecution of Mideast Christians is 'Genocide'," http://cnsnews.com/news/article/lauretta-brown/caucus-co-chairs-call-mideast-christian-persecution-genocide, CNS News, September 10, 2015.

23. Ibid.

24. Douglas Ernst, "Congressmen condemn Obama silence on Christian 'genocide', http://www.wnd.com/2015/09/congressmen-condemn-obama-silence-on-christian-genocide/, WND, September 11, 2015.

25. Ibid.

26. Ibid.

27. *CBN News* Interview, (Ret.) General Jay Garner, Erbil, Kurdistan.

28. Chris Mitchell, "Christians Facing Genocide Need Your Help Now", http://www.cbn.com/cbnnews/insideisrael/2015/September/Christians-Facing-Genocide-Need-Our-Help-Now/, *CBN News*, September 4, 2015.

29. Ibid.

30. Ibid.

31. Ibid.

32. Chris Mitchell, "Abandoned? Mideast Christians Overlooked in the War on Terror," http://www1.cbn.com/cbnnews/insideisrael/2015/December/Displaced-Christians-Ask-for-Prayer/, *CBN News*, December 30, 2015.

33. Ibid.

34. Ibid.

35. Ibid.

36. Ibid.

CHAPTER NINE: ASLAN IS ON THE MOVE

1. C. S. Lewis, *The Lion, the Witch and the Wardrobe;* The Chronicles of Narnia https://bracademy.wikispaces.com/file/view/ The+Lion+The+Witch+and+The+Wardrobe+by+C.S.+Lewis, pdf, p. 39.

2. Ibid.

3. Ibid.

4. Lara Marlowe, "Hooked in Iran, where addition rates are world's highest," http://www.irishtimes.com/news/world/middle-east/hooked-in-iran-where-addiction-rates-are-world-s-highest-1.1834386, *The Irish Times*, June 17, 2014.

5. *CBN News* Story: "Supernatural Dreams Open Doors for Jesus in Iran";

6. http://www1.cbn.com/cbnnews/insideisrael/2015/December/Divine-Encounters-Break-Out-in-Iran, *CBN News*, December 8, 2015.

7. Ibid.

8. *CBN News* Interview, "Susan," Erbil, Kurdistan, September 2015.

9. Ibid.

10. Ibid.

11. Ibid.

12. *CBN News* Story: "Supernatural Dreams Open Doors for Jesus in Iran"; http://www1.cbn.com/cbnnews/insideisrael/2015/December/Divine-Encounters-Break-Out-in-Iran, *CBN News*, December 8, 2015.

13. Ibid.

14. Ibid.

15. Ibid.

16. Ibid.

17. Chris Mitchell, "Jerusalem Dateline: Christians join the fight against ISIS," http://www1.cbn.com/video/jerusalem-dateline/2015/07/10/christians-join-the-fight-against-isis-ndash-july-10-2015, *CBN News*, July 10, 2015.

18. Ibid.

19. Tom Doyle with Greg Webster, *Killing Christians: Living the Faith Where It's Not Safe to Believe* (Nashville: Thomas Nelson, 2015), 41-42.

20. *CBN News* Interview, Fabian, Erbil, Kurdistan, September 2015.

21. Ibid.

CHAPTER TEN: THE IRANIAN NUCLEAR DEAL

1. *CBN News* Interview, U.S. Senator Tom Cotton, R-AR, Jerusalem, Israel.

2. Ewen MacAskill and Chris McGreal, "Israel should be wiped off map, says Iran's President," The (U.K.) Guardian, October 27, 2005, http://www.guardian.com/world/2005/oct/27/israel.iran.

3. Quds Day Speech (Jerusalem Day), Global Security.org, http://www.globalsecurity.org/wmd/library/news/iran/2001/011214-text.html, December 14, 2001.

4. Jethro Mullen and Nic Robertson, "Landmark deal reached on Iran nuclear program," http://edition.cnn.com/2015/07/14/politics/iran-nuclear-deal/, CNN, July 15, 2015.

5.   Ibid.

6.   Ibid.

7.   Ibid.

8.   Ibid.

9.   Ibid.

10.  "Assad Regime, Hizbullah: Iran Nuclear Agreement Is Historic Victory For Resistance Axis, Surrender For Americans, Defeat For Saudis," MEMRI, Special Dispatch 6108, http://www.memri.org/report/en/0/0/0/0/0/0/8666.htm, July 16, 2015.

11.  Ibid.

12.  Ibid.

13.  "Joint Comprehensive Plan of Action," Vienna, http://www.theguardian.com/world/2015/jul/14/iran-nuclear-deal-full-text-of-joint-comprehensive-plan-of-action, July 14, 2015, p. 2.

14.  Ibid.

15.  "The Iran Nuclear Deal: What you need to know about the JCOPA," https://www.whitehouse.gov/sites/default/files/docs/jcpoa_what_you_need_to_know.pdf.

16.  "Joint Comprehensive Plan of Action," Vienna, http://www.theguardian.com/world/2015/jul/14/iran-nuclear-deal-full-text-of-joint-comprehensive-plan-of-action, July 14, 2015, p. 34.

17.  Fredrik Dahl, "Despite nuclear probe progress, IAEA access to key Iran site elusive," http://www.reuters.com/article/us-iran-nuclear-iaea-idUS-BREA4P07B20140526, Reuters, May 26, 2014.

18.  "READ: Full text of secret deal between Iran and IAEA on inspections," http://www.timesofisrael.com/read-full-text-of-secret-deal-between-iran-and-iaea-on-inspections/, *The Times of Israel*, August 20, 2015.

19.  "Joint Comprehensive Plan of Action," Vienna, http://www.theguardian.com/world/2015/jul/14/iran-nuclear-deal-full-text-of-joint-comprehensive-plan-of-action, July 14, 2015, p. 35.

20.  *Jerusalem Post*, "Jackie Mason: NYC restaurants subject to tougher inspections than Iran under nuclear deal," http://www.jpost.com/Middle-East/Iran/Jackie-Mason-NYC-restaurants-subject-to-tougher-inspections-than-Iran-under-nuclear-deal-410203, July 26, 2015.

21.  "Joint Comprehensive Plan of Action," Vienna, http://www.theguardian.com/world/2015/jul/14/iran-nuclear-deal-full-text-of-joint-comprehensive-plan-of-action, July 14, 2015, p. 117.

22.  *CBN News* Interview, Clare Lopez, VP, Center for Security Policy, Washington D.C.

23.  Dore Gold, Foreign Press Association Press Conference, Jerusalem, Israel.

24.  Daniel Pipes, "Middle East Provocations and Predictions," http://www.danielpipes.org/16103/middle-east-provocations-and-predictions, Middle East Forum, September 17, 2015.

25.  *CBN News* Interview, U.S. Senator Tom Cotton, R-AR, Jerusalem, Israel.

26. Ibid.

27. *CBN News* Interview, Congresswoman Michele Bachmann, Jerusalem, Israel.

28. Ibid.

29. Ibid.

30. Tzippe Barrow, "Top Military Brass to Congress: Reject Iran Deal," http://www1.cbn.com/cbnnews/insideisrael/2015/August/200-Ret-Generals-Admirals-Appeal-to-Congress/, September 1, 2015.

31. "PM Netanyahu on UNSC endorsement of Iranian accord," http://mfa.gov.il/MFA/PressRoom/2015/Pages/PM-Netanyahu-on-UNSC-endorsement-of-Iranian-accord-20-July-2015.aspx, July 20, 2015.

32. "Alea iacta est," https://en.wikipedia.org/wiki/Alea_iacta_est.

33. https://www.facebook.com/Netanyahu/posts/10153116482972076:0.

34. Ibid.

35. "Israel should be annihilated,' senior Iran aide says," http://www.timesofisrael.com/israel-should-be-annihilated-senior-iran-aide-says/, *The Times of Israel*, August 25, 2015.

36. "Watch: Khamenei threatens 'criminal America' in chilling new video," http://www.timesofisrael.com/khamenei-threatens-criminal-america-in-new-video, *Times of Israel* Staff, September 18, 2015.

37. Chris Mitchell, "All Eyes on Congress for Showdown on Iran," http://www1.cbn.com/cbnnews/insideisrael/2015/July/Iranian-Deal-Switches-Focus-to-Washington/, *CBN News*, July 16, 2015.

38. "Poll: 47 percent of Israelis back Iran strike following nuke deal," http://www.timesofisrael.com/poll-47-percent-of-israelis-back-iran-strike-following-nuke-deal, *The Times of Israel*, July 17, 2015.

39. Ari Yashar, "IDF Appoints Special Team to Plan Strike on Iran," http://www.israelnationalnews.com/News/News.aspx/197486#.Vo7WNIfUiUk, *Israel National News*, June 30, 2015.

40. Yaakov Lappin, "Senior defense source: IDF preparing for possible covert Iranian nuclear production," http://www.jpost.com/Arab-Israeli-Conflict/Senior-defense-source-IDF-preparing-for-possible-covert-Iranian-nuclear-production-409576, *Jerusalem Post*, July 20, 2015.

41. "Ehud Barak: Steinitz, Ya'alon got cold feet just before Israel was about to attack Iran," http://www.jpost.com/Middle-East/Iran/Ehud-Barak-Steinitz-Yaalon-got-cold-feet-just-before-Israel-was-about-to-attack-Iran-412867, *Jerusalem Post*, August 21, 2015.

42. Ibid.

43. Ben Caspit, "Israel fears return on Persian Empire," http://www.al-monitor.com/pulse/originals/2015/09/israel-fear-persian-empire-iran-shiite-hezbollah-axis-nuke.html#ixzz3wPLs5cBi, *Al Monitor*, September 21, 2015.

44. David Sanger, "Iran Complies With Nuclear Deal; Sanctions Are Lifted," http://www.nytimes.com/2016/01/17/world/middleeast/iran-sanctions-lifted-nuclear-deal.html?_r=0, *New York Times*, January 16, 2016.

45. Elise Labbott, "John Kerry: Some sanctions relief money for Iran will go to terrorism," http://edition.cnn.com/2016/01/21/politics/john-kerry-money-iran-sanctions-terrorism/, CNN, January 21, 2016.

46. David Sanger, "Iran Complies With Nuclear Deal; Sanctions Are Lifted," http://www.nytimes.com/2016/01/17/world/middleeast/iran-sanctions-lifted-nuclear-deal.html?r=0, *New York Times*, January 16, 2016.

47. "Winston S. Churchill Quotes," http://www.goodreads.com/quotes/614924-you-were-given-the-choice-between-war-and-dishonour-you.

CHAPTER ELEVEN: THE RUSSIANS ARE COMING! THE RUSSIANS ARE COMING!

1. Chris Mitchell, "Where are We on the End Times Timetable?" http://www1.cbn.com/cbnnews/insideisrael/2015/November/Where-Are-We-on-the-End-Times-Timetable/, *CBN News*, January 2, 2016.

2. "The Russians are Coming the Russians are Coming (1966) Quotes," http://www.imdb.com/title/tt0060921/quotes.

3. Merriam Webster, http://www.merriam-webster.com/dictionary/d%C3%A9marche.

4. Andrew Buncombe, "Syria bombing: Russian three star general warned US officials 'we request your people leave'," http://www.independent.co.uk/news/world/middle-east/syria-bombing-russian-three-star-general-warned-us-officials-we-request-your-people-leave-a6674166.html, *The Independent*, September 30, 2015.

5. "President Obama: 'We Will Degrade and Ultimately Destroy ISIL'," https://www.whitehouse.gov/blog/2014/09/10/president-obama-we-will-degrade-and-ultimately-destroy-isil, September 10, 2014.

6. "Krauthammer: Obama Administration 'Sputters,' Has No Idea What to Do about Russia, Syria," http://nation.foxnews.com/2015/09/30/krauthammer-obama-administration-sputters-has-no-idea-what-do-about-russia-syria, Fox News, September 30, 2015.

7. Ibid.

8. "Bolton: 'Power in the Middle East is Passing from America's Weak Hands'," https://grabien.com/story.php?id=38111, Grabien, September 30, 2015.

9. Christi Parsons and Michael A. Memoli, "Obama says Syria 'is not some superpower chessboard contest'," http://www.latimes.com/world/la-fg-obama-syria-russia-20151002-story.html, *LA Times*, October 2, 2015.

10. "Comprehensive Infographic about the Russian Intervention in Syria – December 2015 Update," https://www.offiziere.ch/?p=24993, December 8, 2015.

11. "Scars remain amid Chechen revival," http://news.bbc.co.uk/2/hi/programmes/from_our_own_correspondent/6414603.stm, BBC News, March 3, 2007.

12. Ely Karmon, "Russia, Iran and Hezbollah: A Temporary Alliance or Long-term Threat to Israel?" http://www.haaretz.com/opinion/.premium-1.680180, October 13, 2015.

13. Ibid.

14. "Dr. Steven P. Bucci, The Heritage Foundation," http://www-304.ibm.com/industries/publicsector/fileserve?contentid=239350.

15. "Jerusalem Dateline: Netanyahu Pledges To Overcome Upsurge in Palestinian Terror," http://www1.cbn.com/video/jerusalem-dateline/2015/10/9/netanyahu-pledges-to-overcome-upsurge-in-palestinian-terror-ndash-october-9-2015, *CBN News*, October 9, 2015.

16. Andrew Tilghman and Oriana Pawlyk, "U.S. vs. Russia: What a war would look like between the world's most fearsome militaries," http://www.militarytimes.com/story/military/2015/10/05/us-russia-vladimir-putin-syria-ukraine-american-military-plans/73147344/, *Military Times*, October 5, 2015.

17. Chris Mitchell, "Where are We on the End Times Timetable?" http://www1.cbn.com/cbnnews/insideisrael/2015/November/Where-Are-We-on-the-End-Times-Timetable/, *CBN News*, January 2, 2016.

18. Ibid.

19. *CBN News* Interview, (Ret.) General William "Jerry" Boykin, Jerusalem, Israel, November 2015.

20. "Jerusalem Dateline: Netanyahu Pledges To Overcome Upsurge in Palestinian Terror," http://www1.cbn.com/video/jerusalem-dateline/2015/10/9/netanyahu-pledges-to-overcome-upsurge-in-palestinian-terror-ndash-october-9-2015, *CBN News*, October 9, 2015.

21. *CBN News* Interview, (Ret.) General William "Jerry" Boykin, Jerusalem, Israel, November 2015.

22. Yoav Zitun, "Hezbollah is getting the most sophisticated Russian weapon," http://www.ynetnews.com/articles/0,7340,L-4755776,00.html, *YNet News*, January 20, 2016.

23. Ibid.

24. Ibid.

25. Chris Mitchell, "Where are We on the End Times Timetable?" http://www1.cbn.com/cbnnews/insideisrael/2015/November/Where-Are-We-on-the-End-Times-Timetable/, *CBN News*, January 2, 2016.

26. Ibid.

## CHAPTER TWELVE: MIDDLE EAST GAME OF THRONES

1. Caroline Glick, "Our World: In Pakistan they trust," http://www.jpost.com/Opinion/Our-World-In-Pakistan-they-trust-441168, The *Jerusalem Post*, January 11, 2016.

2. Chris Mitchell, "Odd Bedfellow Israel Saudis in Step on Iran" Threat, http://www1.cbn.com/cbnnews/insideisrael/2015/June/Odd-Bedfellows-Israel-Saudis-in-Step-on-Iran-Threat/, *CBN News*, June 8, 2015.

3. Ibid.

4. Dore Gold, Foreign Press Association meeting, July 21, 2015.

5. Ibid.

6. Ibid.

7. Ibid.

8. Jonathan Spyer, "Is it Iran's Middle East Now?" http://www.meforum.org/5622/iran-middle-east, *Middle East Forum*, November 10, 2015.

9. Ben Caspit, "Will Israel, Russia tighten coordination on Syria?, http://www. al-monitor.com/pulse/originals/2015/12/israel-security-syria-russia-coordination-balance-power.html, *Al Monitor*, December 2, 2015.

10. *CBN News* Interview, (ret). U.S. General William "Jerry" Boykin, November 2015.

11. Ibid.

12. Chris Mitchell, "It's the Mideast Conflict That Holds Chaotic Global Implications," http://www1.cbn.com/cbnnews/insideisrael/2016/January/Its-the-Mideast-Conflict-That-Holds-Chaotic-Global-Implications/, *CBN News*, January 7, 2016.

13. Ibid.

14. Ibid.

15. Ibid.

16. Caroline Glick, "Our World: In Pakistan they trust," http://www.jpost.com/Opinion/Our-World-In-Pakistan-they-trust-441168, The *Jerusalem Post*, January 11, 2016.

17. Ibid.

18. Chris Mitchell, "It's the Mideast Conflict That Holds Chaotic Global Implications," http://www1.cbn.com/cbnnews/insideisrael/2016/January/Its-the-Mideast-Conflict-That-Holds-Chaotic-Global-Implications/, *CBN News*, January 7, 2016.

19. Ibid.

20. Ben Caspit, "Israel Fear Return of Persian Empire," http://www.al-monitor.com/pulse/originals/2015/09/israel-fear-persian-empire-iran-shiite-hezbollah-axis-nuke.html, *Al Monitor*, September 21, 2015.

21. *CBN News* Interview, (Ret.) Col. Steven Bucci, September, 2015.

22. Ibid.

23. Dore Gold, Foreign Press Association meeting, July 21, 2015.

24. Ret. Israeli General Yaakov Amidror, "Syria's Unraveling Gives Way to New Regional Order," http://besacenter.org/perspectives-papers/syrias-unraveling-gives-way-to-new-regional-order/, BESA Center, November 1, 2015.

25. Andrew Roth, "Vladimir Putin's massive triple decker war room revealed," https://www.washingtonpost.com/news/worldviews/wp/2015/11/21/vladimir-putins-massive-triple-decker-war-room-revealed/, *Washington Post*, November 21, 2015.

26. David Axe, "Putin Blasts Syria with New Stealth Missile – and Shows the World He can Strike From 1,700 Miles Away," http://www.thedailybeast.com/articles/2015/11/19/putin-blasts-syria-with-new-stealth-missile-and-shows-the-world-he-can-strike-from-1-700-miles-away.html, *The Daily Beast*, November 19, 2015.

27. Stepan Kravchenko, "Putin Tells Defense Chiefs to Strengthen Russian Nuclear Forces," http://www.bloomberg.com/news/articles/2015-12-11/putin-tells-defense-chiefs-to-strengthen-russian-nuclear-forces, *Bloomberg News*, December 11, 2015.

28. Phil Stewart and David Alexander, "Russia is top U.S. national security threat, " http://www.reuters.com/article/us-usa-defense-generaldunsmore-idUSKCN0PJ28S20150709, *Reuters*, July 9, 2015.

29. Maria Tsvetkova and Andrew Osborn, "Russia's Putin lashes Turkey, says Russia's forces inside Ukraine," http://uk.reuters.com/article/uk-russia-putin-idUKKBN0U01KP20151217, *Reuters*, December 17, 2015.

30. Ben Caspit, "Will Syria become Russia's Vietnam?," http://www.al-monitor.com/pulse/originals/2015/12/israel-russia-submarine-syrian-coasts-intelligence-data-iran.html, *Al Monitor*, December 14, 2015.

31. Caroline Glick, "Rubio, Cruz and US Global Leadership, "http://www.jpost.com/Opinion/Column-One-Rubio-Cruz-and-US-global-leadership-437675, *Jerusalem Post*, December 17, 2015.

32. Daniel Pipe, "ISIS' Imminent Demise," http://www.danielpipes.org/blog/2015/12/isis-imminent-demise, *Middle East Forum*, December 5, 2105.

33. Ibid.

34. Jonathan Spyer, "Is it Iran's Middle East Now?" http://www.meforum.org/5622/iran-middle-east, *Middle East Forum*, November 10, 2015.

35. Ben Caspit, "Israel Fear Return of Persian Empire," http://www.al-monitor.com/pulse/originals/2015/09/israel-fear-persian-empire-iran-shiite-hezbollah-axis-nuke.html, *Al Monitor*, September 21, 2015.

36. "Civilians in Syria suffering 'a living tragedy' with no end in sight, UN human rights expert warns," http://www.un.org/apps/news/story.asp?NewsID=51788#.VnaVBofUiUk, UN News Centre, September 3, 2015.

37. Quick Facts: What you need to know about the Syrian Crisis," https://www.mercycorps.org/articles/iraq-jordan-lebanon-syria-turkey/quick-facts-what-you-need-know-about-syria-crisis, MercyCorps, September 2, 2015.

38. Yaakov Lappin, "How Russia's military presence in Syria complicates Israeli affairs," http://www.jpost.com/Middle-East/Security-and-Defense-Under-Russian-cover-432211, *Jerusalem Post*, November 7. 2015.

39. Ibid.

40. Ben Caspit, "Will Israel, Russia tighten coordination on Syria?," http://www.al-monitor.com/pulse/originals/2015/12/israel-security-syria-russia-coordination-balance-power.html, *Al Monitor*, December 2, 2015.

41. *CBN News* Interview, Joel Rosenberg, November, 2015.

## CHAPTER THIRTEEN: APOCALYPTIC ISLAM

1. Ryan Mauro, "The Islamic State Seeks the Battle of the Apocalypse," http://www.clarionproject.org/analysis/dabiq-islamic-state-wants-battle-end-days, *The Clarion Project*, November 18, 2014.

2. William McCants, *The ISIS Apocalypse: The History, Strategy, and Doomsday Vision of the Islamic State*, New York, St. Martin's Press, 2015, p. 102-103.

3. Ibid, p. 103.

4. "The Return of the Khilafah," *Dabiq Magazine*, Issue 1, http://media.clarionproject.org/files/09-2014/isis-isil-islamic-state-magazine-Issue-1-the-return-of-khilafah.pdf, p. 2.

5. Samer Al-Atrush, "Islamic State offensive driven by apocalyptic prophesy," http://www.timesofisrael.com/islamic-state-offensive-driven-by-apocalyptic-prophesy/, *The Times of Israel*, October 8, 2014.

6. *Jerusalem Dateline* Interview with Ryan Mauro, National Security Analyst for the Clarion Project, http://www.clarionproject.org/content/ryan-mauro; http://www.cbn.comr/tv/3832635882001, October 10, 2014.

7. Graeme Wood, "ISIS: What They Want," http://www.theatlantic.com/magazine/archive/2015/03/what-isis-really-wants/384980/, *The Atlantic*, March 2015.

8. Amir Taheri, "Nobody Has Actually Seen Khamenei's Anti-Nuclear Fatwa, Which Obama Often Quotes," http://www.memri.org/report/en/0/0/0/0/0/0/0/7886.htm, Special Dispatch No. 5681, *MEMRI*, March 17, 2014.

9. Reza Khalili, "Iran Supreme Leader: The Islamic Messiah Is Coming Soon To Kill All Infidels," http://dailycaller.com/2014/06/15/iran-supreme-leader-the-shiite-islamic-messiah-is-coming-to-free-the-world/, *The Daily Caller*, June 15, 2014.

10. Y. Mansharof and A. Savyon, "Escalation in the Positions of Iranian President Mahmoud Ahmadinejad, http://www.memri.org/report/en/print2388.htm, *MEMRI Special Dispatch* No. 389, September 17, 2007.

11. Reza Khalili, "Iran Supreme Leader: The Islamic Messiah Is Coming Soon To Kill All Infidels," http://dailycaller.com/2014/06/15/iran-supreme-leader-the-shiite-islamic-messiah-is-coming-to-free-the-world/, *The Daily Caller*, June 15, 2014.

12. "The Failed Crusade," *Dabiq Magazine*, Issue 4, http://media.clarionproject.org/files/islamic-state/islamic-state-isis-magazine-Issue-4-the-failed-crusade.pdf, p. 7-8.

13. Malise Ruthven, "Lure of the Caliphate," http://www.nybooks.com/blogs/nyrblog/2015/feb/28/lure-caliphate-isis/, *The New York Review of Books*, NYR Daily, February 28, 2015.

14. Jessica Stern, "ISIS's Apocalyptic Vision, http://www.hoover.org/research/isiss-apocalyptic-vision, Hoover Institute, February 25, 2015.

15. Joel Rosenberg, "Islamic Extremists are Trying to Hasten the Return of the Mahdi," http://www.nationalreview.com/article/423852/radical-islam-iran-isis-apocalytpic-messiah-mahdi, *National Review*, September 11, 2015.

16. Dale Hurd, "ISIS's First Step: Conquer Rome, Defeat Christianity," http://www1.cbn.com/cbnnews/world/2015/October/ISISs-First-Step-Conquering-Rome-Defeat-Christianity/, *CBN News*, December 31, 2015.

17. Ibid.

18. Ibid.

19. Ibid.

20. Chris Mitchell, *Dateline Jerusalem: An Eyewitness Account of Prophecies Unfolding in the Middle East*, Nashville, Thomas Nelson, 2103, p. 66.

21. Ibid, p. 67.

22. Ibid, p. 66.

23. Lela Gilbert, "The Islamic State: Hastening the Apocalypse?," http://morningstarnews.org/2015/03/the-islamic-state-hastening-the-apocalypse/, *The Morningstar News*, March 16, 2015.

24. Ibid.

25. Graeme Wood, "ISIS: What They Want," http://www.theatlantic.com/magazine/archive/2015/03/what-isis-really-wants/384980/, *The Atlantic*, March 2015.

CHAPTER FOURTEEN: TEN THINGS YOU NEED TO KNOW ABOUT THE MIDDLE EAST

1. *CBN News* Interview, Michael Oren, Jerusalem, November, 2015.

2. Ibid.

3. Ibid.

4. Combat Veterans for Congress, http://www.combatveteransforcongress.org/cand/2763

5. Kate Nocera, "The freshman most likely to _____," Politico, http://www.politico.com/story/2013/01/freshman-yearbook-most-likely-to-085703, January 2, 2013.

6. *CBN News* Interview, Senator Tom Cotton (R-AR), Jerusalem, September 2015.

7. Ibid.

8. Sophie Haspeslagh, "Safe Havens in Iraq: Operation Provide Comfort, http://www.beyondintractability.org/cic_documents/Safe-Havens-Iraq.pdf.

9. *CBN News* Interview, (Ret.) General Jay Garner, Erbil, Kurdistan, September 2015.

10. Ibid.

11. Lt. Gen. William G. Boykin (Ret.) with Lynn Vincent, *Never Surrender: A Soldier's Journey to the Crossroads of Faith and Freedom*, New York, Faith Words, 2008), 350.

12. "Gen. Boykin named FRC executive VP", The Ethics & Religious Liberty Commission, http://erlc.com/article/gen.-boykin-named-frc-executive-vp/, July 17, 2012.

13. *CBN News* Interview, (Ret.) General William "Jerry" Boykin, Jerusalem, November 2015.

14. "About Robert Spencer, http://www.jihadwatch.org/about-robert.

15. Ibid.

16. Ibid.

17. Ibid.

18. *Jerusalem Dateline* with Robert Spencer, http://www1.cbn.com/video/jerusalem-dateline/2015/09/4/obama-secures-support-to-press-on-with-iran-nuke-deal-ndash-september-4-2015, September 4, 2015.

19. "Heroes Caroline Cox: Never Alone," http://www.britsattheirbest.com/heroes_adventurers/h_baroness_cox.htm, Brits At Their Best.

20. Ibid.

21. Ibid.

22. Ibid.

23. Ibid.

24. Ibid.

25. *CBN News* Interview, Baroness Caroline Cox, London, England, November 2015.

26. Jessica Gresko, "Prosecutors Seek 45-Year Sentence for Family Research Council Shooter Floyd Lee Corkins, AP, http://www.huffingtonpost.com/2013/04/22/family-research-council-shooter-sentence_n_3132634.html, March, 22, 2013.

27. *CBN News* Interview, Tony Perkins, Jerusalem, November 2015.

28. Ibid.

29. Ibid.

30. *Jerusalem Dateline*, CBN http://www1.cbn.com/video/jerusalem-dateline/2015/07/10/christians-join-the-fight-against-isis-ndash-july-10-2015, July 10, 2015.

31. Ibid.

32. Ibid.

33. *CBN News* Interview, Joel Rosenberg, Jerusalem, November 2015.

34. *CBN News* Interview, Fabian, Erbil, Kurdistan, September 2015.

CHAPTER FIFTEEN: A TIME FOR WAR

1. Chris Mitchell, "Send Her My Love: Letters from World War II," http://www.cbn.com/special/WW2letters/index.aspx., CBN.com

2. Ibid.

3. Ibid.

4. Ibid.

5. Ibid.

6. Ibid.

7. Ibid.

8. Ibid.

9. Josh Lev and Holly Yan, "Western allies reject ISIS leaders' threats against their citizens," http://edition.cnn.com/2014/09/22/world/meast/isis-threatens-west/, CNN, September 23, 2014.

10. Dada VP Vaswani, "Kill Fear before Fear Kills You," http://timesof-India.indiatimes.com/edit-page/Kill-fear-before-fear-kills-you/article-show/14245889cms, *India Times*, June 19, 2012.

11. *CBN News* Interview, Joel Richardson, Jerusalem, September 2014.

12. Robin Mark, "When It's All Been Said and Done ," http://www.invubu.com/lyrics/show/Robin_Mark/When_It's_All_Been_Said_And_Done.html.

13. Don Finto, *Prepare! For the End-Time Harvest*, Nashville: Caleb Publications, 2015, p. 7.

14. Ibid., p. 14.

15. "Their Finest Hour," The Churchill Centre, http://www.winstonchurchill.org/learn/speeches/speeches-of-winston-churchill/122-their-finest-hour, June 18, 1940.